# THE SECRETS OF
# PALMERSTON HOUSE

PHILLIPA NEFRI CLARK

# THE SECRETS OF
# Palmerston House

Phillipa Nefri Clark

**The Secrets of Palmerston House**

© 2018 Phillipa Nefri Clark

Further the author acknowledges the use of these brand names: Lotus Elite S, Facebook, Pinterest, Range Rover.

**Cover design: Steam Power Studios**
*The Secrets of Palmerston House is set in Australia, and written in Australian English.*

# ALSO BY PHILLIPA NEFRI CLARK

*My love and thanks to Ian, Nick & Alex. No journey is complete without you.*

*To Nas Dean, Jade & Vlad, and Helen. You make my job easier in so many ways.*

# 1

## VANISHING ACT

*C*hristie Ryan peered through the lacy curtains of her bedroom window in Palmerston House as below, in the garden, wedding guests gathered. Each carried a lantern and in a while, they would light Christie's way along the path to the pond where Martin waited. For her.

Heart racing with excitement, Christie longed for the moment she'd see the love in Martin's eyes as she joined him at the arch to become his wife. *Mrs Christie Blake.*

Everyone was here who mattered to them. Her great-aunt Martha, and Martin's grandfather Thomas, reunited recently after five decades apart. Martin's godfather, George, aunt Sylvia, and cousins Belinda and Jess. And dear Angus – who would soon walk Christie down the pathway to Martin – the closest she'd had to a father growing up.

So many good friends joined them this evening. Elizabeth of course, for she owned Palmerston House. Trev Sibbritt, handsome in a tuxedo instead of his customary police uniform. Daphne and John Jones, the very first people to welcome Christie to River's End almost a year ago. Charlotte Dean, who'd come for a sea change months ago and never left.

Where was Charlotte? For that matter, where was Martin?

Christie's eyes roamed the garden, ending up on Thomas, who had one hand on the head of Randall, Martin's golden retriever. Thomas listened to Trev speak on his phone. *What is going on?*

"Christie, may we come in for a moment?" Elizabeth called from the doorway "Angus is with me."

The worry in both their faces made Christie's eyes widen. "What's wrong?"

"My beautiful young lady," Angus reached for her hands. "I'm so proud of you. No matter what."

"What do you mean? No matter what, what?"

Elizabeth took one of Christie's hands from Angus. "Now, I don't want you to worry—"

"Elizabeth, Angus, what's wrong?"

Angus and Elizabeth exchanged a glance.

"Where's Martin? I couldn't see him from the window."

Belinda burst through the doorway. "I'll join the search party!" She stopped in her tracks as all three turned. "Oh no. You haven't told her?"

"Somebody needs to tell me. Angus?" A cold knot formed in Christie's stomach.

"We can't seem to locate Martin."

"Funny. Okay, time to stop joking around."

"No, dear. He should have arrived half an hour ago and there is no sign of him," Elizabeth said.

"Try his phone."

"Thomas has. So did Trev."

"Well, can someone run up to the house? Maybe he lost track of time." Christie's voice faltered as she looked back at Angus, who shook his head.

"Trev sent someone up and he's not there."

*This can't be happening.*

"He probably went for a walk to clear his head. He'll be along."

"Christie, darling, I'm so sorry, but he's not at the house. The front door was wide open. His tuxedo is in his bedroom and the phone is on the bed. He has vanished."

## 2

## HOW IT BEGAN

"*S*top fussing, Thomas!" Martin Blake rearranged the flowers in the middle of a table on the deck right after his grandfather straightened them.

"Ha! Who is fussing now?" Thomas Blake reached into a pocket. "Might have to take a photo of you fluffing up flowers with this fancy phone you gave me."

"Shouldn't you be home with your bride?"

"My bride is having an evening out. A girl's night, so she informed me."

Martin stopped what he was doing to stare at Thomas. "Which means you have nowhere to go."

"Rubbish. I'm an independent man. No need to worry about me, son."

"Go see George."

"Busy."

Martin shook his head. "Then John and Daphne. Barry? Trev?"

"I like the view from up here. And dinner smells good." Thomas turned to gaze across the meadow to the endless ocean beyond the cliff edge. The sun was setting, sending streams of gold across the sky.

"Normally you'd be welcome." Martin joined Thomas at the railing. Sea air drifted up the cliff, mingling with the ever-present jasmine climbing wildly along the desk. Martin smiled. Christie's favourite scent. Sailboats dotted the ocean, heading back to Willow Bay a little further along the coast. In half an hour the sky would be velvet black. "Six months ago, I proposed to Christie."

"How precisely did you confuse her enough agree?"

"Same way you confused Martha."

"Touché. So, no invitation to dinner?"

"Nope."

"Can I take the dog for the night then?"

Randall nuzzled against Thomas' leg. "You and Randall can have a boy's night in. If you leave now, you'll have the cottage to yourself because," he checked his watch, "Christie will be here any minute."

"Nice." Thomas grinned at Martin. "If I leave now. Just as well, young man, that I love you."

"You too." Martin patted Thomas' back. "Now, I really do have to finish dinner."

Thomas whistled as he took the steps onto the grass and Randall shot after him. "Bye, dog." Martin went indoors. He did love his grandfather dearly, but tonight he loved his fiancée a whole lot more. He checked the oven and turned it down, his mouth watering at the aromas wafting out.

From an overhead cupboard he selected wine glasses, leaving them on the counter as he collected a bottle of white wine from the fridge. He stood reading the label. "Perfect."

"Is that the gold medal winner?"

Christie stood on the other side of the counter, head tilted and a gorgeous smile lighting her face. Martin placed the bottle beside the glasses and gazed at her. Dressed in a simple blue dress, hair in loose waves around her shoulders, she was stunning.

"It is."

"The same one we had when you proposed?"

Martin came around the counter. "From the same batch. Seemed appropriate." He gathered her into his arms. "Hi."

"Hi. Something smells wonderful."

"You do." Martin kissed her lips, drawing her even closer until he wanted to forgo the meal and go straight to other more interesting things. But she needed feeding and, with a final kiss, he released her. "Did you pass Thomas?"

"No. Did he just leave?"

"He probably wanted to give Randall a run on the beach first." Martin returned to the kitchen. "He's at a loose end because Martha's out on the town without him."

Christie perched on a stool. "She was quite excited actually, having dinner out with Daphne, Sylvia and Elizabeth. I think there may be a few drinks involved. Hopefully Trev doesn't need to arrest them."

"She's going to corrupt the town. What did you do, getting those two back together?" Martin opened the oven and carefully slid a covered dish out.

"Me? I do recall you had some involvement."

"Only because you were crying and I felt sorry for you."

"Felt sorry for me! I was not crying."

Martin raised his eyebrow at Christie and she giggled. "Okay, so maybe a bit. And I don't regret one minute of it. Thomas and Martha belong together."

"And now they are. Or will be, once Martha gets home."

Thomas and Randall took their time heading home. The walk along the beach always put things into perspective and by the time they reached the top of the stone steps, he'd decided it was good for Martha to have a ladies' night out. An evening with Martin would have distracted him, but the boy deserved his special dinner with Christie.

They cut through the graveyard, walking behind three headstones in a row. Thomas touched those of his son and daughter-in-law. His hand automatically reached out to the headstone of his first wife, but he shook his head and kept walking. There was still a way to go before he could forgive Frannie.

Twilight turned the trees along the road into silent sentinels. How often in his youth Thomas ran along here to get home for dinner after kicking a ball with his friends until hunger overtook them. There might be more potholes now in the old road, but the sense of welcome as the cottage appeared on the other side of the abandoned railway line remained.

Christie's effort over the past few months was astounding, and what was until recently a sad and neglected property, now radiated old-world charm and comfort. There was still some work to do in the sprawling gardens, but the cottage of his childhood was again his home.

At the driveway, Randall stopped, his body rigid as he stared further down the road, where it narrowed and then eventually came to a dead end. A low rumble came from his throat.

Thomas couldn't see anything, but a car's engine roared into life in the distance. Headlights appeared and Randall stepped in front of Thomas. "No you don't." Thomas took him by the collar. "Just a lost driver."

A small SUV approached. Thomas expected it to stop but instead it accelerated past the cottage, throwing up stones in its wake. The windows were heavily tinted, revealing only the glimpse of a male profile. A cloud of dust spread across the road as the tail-lights disappeared around the corner toward town.

With a whine, Randall pulled away and followed as far as the railway track. "Randall, get back here." Thomas whistled, and a moment later, Randall ran back. "Inside. You don't need to protect me."

Thomas turned to the cottage, uneasy. People who were lost normally asked for directions. People around here normally stopped for a chat. But whoever that was made a quick exit. A bit too quick.

# 3

# A STRANGER IN TOWN

*B*ernie Cooper scowled as he touched the brakes of his SUV. Ahead, a police car was parked near a bridge and he was going too fast. Even as he slowed, the door opened and a police officer got out.

The last thing he'd expected at the cottage was an old man and a dog arriving on foot, scaring the living daylights out of him as he peered through the kitchen window. At least he'd made it across a paddock to the car before the dog noticed.

The police officer stepped into the road and gestured for Bernie to pull over. With a curse, he flicked the indicator on and nosed the SUV behind the other vehicle. As the officer approached, he lowered the window, tilting his head out with a smile.

"Sorry, officer. My mistake not paying attention."

"Senior Constable Trev Sibbritt." He flashed his torch into the front seat. "Any reason?"

"Just a bit over excited at being here, sir." Bernard opened his wallet. "Do you need my driver's licence?"

"Yes. Never heard anyone say they were excited about coming into a sleepy little town like this." Trev took the offered driver's licence. "Bernard William Cooper. You're a long way from home."

"Always am. I only get back to Brisbane a few times a year. I'm a photographer. Freelance. Go where the wind takes me, in a manner of speaking."

"Sit tight. I'll be right back."

As soon as Trev's back was turned, Bernard grabbed the smallest of three cameras on the seat and forced it into the glove box. The copper seemed friendly enough and if he could get out of this with a warning, it would be a bonus. As long as nothing came up on the check he presumably was doing at his vehicle.

The moments ticked by. On the other side of the bridge was the township of River's End, which, under the darkening sky, was little more than a couple of streets of shops with a pub at one end. Not a lot happening there, which was going to make the next week or so interesting. Everybody would know each other here and a stranger might create a bit too much interest for his liking. This town had no idea what was coming.

Trev wandered back and Bernie grabbed a folded map from his door pocket.

"Can you tell me which is the best road to take? There seems to be a couple of ways to my destination?"

"Here's your licence." Trev handed it back. "Where you heading?"

"Place called Palmerston House. Going to be staying there for a few days while I take shots for my new book."

"Over the bridge bear left. That avoids town. First fork, go right and you won't miss it. Elizabeth expecting you?" Trev watched Bernie a bit too intensely.

"Thanks for that. That's Mrs White? Sounded lovely on the phone when I booked the other day." Bernie held Trev's gaze, hoping his acting skills held up. There wasn't much he couldn't charm his way out of. Or into.

"Watch your speed. I'm not as nice if anyone causes an accident."

"I'll be more aware. Promise. And thanks, mate."

With a nod, Trev returned to his police car. Careful to indicate and take his time pulling back on the road, Bernie raised a hand to Trev as he passed him. Thank goodness. Not the way to start his visit to town. *Your triumphant arrival.* He took the left after the bridge.

## 4

## AN UNWANTED GUEST

Through the foyer window of Palmerston House, Elizabeth checked the driveway for the third time in as many minutes. "We're going to be late, so you all go ahead and I'll drive myself down soon."

"What if I ring the pub and let them know we're a bit behind schedule?" Martha was reaching for the phone near the staircase as she spoke.

"Oh, Martha, yes please. I am sorry!"

Daphne and Sylvia joined Elizabeth at the window.

"We'll all go together, even if it's a bit late." Daphne wound her arm through Elizabeth's.

"Perhaps I should stay – it doesn't feel right to greet a guest then disappear so quickly. What if he needs something and I'm not here?"

"Then he can ask me." Charlotte emerged from the hallway on the other side of the stairs, with a steaming cup of coffee in her hands. "Why don't you go to your dinner? I'll let your new guest in, show him his room and all that."

Martha replaced the receiver with a smile. "How generous, Charlotte. But we wouldn't want to upset any of your own plans, dear."

Charlotte laughed shortly. "Yup. So many plans. But really, go. I'm sure I can manage one guest on my own."

"Well, if you're certain? His room is all set up, of course. And there's a welcome pack on the bed. If you can just show him around and where... oh, I'll leave it with you." Elizabeth grinned at the face Charlotte had pulled. "Ladies, let's be on our way."

Within a couple of moments, they'd piled into Daphne's car and Charlotte closed the front door after waving until they disappeared. Her coffee finished, she ran upstairs to put on the bedside lamp in the new guest's room and smoothed the already perfect eiderdown. Elizabeth's special little touches made every room inviting.

The sound of a car driving in drew Charlotte to the window. It was a small SUV, hesitating at the fountain as if the driver didn't know where to park. Well, she could point him in the right direction. She left the door ajar and sprinted back down the stairs. By the time she reached the front door, there was a shadow through the frosted side windows.

With a flourish, Charlotte opened the door. The man was leaning down, concentrating on a zip in a large duffel bag on the verandah. "Welcome to Palmerston House."

The man straightened, until he stood before Charlotte with a smile that did not reach his eyes. "Not at all as I expected you to look, Mrs White."

Charlotte's hand flew to her mouth. Colour drained from her face as she took a step back.

Bernie Cooper picked up his bag and brushed past her to go to the middle of the foyer, where he gazed around. "Nice. Just like the photographs. So, where is Mrs White?"

"What are you doing here?" Voice trembling, Charlotte dropped her hands, clenching them into fists at her side.

"Good to see you too, Doctor."

With a click, Charlotte closed the front door. "I said, what are you doing here, Bernie?"

"So, are you working here, now? Bit of a come-down from your old job."

"No I am not working here! Either tell me why you're here, or get—"

"Get out?" He crossed his arms. "I'm a guest. And unless you own Palmerston House, I won't be going anywhere."

"Don't be so sure. Once Elizabeth knows about you, she'll throw you out herself."

Bernie threw his head back in a loud and insincere guffaw. Charlotte glared at him. He wasn't dangerous. At least, he hadn't been. "Have you been seeing someone?"

He stopped laughing. "Romantically? I didn't know you cared."

"Truly, I don't. Psychologically."

With one movement, he picked up his bag and slung it over his shoulder, face red. "I'm here to take photographs. Got a commission from local tourism so simply taking the opportunity to stay here. That's the full story, Lottie."

"But, Bernie, why here? It won't help you—"

"Oh, now you wanna be my psych again?"

"No."

"Let's set things straight. You can't say anything about me. Imagine what it would do to your career, not to mention the law suit I'd file against you for breach of confidence. I'm here to take photos and you can be friendly or stay out of my way. Your choice. Now, are you gonna to show me my room or do I go looking?"

Charlotte stalked past him toward the staircase. "Elizabeth had to go out so I offered to step in, but dammit, had I known it was you..." She stopped and looked back. "You weren't surprised to see me."

He shrugged.

"You knew I was here. Nobody knows where I am, except—"

"Yup. Except your dear old mother." Bernie put one hand on the balustrade and leaned close to Charlotte. "The other reason you'll be keeping my secrets."

Her throat constricted and she forced out the words. "What did you do?"

"Had a lovely chat. Pushed her wheelchair down to that nice little lake at the institute you stuck her in. She was quite happy to talk about her daughter. The acclaimed psychiatrist who took a sabbatical. Her mind is a whole lot better than you think." He stared at Charlotte as if disappointed in her. "I didn't know how else to find you, disappearing like that. Imagine my delight that you came here. To Palmerston House, as if you want what's mine."

Then, as though nothing had happened, Bernie went past Charlotte up the stairs. "Come on, show me around."

Unable to make her legs function, she glanced at the front door. Where was Trev when she needed him? For once, his habit of dropping by unannounced would be welcome. But the reality sank in. She couldn't do anything. Bernie was here on some misguided mission which would fail. What would she tell Elizabeth and Trev? A former patient wanted to see a house that meant something to him. *Hardly a crime.* With a deep breath, she forced her feet to follow him upstairs.

## 5

# STARS THAT GUIDE

*M*artin and Christie swayed as one on a make-believe dance floor beside the table on the deck. There was barely room to turn, but neither cared, their eyes on each other as Norah Jones invited them to come away with her. Her husky voice drifted out to the cliff edge and beyond, filling the night. As the last few notes ended, Martin touched his lips to Christie's. "Time for dessert."

"Mmm." Christie's eyes closed and she leaned against his chest, her arms tight around his waist.

"But you'll need to release me so I can get it."

"No dessert. More dancing."

Martin whispered, "The first layer is chocolate mousse."

Christie opened her eyes.

"Then, a layer of fresh cherries that I soaked in a rather good brandy overnight."

"Yum."

He held her close. "Next is more mousse, this time with some slivers of almonds and grated chocolate. But you don't want dessert so stop wiggling."

"Martin—"

"Where was I? Ah, whipped cream, with just a few more cherries. I might have mine now, and save yours for breakfast."

There was a long silence.

"Have you fallen asleep?" Martin loosened his arms to gaze down at Christie. He grinned at her expression. "Thomas wanted to stay for dinner."

"Thomas is not nearly as nice to dance with as I am."

"This is true." He kissed the tip of her nose. "Why don't I refill our glasses and you can stargaze whilst I get dessert?"

"I'm not going to refuse such an offer, particularly in this lovely weather." Christie dropped her arms and took a seat back at the table. "You don't need a hand?"

Martin poured two glasses of white wine. "I think I can manage. When I get back, we can talk about the wedding, if you'd like to?" He handed Christie a glass and wandered inside, through the open sliding glass door.

With no music or conversation, the soothing sounds from the ocean were carried on a breeze. Christie's eyes sought the horizon, now as dark as the sky above, a clear, black velvet with diamond stars. She recognised the constellations. A little too early in the evening for the Southern Cross, Christie turned her attention to the stars belonging to Carina and Vela. The keel of a boat and sails in the sky. She curled her fingers around the pendant that rarely left her neck.

"Sweetheart?" Martin placed the decadent dessert in front of Christie, then covered her hand holding the pendant with his. "Thinking about your parents?"

Christie blinked to clear what might have been a tear or two. "Thank you, this looks divine."

He released her hand and sat opposite, picking up his wine glass and sipping. His eyes never left her face and after a moment she answered, "I was stargazing."

Now Martin glanced at the sky. "They brought you safely home to me."

"Sometimes, it just feels as though..."

"As though?"

She picked up her spoon. "Where do you find these recipes?"

"Pinterest. I've told you this before. Are you changing the subject?"

"Yes." With a smile, she scooped up a cherry and bit into it with a sigh. "So good. Does Pinterest have wedding pictures?"

"How can such a world-wise person know nothing of Pinterest? Have you never looked at it for inspiration?"

"For make-up? Nope. But I might for the wedding. We are still talking about it, remember." She slid her spoon into the soft mousse and sneaked a look at Martin. He shook his head ever so slightly, not in answer to the question, but at her attempt to divert him away from whatever was worrying her.

"Yes. We are still talking about it."

6
_____

# REFLECTIONS

*H*is solitary dinner eaten, plate washed and whiskey now in hand, Thomas wandered around the cottage. Such quiet used to suit him best. Time to reflect, paint, read. Whatever took his fancy, whenever he wished. After Martin built the house on the cliff, Thomas found himself alone in his cabin in the mountains. Lonely for the little boy he'd raised, for the family he'd lost in the car accident, for the girl he once loved more than life itself. *Martha.* But time changed him and being on his own was all he knew for many years.

Thomas stared at the seascape hanging above the fireplace. Lightning forked into an angry ocean under cover of darkness. His finest work. One born from despair when Martha disappeared the night of their engagement party. He sipped the whiskey. He'd followed her beneath the waves of the storm, finding her only seconds before the sea took her for itself. Either way, she'd been lost to him. Until Christie burst into their lives almost five decades later and changed everything.

He turned his back on the seascape and went to the dining room, where more of his paintings adorned the walls. Martha insisted he hang everything they could fit and he had to admit, it was nicer than having them under sheets. He set his glass on the table and pulled out a chair. As a child he'd rarely been allowed in here where his mother kept her special plates and glasses. The table had been shiny mahogany – so no fingerprints allowed – and only as a teenager had Thomas been included in the occasional dinners she hosted.

The new table was built with local mountain ash and better suited the small room. Martha dressed it with a pretty table runner from her old home in Ireland, and a vase of fresh flowers. He was now welcome in this room anytime. He stretched his legs out under the table, his foot prodding Randall, who grunted and got up for a pat.

"Didn't know you were there, old boy." Thomas scratched the dog's head. "Good thing you've got me to keep you company."

Randall padded out of the dining room and up the hallway to one of the bedrooms. Thomas chuckled. "Yup."

Soon, he'd get up and put the kettle on. Have tea ready to make when Martha arrived home. *Martha.* Her perfect smile filled his heart with warmth and there was not a moment awake or sleeping when her presence left him. Even with her off gallivanting with the other ladies, he knew she was with him. All those wasted, lost years apart. He picked up his glass and drank the rest in one gulp to force those old feelings back to where he usually kept them. The here and now mattered and they had a lot of catching up to do. No more time apart or people interfering with their relationship.

Christie would move out in a few weeks to marry that boy of his. She'd be safe with Martin, particularly with her dangerous ex-fiancé Derek behind bars. Too many strangers in such a small town just spelt trouble and River's End was due for a nice long time of peace and quiet. Hopefully, the SUV up the road earlier was simply a lost driver passing through town. A car door slammed outside and Daphne's loud laughter lightened his mood. Martha was home.

# 7

# MAKING FRIENDS. OR ENEMIES.

Soon after dawn, Elizabeth flicked on the lights in the kitchen of Palmerston House. She blinked a bit at the sudden brightness. Hot, strong tea was first on her list. The kettle heated as she added tea leaves to her favourite porcelain teapot. Perhaps the nightcap at the cottage was one too many. Such a wonderful evening though with Martha, Daphne and Sylvia, and how sweet of Daphne's husband John to come and drive them around once he knew they'd drunk a little more than planned.

Before the kettle could whistle she poured its water into the teapot. As she waited for it to brew, she took two teacups and saucers from the cupboard. *How silly.* She only needed one. With Angus still away in Melbourne, there was nobody to share the first cup of the day with so early. She sighed and went to put back the second cup, halted by a tap on the open door behind her.

"Good morning. Mrs White?"

"Mr Cooper, how nice to meet you!" Elizabeth extended her hand as a tall, young man approached.

"Bernie, please." Bernie shook her hand. "My apologies for arriving so late. I was rather unavoidably detained."

"No problem at all. I'm sorry I wasn't here to greet you, which is quite unlike me. Charlotte was so generous offering to take my place. Now, would you like a cup of coffee?"

"Actually, I love tea and can smell the brew from here."

"Come and sit at the table then."

Elizabeth returned to the counter and Bernie found himself a seat, gazing around at the old but beautifully kept kitchen. "This is a lovely building, Mrs White."

"Indeed it is. And please call me Elizabeth. Everyone does." She poured two cups and brought them to the table. "Please, help yourself to milk and sugar. Do you mind if I join you before starting to make breakfast?"

"I think I interrupted you, so I must insist you do." Bernie smiled broadly, reaching for the sugar bowl. "Have you owned Palmerston House for a long time?"

"Oh, quite some years. More than twenty, yes, because Martha and I met up in London in 1995 for a visit, and it took another year or so for the sale to happen."

Bernie tilted his head in interest. "Martha?"

"Martha Blake – Ryan back then. Her family were the owners of Palmerston House for many generations and she knew the property was sitting idle, boarded up and showing signs of neglect. Her sister was kind enough to sell to us at a fair price. My late husband worked tirelessly to restore it to its previous splendour and since then many wonderful guests have enjoyed its charms, as I do every day."

"Surely you don't run it all alone?"

"I have some part-time help, of course, with the grounds. And the pond. Anyway, I mustn't bore you with my story. You mentioned on the phone you are a photographer?"

"Actually, I'm enjoying hearing about the property here. Its history and all that. I love photographing old buildings so perhaps you'd allow me to do so during my stay? I'm sensitive about the privacy of your other guests, so would be discreet."

"I would be delighted. The grounds are particularly pretty at this time of year, with early jonquils blooming."

"Yes, lots to photograph outside." Charlotte walked in, straight to the table, holding a set of keys out to Elizabeth. "Morning, Elizabeth. Here's the keys you left with me last night."

Elizabeth stood, took the keys and hung them on a rack near the door to the cellar. "Charlotte, dear, thank you for looking after Mr Cooper last night."

"Bernie." He stared at Charlotte. "Yes, thank you for being so... welcoming."

Charlotte kept her eyes on Elizabeth. "No worries, Elizabeth. Would you like a hand getting breakfast made?"

"No, but thanks." Elizabeth picked up her cup. "More tea, Bernie? Coffee, Charlotte?"

"I'd love another which, if you don't object, I'll take up to my room," Bernie said, still watching Charlotte.

Elizabeth creased her forehead as her eyes moved from Bernie to Charlotte. "Coffee, dear?" she repeated.

"I might have a shower first. I'll see you at breakfast, Elizabeth." Charlotte rushed out of the kitchen leaving Elizabeth gazing after her.

---

*C*harlotte ran up the sweeping staircase of Palmerston House. She'd expected to find Elizabeth alone in the kitchen, enjoying her first cup of tea as usual.

Once in her room, she stripped off and threw herself into the shower, turning the water on as high and hot as it would go. As steam rose around her, she forced her emotions to drift with it.

*Let go. One breath. Two.*

Bernard Cooper must not get under her skin. She leaned against the tiles, eyes closed. Fitful sleep, punctuated by long spells staring at the ceiling, had left her exhausted.

What was he really after? His fascination with River's End permeated every session for the first few months she'd treated him in Brisbane, until one day he simply dismissed the subject. He'd refused to discuss it again, after telling Charlotte he'd been wrong thinking his ancestors once owned Palmerston House. All a mistake. Charlotte had believed him.

"Because you wanted to." The torrent of water drowned her words and she opened her eyes.

There was no point in revisiting this. Around the same time her own life hit rock bottom and she was no longer the psychiatrist he needed. That anybody needed. With a savage twist, she turned the shower off. Whatever Bernie's motives, Charlotte's hands were tied.

She reached for a towel and worked on her hair, catching her reflection in the mirror which, streaked with condensation, made her look broken. Like two people. Maybe it was time to move on, find another place to stay. If she gave Elizabeth a week's board to compensate notice, she could leave today. This morning. She'd head along the coast to South Australia.

The idea bubbled up and consumed her. She'd find another small town, and another. Lose herself in the dramatic landscape of the Limestone Coast. Then perhaps she'd be ready for the city of Adelaide where at least she would be less visible.

Dry, Charlotte hurried into the bedroom and dressed. In a few hours, River's End would be behind her. Bernie would probably stay a while then move on as he always did.

She dragged her suitcase from under the bed and opened it on the floor. Inside were a few winter jumpers, a couple of pairs of nice shoes, and the small box that travelled with her. A box of memories, her mother used to say.

With a light tap on the door, Elizabeth called out, "I've brought you a cup of coffee, dear."

"Oh, I'll be right there." The suitcase got shoved back under the bed and Charlotte opened the door. "You didn't need to do that, Elizabeth." Charlotte took the cup. "Thank you."

"Dear, did everything go alright last night? You didn't have any problems with Mr Cooper?"

Charlotte pushed the door wide open so Elizabeth could come in, then closed it behind her. "Why do you ask?"

"Just a feeling."

"I'm just not very outgoing."

"I don't want you upset. Since you arrived, I've grown fond of you, Charlotte. So have many folk in town and the way you looked after Randall and Christie and Martin the night of that awful storm... well, we see you as one of our own. So, you have your coffee and come down for breakfast when you wish."

With a smile, Elizabeth slipped out. Charlotte knew she should have told her she was leaving today. Should be putting down the coffee and pulling the suitcase back out. *They see you as one of their own.* Nobody ever said such a thing before.

## ON THE CLIFF

*I*t was still early when Christie – after a lingering kiss from Martin – followed the track down the cliff face near his house.

Halfway down, Christie paused to watch the sea, shuffling the bag carrying her clothes from last night from one shoulder to the other. How beautiful the water looked today, reflecting the perfect blue morning sky. The tide was still low and the jetty stood high above the calm waves. Further out a yacht sailed toward Green Bay. It was one of the luxury yachts moored in Willow Bay, where her own *Jasmine Sea* normally anchored. But *Jasmine Sea* was all the way up the coast in Geelong in dry dock, being repaired from the damage her ex-fiancé did when he put a hole through the hull and almost sank her, with Christie and Randall aboard.

Her hands clenched.

*I'm safe now.*

Christie uncurled her fingers and rubbed them, the tension draining away as her thoughts turned to today's plans. She had an early meeting with builder Barry Parks at the beauty salon to finalise the renovations, then lunch with Martha and Thomas, so it was time to get going.

A few steps further down the track she stopped again when the crunch of rubble, as if underfoot, caught her attention. She glanced back, expecting to see Martin, but nobody was there.

How odd. Walkers rarely strayed up this track, being narrow and quite steep in parts, winding back and forth across the cliff face. Smaller paths, barely visible, forked off in places but Martin had cautioned her against investigating them alone.

"Hello?"

A rabbit bounded past and she jumped. With a shake of her head, Christie followed the rabbit toward the beach.

---

*B*ernie stepped out from a crevice in the cliff, careful not to make another sound. He watched Christie walk away, admiring how her jeans fitted. Even from this view, she was prettier in person than the images he'd found online.

*Very nice, if you like the descendants of thieves.*

She disappeared from sight.

He reached into the crevice and retrieved a backpack. He took out an almost empty plastic bottle of water and drank rapidly, before crushing the bottle. The lid he returned to the bag, but he tossed the bottle into the undergrowth.

From a pocket he pulled out a compass. Old, of English seafarer design, it glinted as the sun caught its brass outer. Bernie watched it adjust, then took a few steps to his right. There was the faintest track here between chest-high bushes somehow growing at a ridiculous angle over and around the steep cliff.

Compass back in his pocket, he pulled a pair of heavy gloves from the backpack. He worked his way between the bushes, swearing under his breath as his arms were scratched. Two steps in and the ground sheered away. He sat on the edge, one hand on a sturdy branch and the other shading his eyes against sun-glare from the sea.

If he had the right equipment, he could use the shrubs to climb from. Bernie extracted his small camera from a pocket inside his jacket. He spent a few moments shooting images of every inch below and around himself, then sat for a while, staring at the horizon.

# BEAUTIFUL PLANS

*C*hristie let herself into the old hairdressing salon she'd purchased a few months ago and closed the door behind her, leaning against it to survey what would soon be her new business. So far, she'd removed the old sinks, mirrors and reception desk, with some help from Martin.

Barry Parks wandered past the window with a nod and Christie flung open the door with a wide smile.

"Welcome to my new project, Barry!" she waved dramatically inside. "Just when you thought it was safe to expect a normal job."

"This looks a whole lot easier than that cottage of yours."

"Why? Is it the lack of hidden entry ways, or the absence of decades old carpet? Although..." Christie frowned at bright orange linoleum covering every inch of the floor.

Barry grinned as he opened his iPad. "What's the plan? Old-world charm or cutting edge modern?"

"Neither. How many rooms can we fit in here?"

"Rooms?" Barry gazed around. Longer than wide, the shop was an open space, with a door in the back wall. He wandered down and peered through to a small kitchen and tiny bathroom. Beyond was the back door. "What's out there?"

"Well," Christie moved ahead to unlock the door. "That's the other thing."

She opened it onto an enclosed, concrete yard with a broken clothes line. It was about half the size of the shop. Barry looked at Christie with an expression she knew from his days restoring the cottage.

She smiled. "You'll love it."

"Oh dear."

"I've checked with council and as long as we comply with fire safety and some other rules which I forget, they have no issue with internal changes. And out here I can landscape and enhance unless we go higher than the building."

"I'm getting worried now. Since when do you speak to council?"

"Best way to overcome objections is to present a viable proposition."

"To me."

"Well, I didn't want you wasting your time, in case they didn't see things my way."

Barry laughed. "What is it you want me to do?"

In a serious tone, Christie lowered her voice. "Barry, do you have any idea how much the ladies of River's End have been missing out on?"

He groaned.

---

*T*homas and Randall strolled through the meadow to Martin's house, leaving his old four wheel drive on the other side of the gate. There'd never been a driveway to the house and Martin liked it that way. As a young man, Thomas used to set up his easel near the cliff edge and paint for hours. Back then it was council-owned land and accessible to anyone wanting to use it, not that many folk did. Being so high up and with limited windbreaks, once winter came along the land was buffeted and colder here than in town.

Martin didn't care. He'd built the house to suit the seasons and spent most of the winter painting in his studio.

"I wonder what Christie will think about that?" Thomas asked Randall, who looked around expectantly at the sound of her name. "Yep, you love her every bit as much as we do."

"Who are you talking to, Thomas?" Martin came around the corner of the house, holding his mobile phone. "Hello, dog." He patted Randall as his dog circled him with a whimper of delight.

"The dog of course. See anyone else here?"

"I'm more concerned about you talking to yourself."

"Been doing that my whole life. Sign of high intelligence, I'm told."

"Who told you such a thing?"

Thomas feigned offence. "Well, I did. Most intelligent person I know."

"Right. Coffee?"

"Might as well. Got another hour until lunch with Christie. Speaking of which, how was last night?" Thomas dropped an arm over Martin's shoulders as they walked. "Did you burn dinner?"

Martin rolled his eyes. "How was your night? Did you manage to feed yourself without Martha to look after you?"

"Funny. Randall and I enjoyed a nice steak. Cooked the way I like it."

"Black."

"Properly cooked. None of this medium rare business. What's with the mobile phone?" Thomas followed Martin up the handful of steps onto the long deck. The remnants of a candle remained on the table and Martin collected it on his way past.

"Just had a call from Tony, the principal up at Camp Hawk." Martin headed inside, Thomas and Randall behind him.

"Ah. Your special project camp."

"They have a new intake of students in two days and Tony has to attend a funeral interstate." Martin filled the coffee machine with water. "He's also the art teacher and to go a full week without one is not fair on the kids. Not when they're only there for three weeks."

Thomas settled onto a stool at the long bench between the living room and kitchen. "So, they need you."

"I'm getting married in a few weeks, Thomas. There's so much to organise."

With a chuckle, Thomas shook his head. "Son, you just need to show up. Christie is surrounded by people who will help her."

Martin considered this as he watched coffee trickle into one, then the other cup. When he joined Thomas with their drinks, his forehead was furrowed. "It isn't just the wedding."

"I can see that. But you can't watch over her every minute. Christie is safe. She's with Martha and me at night and I'm pretty certain the new project of hers is occupying her at the moment. We'll all help out. You go."

"You're having lunch together?"

"At the bakery. Want to join us?"

"No. I'll give her a call and see if she'll drop round afterwards, so leave it for me to tell her. Unless she's okay about it, I'll say no."

Thomas grinned. "As long as nobody thinks you're skipping out on the big day."

# 10

## KEEPING SECRETS

*C*harlotte lay on her bed, eyes on the same spot on the ceiling for the last ten minutes. Elizabeth's kind words earlier had reminded her of the day she'd arrived.

There she'd been, totally lost going up and down dead end roads. Exhausted from a full day driving, nothing to eat in hours, tears streaking her face, and with a giant map open on her steering wheel, she'd veered out of a side road almost into the path of a police car. Her heart had almost stopped when the patrol car's lights flashed.

After pulling over, she'd brushed the tears away but her hands refused to stop shaking. Everything in her life was out of control and this was possibly the final straw. Agitated, she'd watched the approach of the police officer in her side mirror, his walk cautious and hand on his holster. Oh God, had she broken some laws? Without a thought, she'd flung the door open, wanting to explain she was not dangerous.

"Hold it there, ma'am." His voice was deep. Why she'd noticed was beyond her. She put her hands up for some reason before realising the road map was in one of them. She let go and saw him watch it drift down. He was a little bit older than her, she guessed. Solid but from muscle, not fat. A kind face with keen eyes. He'd gently scolded her for driving and reading the map at the same time, then asked where she was going. Senior Constable Trevor Sibbritt.

*Trev.*

Before she knew it, she was following him to Palmerston House, and he'd stayed to make sure Elizabeth got her settled.

With a sigh, Charlotte sat up, putting her legs over the side of the bed. Trev was a good man and in another lifetime she'd allow him to court her, for that is what she knew he wanted. Old-fashioned the word might be, but it fitted the respectful, if slightly hesitant way Trev usually spoke to her.

She pushed those thoughts away. The bigger problem at hand was Bernard Cooper. His words from last night taunted her.

"Had a lovely chat. Pushed her wheelchair down to that nice little lake at the institute you stuck her in. She was quite happy to talk about her daughter. The acclaimed psychiatrist who took a sabbatical. Her mind is a whole lot better than you think."

Charlotte reached for her phone on the bedside table and dialled. She curled her legs back underneath herself.

"Lakeview Care. Maggie speaking."

"Maggie, it's Charlotte Dean. How are you?"

"Oh, Dr Dean! How nice to hear from you. I'm quite well. You'd like to speak to your mother?"

"Actually, would you have a moment? I would like an update."

There was hesitation on the other end of the line.

"What is it Maggie? Is something going on with my mother?"

"Not as such. But she had a visitor and since then asks about you every day. When you are coming to see her. That kind of thing."

"What visitor?"

"Oh, I thought you'd know. Your cousin, Bernard. He seemed very fond of Angelica and spent a lot of time here. They went down to the lake and had lunch together. She really brightened up."

Charlotte lay back on the bed, eyes tightly closed.

"Dr Dean?"

"Maggie, he's not my cousin, so please make a note he is not to visit again. Okay?"

"Oh my! I am so sorry. He was very convincing."

"Not your fault."

"Dr Dean, when will you be coming to see your mother? Just so I can let her know when she asks."

Her heart felt like it would explode, so fast it beat. *One breath. Two.* This wasn't working.

"Are you still there?"

"Sorry. Tell her I love her. I'm away. I'll call when I'm back."

She hung up and turned on the bed to curl up in the foetal position.

———

*T*rev checked his phone while waiting for his order at the bakery, clearing junk emails and reminders. The latter were of no value anyway, because he missed them time and again. There were two text messages. One from Thomas, asking if he'd seen a speeding SUV. He scratched his head. Cooper. Bernard William Cooper. He'd go see Thomas and find out why he'd asked. The other message was from his mother. The weekly check in.

*When was he coming home for a visit? Would he be bringing a lady with him? Would he ever give her grandchildren?*

He replied with a smile.

*Soon. No. What about a kitten instead?*

Their regular joke. Except deep down she was concerned he'd never marry. She was alone now, since Dad had passed away, and a few hours' drive from here. In spite of his suggestion she move closer, her heart was with the town he'd grown up in. He did need to visit though.

"There you go, Trev." Sylvia handed him a white paper bag. "It's hot, so don't burn yourself."

"Thanks, I'll be careful." He turned from the counter, almost straight into Thomas, who glanced over his shoulder. Trev followed his glance to Martha and Christie, settling down at a table near the window.

"Pretend we're having a normal conversation."

"Hello, Thomas. Normal, as opposed to what?"

"And keep it quick. Don't want to concern the bride. Either of them."

"What's up?" Trev stepped to one side to let other customers past and Thomas followed, his forehead creased. "What are you worried about?"

"Not worried. Curious. Have you seen anyone in town with a darkish kind of SUV? One of those smaller ones."

"Ah. I just read your message. Yes. Had a chat to someone last night about going too fast."

"Good. Good. Who?"

"Why do you ask? What do you know about him?"

Thomas raised a hand to wave at Martha. "Supposed to be ordering lunch. He was up the road from the cottage in the dark last night. Went hurtling past spraying stones all over."

"Probably just lost."

"Then he should have asked me for directions."

The heat from Trev's pie seeped uncomfortably into his hand and he moved it to the other one. "It's normal to be a bit suspicious, a bit worried after what happened to Christie. He's just a visiting photographer. Seems harmless."

Relief flooded Thomas' face and Trev patted his arm. "Have lunch. Relax and enjoy your family, okay? I'll keep a watch out."

With a nod, Thomas got back in line. On his way out, Trev waved to Martha and Christie. The events of a few months ago stayed fresh. Only time would settle everyone back down. No more break-ins, vandalism, and attempted murder, thanks very much.

# IMAGES OF THE PAST

"Oh! You captured the pond perfectly!" Elizabeth sat at the kitchen table next to Bernie, looking at a series of photographs on a small laptop. Both had empty teacups pushed to one side.

"I love the old trees around it. Makes for a pretty backdrop." Bernie clicked his mouse and a close-up of a duck appeared. "Can't resist these fellows. See the colour on his wings?"

"Hers, actually, but yes. How did you learn to take such beautiful photographs, if you don't mind me asking?"

"Just have a good eye, really. Did a course and got a lucky break. Now, see this one?" Bernie clicked again, eyes not leaving the screen. "It almost looks like the garage was once a stable block."

"Well, it was. A long time ago of course before cars became the new horse and buggy, I imagine."

Bernie sat back in his chair, his attention now on Elizabeth as she continued. "There were always horses kept here, right up until the Ryans left, but those stables were changed into a garage, and ground-keeper lodgings, long before then. New sheds went out in the paddocks for the pleasure horses."

"You said the Ryans. You mentioned a Martha Ryan earlier." He reached for his teacup.

"Let me refill it, dear." Elizabeth poured more tea for them both. "Martha's great-great-grandfather was the first Ryan to live here. I don't know all the history – George Campbell is the best one for local knowledge – but I believe they moved here in the middle of the nine-teenth century."

"Thank you. The tea is lovely. So, who built the house?"

"You really are interested? Come with me and I'll show you a bit of history," Elizabeth took a quick sip of tea before getting to her feet. "We have a few photographs of our own here." She led Bernie to the long hallway in the direction of the foyer. Normally it was dimly lit, but Elizabeth flicked a switch and a row of downlights came on above a series of photographs on one wall. She went to the farthest one.

"Starting with more recent times, this is Patrick and Lilian Ryan, and sitting in front of them a very young Martha and her older sister Dorothy. Martha lives right here in River's End."

Bernie peered at the photograph. "Didn't you say the Ryans left though?"

"Lilian and Patrick moved to Ireland a long time ago. A few years later, Martha followed them and only came home last year. Quite a story on its own."

"But she doesn't live here. At Palmerston House."

"No. Over time all the Ryan properties were sold, except the orig-inal stationmaster's cottage up the hill. Thanks to her great-niece, Christie, the cottage is now hers, all restored and beautiful. Now, let me show you the next photograph."

Elizabeth progressed down the hallway, telling Bernie little snip-pets about each one, until reaching the final frame. The family in this photograph were serious, dressed in black finery in a formal pose.

"That is Eoin Ryan and his wife, Mary. The first Ryan family to own Palmerston House."

"He built it?" Bernie ignored the photograph, staring intently at Elizabeth.

"No, although I believe his timber company provided part of the structure."

"Then who did?"

"I'd suggest having a chat to George, or popping into the library at Green Bay if you want a lot of detail."

Bernie kept his eyes on Elizabeth, smiling with his mouth only. "I love history. Nothing like knowing who forged this country. So, do you know the name of the man who built it?"

"Henry Temple did. Built it and lived here for a few years, I think."

"Sold it to the Ryan family, I guess."

"Oh, no, he didn't sell it. We need more tea. You'll love this part!"

# A HOUSE LOST

*1* *853*

Harry Temple staggered through the open gates, his horse wandering behind, its reins dragging on the ground. Moments earlier he'd fallen into whiskey-induced sleep on its back and slipped off with a thud. Unhurt, he couldn't work out how to mount again, so walked. Or stumbled.

Ahead of him was Palmerston House glowing under the midnight moon, an extravagant show of his wealth and his greatest achievement. A mere three years ago he'd finished building it. A testament to how far a man can come with grit and courage. Dedicated to another man, his namesake.

"Remember him. He was a good man." The voice of his late father, William Temple, came from nowhere to confuse his drunken mind.

How often had his father recounted the tale of his own poverty-filled youth, of a group of older boys chasing him until, in terror, he'd run headlong into a young, impeccably dressed man. Instead of the blow he expected, William was lifted back to his feet and the group sent packing by Henry John Temple. Viscount Palmerston, the man who would become Prime Minister. Their shared surname inspired the labourer to do better for himself.

The horse nudged Harry, who swayed on his feet. His father would be proud of the mansion he'd created out of timber and limestone. He might not be a viscount, but this Henry John Temple believed in repaying a debt, and bestowing the name of Palmerston House on the grand homestead was his tribute on behalf of William.

Inside, his wife and daughter slept. House staff kept watch for his return, no doubt waiting with a glass of whiskey. Under the full March moon, life was as perfect as a man could want.

His legs buckled and Harry landed on his behind. The horse snorted and trotted off to stables beyond the recently dug, sprawling pond. Harry stared at Palmerston House through hazy vision. How would he tell them? How would his sweet Eleanor react to such news? What manner of a man throws away their life work, all for one more shot at a win?

Not an hour ago, he'd swallowed another glass of whiskey and fallen into the trap set by Eoin Ryan, the local timber merchant who'd supplied the mountain ash for the homestead. How many times had Eoin admired his property, even helping build parts of it? Their regular poker games were friendly. Sort of. Until tonight, with Eoin egging him on.

"One more hand. Ye can't lose."

Arms wrapped around himself, Harry rocked from side to side. He'd wagered Palmerston House. Twenty years growing his wealth, all gone in a game of poker. He'd been tricked and there was no way to change it.

---

*L*ess than a week later, Eleanor took their daughter and left. Her initial disbelief at his terrible news turned to fury and finally, despair. Harry gave her flowers. She pulled the petals off each rose whilst silent tears soaked her cheeks. He followed a trail of red and yellow through the house and out to the stables. Eleanor stroked the velvet cheek of her favourite horse as it snuffled at what was left of the bouquet.

"Can we keep the horses? The carriages?" Her voice was barely above a whisper.

He grimaced. "The lawyer will come in a fortnight to list everything. Whatever is here will belong to Eoin Ryan within a month."

Eleanor nodded without looking his way, holding out the remains of the flowers for him to take. Then, she threw her arms around him. Shocked, Harry squeezed her tightly, but when he would kiss her, she pushed herself away and ran back to the house.

After an evening at the hotel drinking, Harry came home to a silent house. No servants, for they left when he could no longer guarantee their employment. Somehow, Eleanor had packed a trunk, harnessed the horse she loved to the largest buggy, and left with their daughter.

He finished off a bottle of wine in the living room, cursing the name of Eoin Ryan with every mouthful. That consumed, he went in search of another. Legs wobbling, he made it to the cellar where he sank to the stone floor. Propped against the wall, he pulled the closest bottle from the rack and opened it by smashing the corked end.

Harry toasted himself. "To Henry John Temple, self-made man."

He spat out a mouthful of shards and threw the bottle at the far wall, where it disintegrated. The wine leeched into the stone, leaving a dark red stain.

"Like my blood. My blood you took from me, Eoin Ryan."

Instead of pooling, the wine trickled under the door to the next room, a small utility space. In there, Harry stowed things he didn't want Eleanor to know about. A stockpile of his favourite whiskey. Ammunition she refused to have in the house. His gun collection. She hated the room for its coldness. What she didn't know, what nearly everybody didn't know, was why it was so cold.

"Mother of God." Harry pushed himself back to his feet. "You might have my blood, Eoin Ryan, but you will not have my whiskey or my treasures."

How had he forgotten? With a hand on the wine rack to steady himself, Harry staggered to the door and pushed it open. Set into the far wall of the storage room was a small stone door. Heavy, very thick, and locked.

The key was where it always was. In plain sight of the family and he knew it was still there. Eleanor might have taken his beloved little girl and her most precious possessions, but not the key. He had a way to redeem himself. Hide everything before the lawyer arrived, then retrieve his goods and find his family.

*I*n the sober light of day, Harry's plans changed. It wasn't as simple as stockpiling everything of value. Some of the paintings he'd brought from England – at great expense – were too large to carry alone. The grandfather clock was simply too bulky. Instead, he spent the morning making a list in his diary of what he could hide.

There was a strange comfort writing in the leather bound book, given to him by Eleanor for Christmas. "So you remember every important thing." She'd known how much he liked order and this beautifully crafted diary went with him everywhere. From room to room he took inventory.

Small artwork

Silverware

Crystal decanters and glasses

Remaining jewellery and knick-knacks

After three rooms, he stopped to lean against a wall, eyes closed. If it hadn't been bad enough wagering Palmerston House, why on earth had he taken the bait on the contents? Eoin's calm offer came as chaos descended on Harry at the loss of his home.

*"I will give ye a chance to win it back. One more hand. Winner takes all. Ye win, then Palmerston House stays with ye. I win, I get everything inside and outside as well."*

*"The carriages? Eleanor's china?"*

*Eoin had pushed a fresh glass of whiskey across the table. "Or ye might win the lot back."*

It took all of ten seconds for Harry to drain the glass and nod.

*Fool.*

He opened his eyes. Well, he wasn't about to let Eoin Ryan walk in here and steal everything away. His head lifted, imagining Eleanor's delight seeing the treasures she loved so dearly. It might take months, waiting on the right tide, the optimum conditions for retrieval, but he'd do it. Then he'd find Eleanor and their daughter and they'd start anew.

Harry opened the diary and continued his list, smiling to himself. Nobody stole from Henry Temple and got away with it.

## 13

## A MODERN INTERLOPER

*I*n the third bedroom of Palmerston House, which once belonged to Martha, Bernie stood with one hand on the window. The front grounds of the property sprawled across an acre or so of perfect lawns and a mix of manicured English plants and native trees. Somehow it all blended into one magnificent garden.

Below, the circular, red gravel driveway was centred by a fountain. At night it changed colour. Quaint. At the far end was the wide entry, flanked by perpetually open gates. Built for horse and carriage. And prestige. Palmerston House was still the largest homestead in the region, and the oldest of any note. A car turned in, a white Lotus with the top down.

Bernie watched it drive around the fountain then pull over to one side. Christie Ryan. Squeezed onto the narrow back seat was a large dog. Looked like the one his headlights picked up last night near the cottage.

She climbed out, grabbing a small box from the front seat and then letting the dog out. Dark sunglasses masked her eyes but when she glanced up at the window, Bernie was certain she'd looked straight at him. He stared back. The moment passed. She went up the front stairs, the dog close behind.

He knew all about her. Miss Rich and Perfect. Might have lost her parents young but landed on her feet at her grandmother's Toorak mansion. Some sort of international make-up artist with a list of film credits to her name. He even knew she'd almost died a while ago in a boating accident caused by an old boyfriend.

*Pity he didn't do his job properly.*

Bernie turned his back on the window. There were still too many Ryans alive for his liking, even if one was an old lady and the other an interloper.

Bernie reached under his mattress and slipped out a dark brown, leather bound book. He sat at a small desk against the wall, running his hand over the old cover of the diary. He opened it to midway and read the neat cursive script aloud.

"Today the lawyer and his leeches spent six hours infecting my air. I sat on the verandah with a glass of something good. They even noted how much was left in the bottle and I laughed in their faces. And they warned me not to attempt to leave with anything. Little do they know. Damned be the Ryan family and all that follow them."

Bernie closed the diary and leaned back in his chair. "Damned be the Ryans. And all that follow them."

# 14

## DREAMS AND HOPES

On the porch behind the cottage, Martha and Thomas shared the love seat, hand in hand. The seat rocked gently back and forth and Martha sighed, her eyes half closed.

"What are you thinking?"

"How clever Christie and Martin are."

"Depends."

"No, it doesn't. Between them, they came up with putting this lovely seat here. Just like the one you used to have."

"My goodness, woman. You remember that old thing?"

Sideways, Martha flashed a knowing smile. "I remember us sitting here at night-time, after your parents went to bed and before you walked me home. More than once, in fact."

"Do you now." Thomas released her hand to put his arm around her shoulders. "I'm listening."

"I told you of my dreams. In the dark, it seemed alright to share my deepest wishes."

Thomas inched closer.

"In my youthful silliness, I wanted to roam the world and write wonderful stories about it. You believed in me."

"And you, my love," Thomas touched her face with his free hand

and she turned to him, "always told me I could paint. And it is the only reason I never stopped," He kissed her lips, just a soft caress. "So then, why did you not pursue your own dreams?"

Her eyes darkened, the way they always did when powerful emotions arose. Thomas kissed her again, a lingering, sensual reminder of their connection. When he sat back, her eyes were still dark, but now there was a subtle longing. For him, probably. For their lost past. Definitely.

"I did write, Thomas. But none of it ever made its way to a publisher. Too personal. Too..." She trailed off, looking away.

"Is that what's in the box you refuse to unpack?"

Martha shot him a glance. "Yes. And don't you go looking."

The familiar sound of the Lotus interrupted.

"We'll shelve this subject. For now. But be certain of this, Martha Blake, when Christie weds Martin and we are alone, you will talk to me about this."

The sudden arrival of Randall stopped any further discussion. The dog threw himself at Thomas' feet, tail wagging madly. Christie wasn't far behind and stopped abruptly when she saw Thomas and Martha.

"Whoops. Sorry to interrupt."

"You didn't," Martha said. Thomas squeezed her shoulder but she ignored him. "Whatever is Randall doing with you?"

"Should have mentioned we'd have a visitor for a few days," Thomas said.

"Yes, Thomas." Christie did a poor job of sounding cross. "We had lunch together and you already knew Martin was going away."

"Not my place to tell you."

"Where is he?" Martha asked, getting to her feet and stepping around Randall.

"Gone to help out at the camp he works at sometimes."

"When he's getting married in a few weeks! Does he have any idea how much preparation there still is?" Martha put her hands on her hips. "I don't even know if you're having a hen's night here in River's End, or going back to Melbourne to have it with whoever will be your chief bridesmaid."

"Auntie, I've just heard all of this from Elizabeth, who has scolded me for being disorganised. So, I'll use the time Martin's away to sort out lots of outstanding details and the most important one needs sorting right this minute." She held out both hands to Martha.

Unable to stay cross at Christie ever, Martha took her hands.

"Okay, Martha Blake, I don't know about a hen's night, but I won't be needing a chief bridesmaid because I want a matron of honour. Will you do this for me? Please?"

Martha squeezed Christie's hands, eyes shining. "Are you sure? Wouldn't you prefer someone your own age—"

"Goodness me, woman. Say yes." Thomas surrounded them both in a bear hug. "She'll do it, Christie."

For once, Martha didn't object to Thomas speaking on her behalf.

---

*C*hristie sat cross-legged on her bed as she texted Martin. He'd arrived safely at the camp in spite of taking his old motor-cycle and having to navigate deep into the Otway Ranges. If anything, it was a surprise he had phone coverage.

Randall appeared in the doorway, ears raised.

"You can sleep in here if you want. Martin will be back soon."

"Or he can sleep in with us." Thomas stuck his head around the door, hand reaching for Randall's head. "Either way, dog, you won't be lonely."

Randall lay down between the two bedrooms and Christie and Thomas laughed.

"I came to see if you'd like a glass of something? Port? Whiskey?" Thomas asked.

"I'm fine thanks. I might spend a bit of time sketching some ideas up for the salon. But, once Barry gets things underway, I'll need all the decorative pieces."

"Artwork?"

"I wonder where I could get some. Maybe some prints from the internet?"

Thomas kept his face stern, which made Christie laugh some more. "Or I could try painting some."

"Stop now or you'll have two cranky artists to deal with once Martin hears about it." Thomas glanced at the access door above him.

"There's not a lot up there now." Christie got to her feet and joined him. "How long since you've been up there, Thomas?"

"A long time." He turned to stare at Christie. "What is there?"

"An old armchair near the window. There's a small blanket on its back, made me wonder if anyone would sit there in the sunshine and read."

"Anything else?"

"The trunk where I found... you know." She didn't want to upset Thomas with old wounds from his past and his eyes flickered down and then back to hers.

"Tell me about the trunk. My parents had no such item."

"Old. Very old in fact and quite beautifully crafted out of some kind of hardwood. You'd know better than I do. Curved top. Would you like me to bring it down?"

"You like your mysteries, Christie. I'm surprised you've not put your mind to why those letters and rings were locked away here. In an empty house."

"Empty? I thought... well, I assumed you lived here. After your parents moved."

"You mean after I married Frannie?" Thomas turned around, keeping his voice down as he gazed toward the kitchen where Martha was singing softly to herself as she followed her nightly routine of cleaning down the table and benches. "The day my parents left was the last day I stepped foot in here. Helped them move out, then turned my back on the cottage until I came to retrieve my letters from a certain obstinate young woman."

"I was rather persistent." Christie put her hand on his arm. "Thomas, if nobody lived here, who on earth stowed the trunk in the attic?"

"Maybe it doesn't matter anymore."

"Perhaps not. Tomorrow I'll get it down, just to take a look in proper daylight. Okay?"

He nodded, eyes still on the kitchen. "Sure you don't want a nightcap?"

"I'm sure. Are you okay?"

"Might give my bride a hand. Goodnight."

Thomas wandered away and after a moment Randall followed.

*It still hurts him.*

Frannie's deception helped keep Thomas and Martha apart for decades. She shot a look up at the access door. All of a sudden, she really did want to get the trunk down.

---

*M*artha lay beside her sleeping husband, listening to him breathe, with a sense of wonder that occasionally filled her. A lifetime apart might have been a dream. A bad dream going on for too long. She'd lived well, a happy enough life in Ireland, with yearly travel to different parts of the world. Being here, right here where their lives belonged, was more than she'd dare hope for. A miracle happened in the form of a beautiful, determined young woman. Her great-niece, Christie.

Eyes open, Martha smiled. The discovery of a relative was a joyful one indeed. Dorothy shared nothing with Martha over the years, apart from one brief discussion when their parents died. How sad not to have known Dorothy's daughter, Rebecca, and her husband Julian. Lost so young and tragically, leaving their beloved little daughter to the mercies of her cold grandmother.

*Why am I thinking about this?*

Martha turned over and closed her eyes tightly.

She knew why. She'd heard Thomas and Christie earlier. Only a snippet of a conversation but one with the name of the woman who once was her own best friend. Frannie. Afraid to hear more, Martha had begun to sing to herself, a song from her childhood. Dorothy used to love the song and sometimes joined in. She missed her sister. The one of her childhood, not the one who'd ripped her world apart.

Why were they talking about Frannie? Thomas never spoke her name and Martha always thought it was because the truth had cut him so deeply. But perhaps it was because he didn't want to discuss her with Martha. Yet there were many unanswered questions, and if only he'd talk to her about his decision to marry the woman who'd helped Dorothy destroy their love, then maybe she'd find a way to forgive.

Forgive who?

*Frannie and Dorothy.*

But a little voiced nagged at Martha. Those two woman might have conspired and set things in motion, but ultimately, she was the one who'd walked away from Thomas. Over many years she'd found a certain peace. Acceptance. Except tonight the feelings flooded back. Thomas moaned in his sleep. Was he dreaming about Frannie? As if sensing Martha's growing distress, Randall came to her side of the bed, his muzzle seeking her hand. She stroked his velvet ears, forcing the emotions back into their box.

## 15

---

## LOCKED

*B*efore dawn, shoes dangling from his fingers, Bernie headed down the staircase, taking great care to avoid the creaky boards he'd identified and memorised yesterday. He figured he had half an hour, perhaps less, to explore. Once the house stirred he'd have no hope, unless everyone went out at the same time.

In darkness, he reached the kitchen and stood for a moment in the doorway. He could just see the neat row of keys hanging beside the doorway on the other side. Six if his memory was correct, based on the quick look he'd had. From a pocket he took a small torch and flashed its light on the keys. Six. Of course he was right. Only the master set was missing, presumably with Elizabeth.

On closer inspection, four of them were modern keys.

*Useless.*

One might work, with its elongated teeth, but it was tagged as the garage key. Thank goodness the final one had potential and he dropped this into a pocket in case he needed it later. He held his breath, listening to the house. Still no movement but he needed to hurry up. Bernie opened the door and stepped through.

It was cooler on this side. He was in a narrow hallway. In half a dozen strides, he reached the top of a set of stairs, so he took them, wincing when they groaned under his weight. From the bottom it was merely an arm's length to another door. He expected it to be locked, but it wasn't, opening with an alarming creak to reveal a cellar with wine racks.

He left the door open behind himself. On the opposite wall was yet another door and again, unlocked. Harry Temple sure liked his doors. This room was small. Boxes and shelves cluttered it. It was cold in here. The shelves on the furthest wall were a complete unit, housing a collection of boxes. One by one, he moved them off. He tested the weight of the unit and then, grunting, lifted it enough to bring it forward on one side.

Behind it was another blank wall. He swore under his breath and leaned against the wall, head down. The plaster moved against his body and he reached a hand out to feel where he thought the door might be. A thin straight line gave way as he pushed on it, plaster falling to the ground in small pieces. Bit by bit, he worked at it until he found a keyhole.

Once it was clear of debris, he took the key out and slid it into the keyhole. It didn't fit. Not even close. He moved the unit back against the wall and replaced the boxes. This was just a reconnaissance anyway. Once he had the house to himself, he'd find a way to get through it.

## 16

# GOING FORWARD. LOOKING BACK.

The first rays of sunlight woke Martha from fitful sleep and for a few moments, she lay with her eyes closed, listening to the morning calls of the resident magpie family. Thomas was up already; she'd heard the tap turn on in the kitchen to fill the kettle. With daylight came a more logical thought process and by the time she opened her eyes Martha was past her night-time fears. What mattered was the here and now, not the events of half a century ago. She was happy and nothing would change that.

"Did I disturb you?" Thomas watched her from the doorway holding two steaming cups. "I was going to tiptoe to the porch if you were asleep still."

"As long as you bring me coffee, you are always welcome to disturb me." Martha sat up, smiling when Thomas came over to sit on the edge of the bed.

He leaned over and kissed her cheek. "Then I shall make sure I do so every day. The earlier you're awake, the longer we have together." He handed her a cup, and sipped from his own. "Christie's long gone."

"Running? And Randall?"

"In the garden. Shall we get a dog?"

"Where do we find one like him?"

"Good point."

"Besides, he's over here almost as much as with Martin. And when they go on their honeymoon, he'll be staying again."

"They're going on a honeymoon?" Thomas put his cup on Martha's bedside table. "Since when?"

"Well, most newlyweds do." Martha put her cup beside his and shuffled in the bed. Thomas stood up to let her legs swing over the side. "There's a travel agent in Green Bay."

Thomas offered her a hand and once she was on her feet, put both arms around her. "Are you suggesting we go for a drive?"

She gazed up at him. "I am. After all, I'm the matron of honour, so getting some brochures on honeymoon locations is surely one of my jobs. And I'd like to get some ideas for wedding gifts, because I've already been asked by half a dozen people."

"What are we getting them?"

"Let me have a shower and we'll work on it."

"I might cook us some breakfast in that case. Sustenance for the day ahead." Thomas released Martha, collected both cups, and wandered out as she straightened the bed.

On his bedside table was a photograph from their wedding. The two of them exchanging vows on the end of the jetty.

*How I love you.*

This wedding of Christie and Martin's was yet another thing to be grateful for. Her life changed for the better the day she met her great-niece, and she intended to do everything to make Christie's special day as wonderful as her own was.

---

*E*lizabeth prepared breakfast trays for Charlotte and Bernie. Cooking for two was no trouble at all, but Elizabeth loved to prepare beautiful meals no matter what the time of day, with special touches to show her appreciation for their patronage. Most Palmerston House guests were tourists, here for a night or two as they explored the town and beach, or drove up the mountains. But long term patrons were special. She'd get to know their likes and dislikes and be able to fuss over them a little more as they became part of her extended family.

With the upcoming wedding, she was expecting a full house. Christie had friends in Melbourne she would invite and, most likely, would stay here as well. The prospect of the place being filled was delightful.

*As long as Angus is here.*

She pushed the thought away. He had business to attend and would be back in time to walk Christie down the aisle. Well, down the path to the pond.

Elizabeth picked up Charlotte's tray before seeing her at the doorway, peering in as though not sure of herself.

*Like you used to be.*

Whatever was bothering Charlotte, Elizabeth was not about to let it get any worse.

"Well, good morning, dear." Elizabeth put the tray down again. "You know you're welcome in here anytime. Day or night."

"I didn't know if you were alone." Charlotte stepped in, her eyes darting around the room. "I mean, I didn't want to interrupt if you were... umm talking to anyone."

"Just me, myself and I. And now you. I was about to bring this up, so would you like it in the dining room? Or perhaps outside? It's nice this morning."

"Actually, I might eat out on the verandah with my book, but no need for you to take it."

"Well, it's warm under the cloche and the kettle just boiled, so would you like a coffee to take with you?"

Charlotte smiled at last. "Sounds lovely." She pulled the tray across the table and lifted the cloche a bit. "Those eggs look delicious."

"Good. This will just be a moment."

"Did I see Christie driving out yesterday, with Randall in the car?" Charlotte replaced the cloche.

"Oh yes, you would have. He's staying at the cottage until Martin comes home. Now, here you are, I'll make a bit of space for it on the corner."

"Thank you, Elizabeth. I didn't realise Martin was away?"

"I think a few days at most."

Charlotte lifted the tray. "Well, I don't think I can wait much longer to eat this. All those wonderful smells!"

"Enjoy. I might take Bernie's up to his room seeing as he hasn't been down yet." Elizabeth picked up the other tray and followed Charlotte out of the kitchen.

*A*t last!

On the other side of the door to the cellar, Bernie pressed his ear against the timber, willing the women to keep walking. Their voices faded and with a cautious turn of the handle he opened the door a fraction. Through the crack there was no sign of movement so he swung it enough to fit through.

For more than an hour he'd been stuck on the other side, afraid to go back down the creaky steps and tormented by enticing smells of bacon and coffee. Much nicer than the insipid tea he'd shared with Elizabeth last time.

The last two minutes of the long wait were worth every second. Martin Blake was away and what's more, the dog was away as well. Time to have another look around the cliff.

Approaching footsteps dragged him from his thoughts and he pulled the key from his pocket. He threw it back over its hook and grabbed the first thing on the counter he saw. A teapot.

"Oh there you are!" Elizabeth carried a tray.

"Morning. I went for a walk and popped in to see if I might persuade you to share a cup of your lovely tea with me." He put the teapot down.

"Of course. But look, here is your breakfast, so take this and find a spot in the dining room. Well, any spot as nobody else is there." She handed him the tray. "I'll brew a pot and bring you a cup in a few moments."

"Sounds wonderful. Thanks, Mrs White."

"Elizabeth. Off you go."

She turned to the stove and picked up the kettle to refill as Bernie left with his tray. At the door he glanced back. Elizabeth stared at the other door. No, not the door. The key rack, where the key he'd so carelessly thrown there still swung from side to side.

17
―――

# THE ATTIC AND THE STATION

*S*tep by rickety step, Christie climbed the old pull-down
ladder to the attic. Below her in the hallway, Randall
whined. "Seriously, dude. I'm okay. Go hop on my bed." Once through
the open access door, she sat on the floor and peered back at the dog.
He still stared at her, his tail flicking at the end. Well, she wouldn't be
long and then she'd give him a nice long brush.

Last time she'd been up here, inappropriately dressed in the
narrow-skirted dress from Gran's funeral, she'd used the torch on her
phone. This time, she knew about the light switch to one side of the
long workbench where Thomas once kept his paints and brushes. On
her feet again, she followed his earlier instructions and was rewarded
with a surprisingly bright light from high in the pitched roof.

She checked the workbench in case there was anything left behind,
but Thomas had been thorough when he'd packed his belongings all
those years ago. He'd told her there was nothing to find, nothing of
his anyway.

It hadn't occurred to Christie to wait until Thomas and Martha
returned from their shopping trip, or see if anyone was around to give
her a hand. Almost as soon as the old four wheel drive was out of
earshot, she was on the ladder.

The atmosphere of the attic was different from her first visit. Then, with the rain thundering down on the metal roof, and dull light through the dusty window creating an aura around the old armchair beside it, she'd wondered if she'd been sent back in time. Perhaps she had. To a forgotten place in the 1960s, harbouring spiders rather than a talented young artist.

She stood at the window, brushing some grime away. The morning sun highlighted the vibrancy of the garden. Trimmed trees and bushes, flowers, pathways. A lovely meandering wonderland. Hers for a while and now, for the first time ever, owned by a Blake. The cottage might have been built for the Blake family to reside in – generations of stationmasters – but it was owned by the Ryans and eventually the only property left in River's End with a connection to the once dominant family of the region.

Randall yipped, checking on her. "Soon, buddy." The trunk was where she'd left it last November, pulled far enough out from below the lowest part of the roof for her to be able to open it. She'd remembered it was well-made but now, with proper lighting, saw she'd underestimated its quality.

It was in nearly perfect condition, apart from a few scratch marks around the keyhole. She touched these, remembering how careful she'd been when she'd used the skeleton key left by Gran to open it. How she'd lifted the lid, holding her breath in anticipation of what might be inside. At first, seeing there was only an old shoebox, she'd been disappointed. Yet its contents led to the reunion of Thomas and Martha, and the end of the fifty-year-old mystery.

Well, now she had a new mystery. Why was the trunk here? Who hid it in the attic, and when? Christie tested its weight, deciding it was light enough for her to carry. Now she had to work out how to get it down the steps safely without dropping it, or losing her own footing.

*T*he old police station in River's End was a one person outfit with the station at the front and a one bedroom residence accessed through a common door. Until thirty or forty years ago it was a family home on the edge of the little shopping precinct. When it came up for sale, it was split almost in half and redesigned with a couple of offices, a counter, lock-up, and not much else on one side, and accommodation on the other. Just the basics. Nobody wanted to work there. Not because of the relative isolation from other police, but because one bedroom meant a single person or couple only, no kids.

When the job came up yet again, Trev Sibbritt took a drive to River's End and fell in love with the town. He was single then and single now, so the little place suited him well. Despite the low crime rate his days were busy as he serviced a wide area outside the town.

In all the years he'd been here, the most crime was earlier this year when Derek Hobbs sent his thug, Rupert, to shake up River's End and specifically, Christie Ryan, in his warped attempt to get her land. Trev managed the situation, but only with the help from the locals, who rallied on the beach in a storm to bring Christie, Martin and Randall back to safety. He'd never been prouder of his job than that night.

His early morning duties done, Trev wandered down to the letterbox with a coffee in hand. From the outside there were few signs this was not still a family home. In a large garden with roses, a couple of gum trees, and a veggie patch at the back, only the signs 'Police' at the beginning of the driveway and on the building itself, plus the heavy duty security bars on the doors and windows, gave away its purpose.

The letterbox was empty, so Trev leaned on the fence to watch the street as shopkeepers opened their doors, sweeping the pavement and calling to each other. The morning routine. Quick footsteps approached and he turned his head. It was Charlotte, hurrying along, her eyes flicking across to the other side of the road. When she noticed Trev, the oddest expression crossed her face and she slowed.

"Morning, Charlotte."

She stopped a few feet away. "Hi, Trevor."

"Nice day for a walk."

"I'm not walking. I mean, I'm not just going for a walk. I have to see someone." She glanced up the road, across at the far corner. Trev followed her gaze. Bernie Cooper was talking to George outside the jewellers. Was it George or Bernie who had her interest?

"Like a coffee? I'm about to get another."

Her eyes shot back to his and her expression softened. "Thanks. But I have somewhere to go."

"I see."

"No, really, I umm, er, I'm going to see Christie."

"Want a lift?"

She smiled. "Two good legs. Mum always said use them, or lose them. But thanks. Really."

"Your mum sounds like a sensible lady."

Charlotte's smile disappeared. "I've got to go."

Her eyes went back to the corner, then to Trev's and for an instance, something like a silent request for help was in those gorgeous eyes. Something wasn't right and he opened his mouth to ask her but she started walking and the moment was gone.

He watched her until she disappeared around the other corner, heading to the bridge. Had he imagined the look in her eyes? Bernie Cooper had gone into the jewellers with George. Might pay to run a bit more of a background check on him.

"I'm particularly interested in any artefacts from the 1800s." Bernie wandered around the jewellery shop.

From behind the glass counter, George Campbell glanced up. "Any particular decade?"

"Dunno. About 50s to 60s? Isn't that around the time the town began to grow?"

"Palmerston House was built in 1850, but I imagine you know this already."

"Why do you say that?"

"Aren't you staying there? Elizabeth talks to all her guests about the history of the building." George put both hands on the counter, tilting his head slightly. "You're a photographer?"

"Small towns. Of course, everyone knows everyone's business." Bernie smiled. "I am. This town intrigues me. Still has old charm and some of the buildings are in virtually original condition. This shop for example," he waved a hand at the front windows, "is almost like stepping back in time. Nothing modern or cheap, just quality from ceiling to floor."

A small smile crept onto George's face. "Thank you for noticing. Most people these days seem to want the latest watch or the cheapest ring. But they don't last."

"I'll bet yours do. Not that I'm a betting man, but what you make probably gets passed down through each generation."

"Indeed. Now, to your request. Are you interested in buying, or photographing? Either is perfectly fine of course, but it might help to know."

"Bit of both. I always keep… mementos, if you like, of places I visit. If you had a keepsake of some sort from those years, I'd be most interested in obtaining it. I do like a fob watch."

"I'm not an antique dealer but may have a couple of pieces of interest. Let me find my spectacles and I'll show you. Please excuse me a moment."

As George opened the door to the back room, Bernie wandered off again. There was a grandfather clock in a corner. He stood a few feet away, admiring its design. Dark mahogany inlaid with gold, taller than his six feet and a bit. Its heavy pendant swung and he watched it go left, right. Left, right.

"This one isn't for sale, I'm afraid." George joined Bernie.

"It must be worth a mint. Surely, for the right price?"

George shuffled forward and ran his hand down one side of the clock. "There is no right price, she belongs with me."

"Family heirloom?"

"Something along those lines."

"When was it made? It's English."

"You know your clocks. She is, but there is really nothing else to say. I've put some rather interesting pieces on the counter, if you'd care to join me there?"

Bernie scowled as George made his way to the counter. There was something about this clock. Something he needed to understand.

# 18

# THE COTTAGE

*a*ll the way up the hill to the cottage, Charlotte replayed her brief conversation with Trev. He was all too good at seeing through people. Seeing through her. Much as she wanted to deny it, they had a connection.

For now, her focus was Bernie Cooper and what he was up to. She hadn't planned to follow him this morning, it just happened he'd left the house as she came downstairs and something made her run back up, grab her bag, and take off after him. He didn't have his cameras, which made her suspicious. When he headed straight for George's shop, the hairs on the back of her neck stood up. The only reason he'd have to see George was to ask questions about the past.

The truth was she'd rather have accepted Trev's offer of coffee. Sat with him in his small kitchen or wandered around his garden. He was a simple man in the very best sense. A person with strong values, who saw things as they were, without the cloud of suspicion and doubt colouring her world. He'd do anything for those he cared about and was strong, inside and out. A good man she'd love to know better.

*But you lied to him.*

What possessed her to say she was visiting Christie, of all people?

She reached the road leading to the cottage and hesitated. This was a woman she admired on a lot of levels, but they weren't exactly friends. Acquaintances who'd been through a bad experience. Bonded in an odd way. How would she explain her appearance on Christie's doorstep? Charlotte glanced back toward River's End. What if Trev asked about the visit? She didn't want to keep lying to him. With a sigh, she kept walking.

This was her first visit to the famed cottage. She'd heard all the stories about Christie inheriting it from her grandmother, coming for her funeral and falling in love with Martin. And she'd been here in River's End when Christie's ex – Derek Hobbs – damaged the yacht and almost claimed Christie's life. What a way to get to know people!

Charlotte turned into the driveway and stopped to admire the beautiful cottage. Freshly painted, the roof restored and an inviting path leading to a pretty front door, it was a picture. No wonder everyone talked about it. The garden celebrated the early signs of spring with new leaves on deciduous trees, jonquils and daffodils popping up everywhere, and, in what looked like a new birdbath, rainbow lorikeets taking turns washing themselves.

*How peaceful this is.*

"Aagh!"

Thud.

Charlotte raced to the front door and pounded on it. "Christie! Martha?"

Nothing. She turned the door knob but it was locked. She peered through the glass panels. Randall stood over a jean-clad leg, his tail down. The rest of the person was around the corner.

"Christie! It's Charlotte!"

Randall bounded to the door, whining.

Charlotte raced around to the back of the cottage and onto the small porch. This door was unlocked and she pushed it open.

"Christie?"

There was a moan from the other end of the cottage and Charlotte followed the sound, met halfway along the hallway by a frantic Randall. "I'm here."

Her heart sank at the sight of Christie, lying motionless on the floor.

Charlotte dropped to her knees next to Christie. She breathed an audible sigh of relief to see her eyes open and recognition in them. Randall threw himself on the ground at Christie's feet.

"I want you to stay still for now. Can you speak?"

Christie opened her mouth but nothing came out. Her face was pale and eyes distressed. Charlotte put a hand on her back and rubbed in slow, circular movements.

"I think you're winded. The air will come back but you've got to stop panicking. Now, little gasps, okay. You want the oxygen in a bit at a time to open up your lungs. Understand me?"

With a nod, Christie began a series of small attempts at sucking air in. Charlotte kept rubbing her back, whilst taking her pulse with her other hand. "When you get some air, just shallow but longer breaths, yup, like those. Good girl."

Charlotte adjusted herself to sit cross-legged and Randall moved immediately to her side, dropping his head onto her lap. "Once you're breathing okay we'll sit you up, but take as long as you need." She glanced up at the open access door. A shape was just visible, something like a large box. "You weren't trying to lift something down on your own?"

"Imp... important," Christie managed to gasp.

"Right. And what if it fell on top of you? And I wasn't here? I think you are a bit more important."

"Sorry." Her voice was a little stronger.

"What would I tell Martin?"

Christie's eyes widened.

"His bride-to-be was squashed under a box because she didn't have the common sense to get someone to help her. Okay, let's sit you up." Charlotte supported Christie's arm as she gradually sat upright, then leaned against the wall. For a moment her eyes closed and then she drew a normal breath, expelling it slowly. Randall wagged his tail at her, but stayed where he was.

"Thanks."

"Better?"

Christie nodded, prodding herself for damage.

"I'm not about to tell you how lucky you are. Only winding yourself, not breaking bones or hitting your head. Mind you, I think a proper check-up is in order."

"No. I'm okay." Christie grasped Charlotte's hand. "Thank you. Thank you so much."

"What's so important about the box?"

"It's a trunk. The one I found Thomas' letters in."

"I don't know much about it, only about him losing Martha for most of their lives and then you reunited them somehow. Even so, if it's been up there all this time, why try to manage it on your own now?"

"Because Thomas finally wants to see it and I'd rather he doesn't go climbing this old ladder."

"So, we'll get it down between us. But safely."

"You'll help me?"

Charlotte rolled her eyes and after gently moving Randall's head, got to her feet. "I'm not leaving you alone at the moment so I might as well do something. But I want to see you steady on your feet, or we're heading to a doctor."

"You're a doctor." Christie let Charlotte help her up.

"I'm a psychiatrist, not a practising MD."

"But you have to qualify as one first."

"Stop arguing. Okay, are you dizzy? Any vision problems." She watched Christie's face closely.

"Do you know how bossy you are?" Christie smiled. "I feel okay, just a bit sore where I landed. Thank you, Charlotte, I thought I was dying."

"Not nice being winded. Did it myself falling off a horse as a kid. Are you fine to come to the kitchen? I'll get you a drink and keep an eye on you for a bit."

"I'm fine, really, but a coffee would be nice, if you'd join me?"

Christie led the way along the hallway, her steps deliberate but steady. "Poor Randall, I seem to give him so many scares."

Randall padded along behind Charlotte.

"He's fine. You sit for a few minutes, please. Point me in the right direction and I'll make us a coffee."

# 19

## TRAVEL PLANS AND DISCOVERIES

"*O*ur grandson doesn't have a passport, so it must be in Australia." Thomas insisted for the second time, hoping the rather keen young man sitting opposite at the travel agents would listen this time. So far, almost every honeymoon destination in the world had been offered, except something suitable.

"It won't take long to get a passport, so how about New Zealand? It's only a few hours away and Queenstown is gorgeous at this time of year."

Martha put her hand onto Thomas' before he could get up, leaned forward a little and smiled across the table. "Dear, what about Uluru? Or perhaps Broome?"

"Oh. I can look at those." The young man clicked on his computer. "Here's an idea! What about Lizard Island? It's perfect for couples and there's a special package... no?"

"No. Not Lizard Island. Or New Zealand, Rome, Paris – which is very lovely by the way – nor Alaska." Thomas kept his voice under control, aware of increasing pressure from Martha's hand. "Now, as Mrs Blake suggested, what is available for Uluru or Broome?"

A few moments later with a pile of brochures under Thomas' arm, he and Martha stepped out of the travel agents. "Do they not teach young people how to listen these days?"

Martha smiled and nodded toward a cafe across the road. "Perhaps we need some morning tea. I could use a coffee."

"Are you telling me I'm being grumpy?"

"Never."

They crossed over and went inside. After ordering coffees and some delicious looking cupcakes, Thomas ushered Martha to a table near the window. "This shouldn't be so difficult."

"At least we've got lots to look at. I rather enjoy brochures."

"Truth be told, they'd probably prefer to sail off down the coast."

"I don't know."

"You're worried about Christie?"

Martha nodded. "She doesn't say anything but I feel she's reliving that night sometimes. How terrified she must have been."

"How brave she was." Thomas took Martha's hand. "She'll be right once she's back on board. Not that the dog will leave land again, if I have my way."

"I wish…"

"What, my love?"

"I'm being silly." Martha looked at the steam rising from her coffee. "I've lived two lives, it feels. Both matter."

"You miss Ireland?"

"Probably all this talk of travel. So, if you were Martin, where would you whisk your new wife for a romantic honeymoon? In Australia." Martha sipped her coffee, squeezing Thomas' hand like a lifeline.

"My cabin up the mountain."

"Oh dear. Any other suggestions?"

"A long time ago, when Martin was off somewhere and before Randall came along, I went to Sydney. Stayed on the harbour and spent a few days exploring the art galleries. I think he'd like that."

Martha's face lit up. "Perfect! We'll find them a wonderful hotel with a view of the harbour and send them off to the theatre, or whatever might be on. Did we get a brochure?" She freed up her hand and flicked through the pile. "Might need to pop back in and see the young man again."

Thomas groaned.

"Which I will do. You, my husband, can head off to the department store and start making a gift list."

He groaned again and Martha giggled. "I love you."

"Are you certain? Sending an old man gift shopping alone is not what I'd call an act of love."

"And I'll be all of five minutes behind you. Or you could go back to the travel agents?" Martha's eyes twinkled.

"Shopping it is. But if I buy anything before you arrive, don't complain." He captured her hand again and lifted it to his lips.

---

"*I* love the cottage, Christie. This kitchen is gorgeous."

"I had lots of help from Barry. Once he knew I wanted the old-world feel to remain, but with modern appliances and an improved view of the garden, he got going."

"Well, it's a credit to you both."

"Thanks. Now poor Barry wishes he'd never met me."

Charlotte finished making the coffee and settled opposite Christie at the original kitchen table. "How so?"

"I met with him this morning at my new salon. I may have scared him with my Zen concepts. Some rooms for private massage and personal beauty visits. Then, out the back I want a really cool area, a bit like a resort. Somewhere women can get together and talk, or just lay in the sun, or relax. Around a spa."

"Well, it sounds nice. I'm not really a spa sort of person, but they seem popular."

"I shall invite you to the VIP opening and you can try out some stuff. Then tell me you don't do spas." Christie grinned.

Charlotte shook her head. "Wasted on me. How are you feeling now?"

"Hurts a bit around the ribs, and where I landed on my thigh, but nothing bad. Promise. And if it gets worse, I'll see a doctor. You know… a real one."

"Ha ha. I'll remember that if you ever need psychiatric help." Charlotte smiled to herself, finishing the coffee. Christie didn't respond. Her thoughts were elsewhere and Charlotte watched her closely. "That was a joke."

"Oh, I know. But, would you see me that way. I mean, if I needed to talk about… concerns."

"Of course. Well, as a friend. Do you want to chat now?"

"Now? No, but thanks. I'm not sure if I even need to but I trust you. If I do need to."

"Okay. Would you like a hand with the trunk? Before you answer… do you have a decent ladder anywhere?"

*B*y the time the four wheel drive turned into the driveway, Charlotte had been gone for an hour. As it turned out, bringing the trunk down was not a difficult task with two people working together and Christie standing partway up a new and very stable aluminium ladder. Charlotte refused to let her back into the attic, climbing up there with a confidence Christie found surprising.

"Wanted to be a boy growing up." She stuck her head down from the access hatch to grin at Christie's expression. "Love climbing."

Five minutes later, the trunk was in the hallway, hatch closed, and the ladder back in the garage. Charlotte helped Christie carry it into the lounge room and place it in front of the fireplace. They stood back.

"It's very old." Charlotte took her phone out. "May I take a photo? I know someone in antiques and she might be able to shed some light on its history… unless you'd rather I don't?"

"Go ahead. I've only seen it once before and have no idea where it came from or how it got up there in the first place. Now, I'm not even sure Thomas will be pleased with me."

Charlotte took photos from a few angles, then patted Christie's arm. "He'd never be cross with you."

She thought about those words later, as Randall rushed to the front door to wait for it to open, his tail wagging. Thomas most certainly had been cross with her in the past, when she'd chased him along a country road and virtually demanded he return with her to see Martha after almost fifty years. He didn't know her then, didn't love her the way she knew he did now. But what if this trunk stirred up too many painful memories?

"Hello!" His voice called through the front door. "Left my keys behind."

Christie hurried to open the front door, blinking at the pile of brochures he had in his arms. "Whatever—"

"Going to Paris and Ireland gave me the travel bug." He winked as he stepped aside to let Martha in first.

"Oh, Thomas." Martha chided him gently and he grinned. "I could use some tea," she told Christie in a tone of voice that made her wonder what they'd been up to.

"I'll put the kettle on."

"Thank you, dear. I might change my shoes."

"And I might find a spot to put these." Thomas commented a bit loudly. "Can you close the door, dog? No?"

Almost at the kitchen, Christie glanced over her shoulder with a smile. Randall sat at his feet, head tilted to listen. Martha had vanished. She refilled the kettle and flicked it on, then took three cups out. It was a day for hot drinks and conversation, so it seemed.

"Oh my!"

Christie frowned at Martha's exclamation, and peered into the hallway. Martha stared into the lounge room, her hands on either side of her face.

*The trunk.*

She hadn't moved by the time Christie, and Thomas – who emerged from the dining room – reached her.

"What is it?" Thomas put his hand on her shoulder then followed her line of sight. "Christie. Is that what I think it is?"

# 20

## AN ANGRY MAN

*B*ernie threw himself into his car and slammed the door. Then reopened it and slammed it again for good measure. With a scowl, he tried to ignore the appearance at the window of a startled woman inside the shop he was parked outside. A real estate agency. He drove off as she stepped onto the footpath. He glanced in his rear vision mirror. Didn't she know how stupid she looked at her age with red streaked black hair and too tight clothes? He wanted to yell at her. Yell at George. Yell at the thieving Ryans.

Instead, he gripped the steering wheel and followed a narrow road up a hill.

*Calm down.*

It was bad enough Lottie was against him. At least she'd behave herself. Keep her thoughts to herself. Did she believe he'd go back to Queensland and harm her mother? He quite liked her mother, more than Lottie. No opinions or demands.

He found himself at the top of the cliff outside Martin Blake's house. The motor off, he sat and watched the ocean. Decades ago, his ancestors arrived here on this ocean, disembarking only a few hours away. With hope in their hearts, they'd settled in River's End, hard-working people who'd made this town what it was today.

*And been ruined for their effort.*

Everything stolen by Eoin Ryan.

The grandfather clock was a tangible link to Harry and Eleanor. He needed to read the diary again to understand how it got into the hands of George Campbell's family. Was it a gift? Or another theft? The old man had clammed right up about it so Bernie had backed off because he wanted to photograph it, take a much closer look. Keep everything nice until he'd done so.

The incessant cawing of seagulls bore into his thoughts and he turned the ignition key. Before driving away, his eyes were drawn to Martin's house. Where did the Blakes fit into all of this? Were they even here back then? Apart from some sketchy information about the railway line servicing the timber industry, he knew little. Another bit of the puzzle. He nosed his car down the hill.

When he drove through the gates of Palmerston House, its beauty kicked him in the gut. Elizabeth White was a good caretaker. She'd lavished love onto the property and kept it from falling into disrepair after its long years boarded up. How could anyone leave here? He slowed the car to a crawl. He'd live here forever. Treasure its gracious rooms and splendid gardens as Harry Temple once did.

Once the car was parked, he hurried inside, glad nobody saw him. All he wanted was to open the diary. Somewhere in there he'd find out what happened to the grandfather clock and maybe work out how to get it back again.

# 21

# HIS SOLEMN VOW

*1* *853*

    Tomorrow, Eoin Ryan and his lawyer would be here again, this time to take his keys. Throw him out. Ruin his life. So they thought, but every waking moment of the past week saw Harry a little bit happier as his plans fell into place.

Most of the precious things he'd secreted were hidden before they'd come here the first time. Except two. Eleanor's timber trunk, and the longcase clock. The trunk would come with him but not the clock.

Harry opened the front door at the first knock, swinging it wide to let Sam and Walter Brown through. Hardworking brothers, they'd made their way to the sea instead of the goldfields. They'd helped Harry out with his secret project as he'd built Palmerston House, and in return he'd gifted them a small parcel of land. He trusted them.

"Lads. You weren't seen?"

"No, sir," Walter's glance went to the clock against the wall. "But, it is too fine for us. Let me sell it for you and bring you the takings."

"It's not for sale, lad. Remember that please. Once in your family it stays there and for this I need your solemn vow."

Walter and Sam nodded at each other, then Sam spoke. "As long as our family lives, it will never be sold."

"Let's get it out onto the dray. No point risking being seen."

After wrapping the clock in blankets from his own bed, with great care and a fair degree of groaning, the three men carried it out to the waiting dray. Laid gently onto a bed of hay, it was covered by an old sail and tied in securely.

Harry sat on the top step and watched until the boys were out of sight. It hurt. A perfect timekeeper, the longcase clock was admired by all who saw it and he never would again.

*Nor will Eoin.*

Now, there was only the trunk.

---

*A*t exactly one minute past midnight, Eoin Ryan pounded on the front door of Palmerston House.

Shocked and a bit drunk, Harry stumbled down the staircase, brain hazy. They weren't meant to be here until much later to let him vacate alone and with dignity. He hadn't finished packing his one case. Open on the floor upstairs, he needed to take the last of his clothes from the cupboard. His shoes. Best suit. Eoin surely would let him stay until morning light?

He opened the door and Eoin brushed past Harry, followed by two of his burly men. Thugs, who'd stood silent at every poker game, ready to throw out anyone who disagreed with their master. "Where are the keys?"

"They're on the kitchen table. All of them. But come back in the morning, Eoin. Let me sleep here until dawn."

"Go to the kitchen. Get them." Eoin directed one of the men. Then he stood in the centre of the foyer and slowly turned to view it. "Ye did a good job, Harry. She's a beautiful house and a credit to ye skills."

"Eoin—"

"Where's ye personal things?"

"My case is half packed. I thought you'd be here this evening."

Eoin waited until the first man returned from the kitchen, keys in hand, then he looked directly at Harry for the first time. "Get dressed." He held his hand out for the keys, pocketing them immediately. "Go with him," he addressed his men. "Throw whatever clothes he has into a case. Stay with him and escort him out once that is done."

"But—"

"Move." One of the men stepped toward Harry and he backed away.

"Listen, I haven't finished... Eoin? Have a heart, man."

Eoin turned away. His men flanked Harry and he shot up the staircase. Damn them. No time to walk through Palmerston House once more. To say goodbye. No chance to check he'd locked his hidden door. Where was the key? He stopped in his tracks outside his daughter's bedroom. The door was ajar and he could see the trunk. The key was in it.

"Move or I'll carry you." One of the thugs pushed Harry.

"Wait! I left something in my daughter's room. Something personal, not on the list."

"Should have got it earlier. Last chance, Temple."

He wanted to push back, to run into the room and grab the precious key. Instead he walked to his bedroom, back straight and head up. No one would manhandle him. He was a gentleman and would teach these three how an Englishman behaves. Scurrilous, underhand miserable thief. Eoin Ryan's name would be known throughout history and his descendants would bear the cross of his evil deeds. A day of reckoning would set right what was being done to him this moment.

Harry hummed as he dressed. Brown suit, fob watch with a photograph of his wife and daughter. Shiny leather boots and suspenders. His hat. An overcoat. By now, the case was squashed shut. He'd need to find someone to sort the clothes out. Like this he wouldn't even get a job interview and that, it suddenly hit him, was what he'd need to do.

Still humming – which was clearly bothering the other men – Harry strode past his daughter's bedroom without a glance. He'd find a way. Eleanor would forgive him leaving it behind once she heard about Eoin's behaviour. The key didn't even matter. He knew other ways in to his stash.

# 22

# A BEAUTIFUL GARDEN

"*B*ut the key will make it easier for me, you idiot!" Bernie muttered at the diary as he closed it. He leaned against the bed head, legs stretched out on the eiderdown. Harry Temple was beginning to annoy him.

At every turn there was a new problem. A valuable grandfather clock apparently handed over to newcomers with the directive to keep it in the family. Not sell it. Well, somehow the Browns managed to offload it to George Campbell, who obviously knew the clock didn't belong to him. If Harry wanted to stop Eoin Ryan enjoying the clock, why not rip out its mechanism?

*I'd have spoilt your little victory.*

Yes, he'd have set fire to the house and left nothing but ashes.

What was so special about the trunk? Of all the household goods, this was the one Harry wanted to take with him. For Eleanor. Out of a sense of guilt or sentimentality? There was no description other than it coming from England with them and being in his daughter's bedroom.

Bernie opened the diary at the page he'd just read, his finger underlining the sentence as he read aloud. "So close. If only I'd run in there before the thugs reached me I could have pocketed the key with them none the wiser." He closed the diary and swung his feet onto the floor. "That's where you are." After sliding the diary under the mattress, he slipped his shoes on and went looking for Elizabeth.

The back door was open and he wandered into the sunshine. Directly behind the house was a strip of grass with a clothes line and vegetable patch. Just like a suburban backyard. Trees bordered the farthest boundary. Claret ash, golden elms, and Japanese maples were interspersed with gums. In a direct line from the back door, a path disappeared between the trees. Bernie followed it.

Sunlight filtered through the leaves and birdsong filled the air. The path curved through the trees until opening on a large pond. It was almost a small lake, with all manner of plants around its banks and in the water, a riot of colour and scents. Bernie stopped at the edge, his artist's eye appreciating the beauty of clouds reflected in the calm water. Ducks swam and squabbled.

To one side of the pathway, a comfortable bench at its base, an oak tree stood strong. This would have been planted when the house was built. Bernie stared up at its highest branches.

"Impressive, isn't it?"

Bernie jumped as Elizabeth stepped from behind the tree, a pile of weeds in her arms.

"Oh, I'm sorry to startle you. I thought you would have seen my tools here." She dropped the weeds into a small wheelbarrow with a smile.

"Actually, I didn't. I think I was miles away, wondering when this was planted."

"The oak? The Temples were responsible. They brought several saplings with them from England, though goodness knows how they kept them alive on those old ships! Martha told me about it before Keith and I came to inspect Palmerston House. We came right here to the pond first, even before going inside. Once we saw the poor pond, all choked with algae, and this wondrous tree… well, we fell in love."

"Martha?"

Elizabeth sat on the bench and Bernie joined her. "Martha lived here until she was about twenty-one or so. You seem so intrigued by this place."

"I am." Bernie stared at the pond. "Perhaps it is the same as you. Falling in love with it. As if I'm meant to be here."

"I understand and am so glad I never have to leave."

*Don't get too comfortable, Elizabeth.*

He forced himself to smile at her. "In fact, I want to do more than photograph the region. I spoke to my publisher and got the go-ahead to do a pictorial on Palmerston House. History, mix of old and new photos. With your permission, of course."

Elizabeth beamed. "How delightful! In that case, you'll need to speak to Martha and go to the library."

"And you'll help me?"

"Of course. Well, with the little I know."

*Like where the trunk is.*

And how to get the house to himself for a few hours. All in good time.

# 23

# ONE MYSTERY LEADS TO ANOTHER

*M*artha sat on the sofa, Thomas at her side holding her hand. Christie ran in with a glass of water and knelt beside Martha, worry creasing her face.

"Here, some water for you." Christie offered the glass. "I'm so, so sorry."

Martha stared at the trunk, not taking the water, so Christie put it on the coffee table and took Martha's other hand. "Please stop shaking, Auntie. I'll get rid of the trunk straight—"

"No! You don't understand." Martha gripped Christie.

"It's my fault," Thomas said. "I was curious about it. How it got into the attic in the first place. But as Christie says, it can go. I don't want you upset, my sweetheart."

"This is where your letters were hidden? And my rings?"

Thomas exchanged a puzzled look with Christie as Martha continued. "This is what was in the attic? Tom?"

"Is that why you're so agitated?"

With a deep sigh, Martha shook her head. "I'm not some silly girl holding grudges. I'll have the water now, please."

Christie passed the glass. The shock drained away and the shaking ceased. Martha handed the glass back. "Would you open it?"

"It's empty."

"Please."

"I'll get the key." Christie got to her feet and headed for the kitchen.

"Please don't blame Christie. I was curious because I know my parents never had such a thing and couldn't work out how it got up there in the first place. Her love of solving old mysteries must be rubbing off on me."

Martha suddenly smiled at Thomas. "I'm about to complicate things further." She released his hand as Christie returned with her house keys. "Now, dear, open the lid and read the inscription on the floor of the trunk."

"Why do I feel as though I'm in a magician's show?" Christie inserted the skeleton key and turned it. With a click, it unlocked and she opened the lid. "Oh, I never saw that before. Though I only had my torch light last time."

"Christie!"

"Sorry, Auntie. It says London—"

"1840," Martha finished.

Thomas and Christie stared at her, open mouthed.

"It belonged to Dorothy." Martha spoke softly. "Mother gave it to her when she turned thirteen because she loved it so much. Before then, it was in the first guest room."

All three stared at the trunk in silence. Christie reached in to trace the carved inscription. The interior was smooth apart from the words and numbers.

"Martha, when Dorothy left home, did she take this with her? Do you recall?"

"No, Thomas. By then she wanted only modern furnishings and left this behind in her room. I'd quite forgotten about it and didn't consider the one hidden in our attic here could possibly be the same trunk. How did it get here?"

"And how did it get up there? Actually, for that matter, Christie, how did you get it down?" Thomas frowned. "You should have waited."

"It isn't very heavy."

"Beside the point. If you'd hurt yourself... what was that look for?"

"Nothing. Anyway, Charlotte dropped by and she gave me a hand so no need to worry." Christie bit her lip as she closed the lid.

"Well, a mystery indeed. Will you solve this one, Christie?" Thomas asked.

"I have a wedding to plan and a business to create, so mysteries might have to take a back seat for a bit. Shall I make some late lunch, if you haven't eaten yet? We can work out what to do with this later."

"I'll come with you, dear." Martha pushed herself onto her feet and followed Christie out.

Thomas watched them leave and turned back to the trunk. It had to be Dorothy who'd put it in the attic. But why?

---

"Well, I never saw such a thing!" Daphne stomped around the counter. "Open shut, open shut. Not even shut, mind you, but slam. Slam!"

John Jones smiled faintly at his wife from the window, where he was updating real estate For Sale notices. "Love, there's no point getting riled about a complete stranger. Maybe the car door doesn't close properly."

Daphne came to a stop, hands on her hips. "It was an almost new vehicle, so why wouldn't the door close? Unless he always slams it with such force and broke it."

"Let it go. You'll probably never see him again."

"We can't be complacent, doll. Not after those horrible people breaking in to our homes. And trying to murder our Christie! And... and attempting to blackmail you!" Daphne burst into tears. John dropped what he was doing and hurried to Daphne, wrapping his arms tightly around her.

"Hey, what's brought this on?"

"I thought I would lose you."

"Me? Never happen. Come on, let's go and make a cuppa." John leaned back to look at Daphne. "Oh, you've made your mascara run. Go wash your face and I'll put the kettle on."

Daphne nodded, not trusting herself to speak. One more firm squeeze from John and then he released her. "Go on. I'll see if some of those ginger biscuits you made are left."

John went off to the little kitchen out the back and Daphne headed for the bathroom, sniffing back tears. What was wrong? Months since dealing with Derek's thug Rupert breaking into their home and destroying a room full of collectables, and every day since she'd been strong and positive. Now, one silly incident and she was a mess.

She stared at herself in the mirror. Tears streaked her make-up, not just the mascara. Her eyes were alien. Wide and startled.

*Get a grip, Daph!*

My goodness, poor Christie was the one who'd nearly perished yet here she was, making a silly fuss over nothing.

*Time to count your blessings.*

Just like her mother taught her to do when all seemed lost – their house, Dad's job, and sick siblings.

"John loves me and I love him." Without a doubt, her greatest blessing and joy. Such a wonderful man, with his handsome face and way with words. A good provider who treated her equally in all things.

Daphne attempted a smile. It failed. "Fine. I have a comfortable home and a wonderful job." This was true. Their house was indeed a home, filled with their memories, plans, and promises. They'd been in this little town for over twenty years and loved every minute of it. Except, some of those memories were shattered. Beautiful crystal from their wedding. Keepsakes from their honeymoon. Tears welled up again, glistening in her eyes. Cold water on her face helped a lot. Things were just things. People mattered.

"My friends are my rock and support." She said it with force. Elizabeth, Martha, and Sylvia were her close friends now, ever since that night on the beach. Christie was super special. A gorgeous girl who'd been fragile at her grandmother's funeral, but as hard as stone standing up to her nasty ex-fiancé. Yes, friends mattered. Trev, Barry, George, all the local traders really.

"Tea's ready, love." John called.

"One more!" Daphne told her reflection. "I have a big heart. It's a blessing to me and those around me." Her mother's words, heard over and over growing up, and echoing across the years since she'd passed on.

With a sense of calm, Daphne turned off the light and went to find her husband. Her smile was wide but deep down the pain lingered.

---

*T*ired from the events of the morning and the walk to and from Christie's cottage, Charlotte longed for a glass of Elizabeth's ice cold lemonade as she arrived back at Palmerston House. Then she'd send the photos of the old trunk to her friend in Brisbane, see if she could help Christie uncover some of its past, or at least, origin.

There was no sign of Elizabeth, so Charlotte took a tall glass from the cupboard in the kitchen. A sound stopped her, a creak. Another creak. She stood still, glass in hand. The door to the cellar opened a crack, then more, and Bernie appeared, not seeing Charlotte. He closed the door carefully behind himself then turned. "Holy—"

"What are you doing, Bernie?"

Hand on his heart, he leaned against the door. "You shouldn't sneak up on people like that!"

"Why were you in the cellar? Is Elizabeth with you?"

"She's gardening. And don't get yourself all twisted." He walked to the window and looked out. "She's been sharing the history of Palmerston House and is quite happy for me to look around and take whatever photos I want. For my new book."

"I don't see a camera."

Bernie left the window, pushing past Charlotte to get a glass for himself. "None of your business, is it?"

"I'm warning you—"

"Warning me?" He leaned in close, trapping Charlotte against the table. "I'd be careful, Lottie."

"These people don't deserve your lies, Bernie. Why not tell them why you're really here?" She glared at him, her fingers digging into the wooden table.

"Why don't you tell me why I'm really here, seeing as you know so much?" With a sneer, he stepped away. "What is it you think you know about me?"

Heart pounding, Charlotte put the table between them. "You were my patient for a long time. You talked a lot about this town and this property."

He opened the fridge and stared into it. "Exactly. You need to remember I was your patient. Which brings a certain privilege. Doctor." Without taking the lemonade out, he slammed the door. "I'm done reminding you."

"Are you threatening me?"

"Take from it what you want. But stay away from me, Lottie."

Charlotte put her glass onto the table. His temper was short, she knew from past experience, but he'd always regained control quickly and apologised. His upbringing affected his choices even now and part of her was fascinated by his deeply held sense of entitlement.

"Lemonade sounds nice, some tea?" Elizabeth – still wearing gardening gloves, hat and sunglasses – wandered in. And stopped. She looked from Charlotte to Bernie, then peeled off the gloves and removed the sunglasses. "Everything okay in here?"

"Have a headache coming on. Might go to my room for a while." Bernie put his glass back into the cupboard and left.

"I might have a shower, Elizabeth. Long walk today. Sorry." Charlotte tried to smile.

*I so want to talk to you.*

What would she say? Bernie believes he owns Palmerston House?

"Charlotte, have your drink first. You don't want to get dehydrated on a warm day."

"Okay. I'll just take a lemonade with me if you don't mind?" Without waiting for a response, Charlotte picked up her glass and opened the fridge. Talking about this would be a mistake.

# 24

# TREV AND CHARLOTTE

*T*rev pushed himself back from the desk with a frustrated sigh. Nothing on Bernard William Cooper. Yet something was wrong. His senses told him so, even though it was the sudden plea in Charlotte's eyes he based the feeling on. The other night when he'd pulled young Cooper over for speeding, nothing was amiss. Bit of a charmer, but no warrants or alerts on his licence or car. He'd spotted him a couple of times since, on foot and with several cameras around his neck.

He scratched his head. Unless Charlotte felt like explaining herself, there was little to be done. Was he being over-protective and imaging things? He liked her so much and all it would take was one tiny invitation from Charlotte and he'd fall for her heart and soul.

*Idiot.*

She didn't see him as a future partner. Not even as a friend, really. Always something held her back.

What did he really know about Charlotte Dean? Practising psychiatrist from interstate somewhere. She loved dogs. He smiled, remembering the night on the beach in the storm when she'd bossed him around as she treated Randall for exhaustion. She had steady hands and a no-nonsense attitude he'd appreciated in the face of near-panic around them.

"You look worried."

Trev jumped at Charlotte's voice from the other side of the counter. So deep in thought, he'd not heard her come through the front door. How long was she there? "Hi. Didn't hear you come in." He got to his feet.

"Good thing I'm not some bad guy." She leaned on the counter, something like amusement in her eyes.

"Oh, I've got a special radar for bad guys." Those eyes were gorgeous. Trev found himself opposite her, aware of a goofy smile on his face. "How did the visit go?"

She frowned.

"With Christie?"

"Oh. Oh, it was interesting. Good timing actually, as she'd decided to fall out of the attic and poor Randall had no idea how to use the phone to call for help."

"She what? Is she—"

"Just winded. Probably bruised, but we didn't get that personal. Anyway, I'm not here to tell tales on Christie. Would you have a few moments to talk?"

"Is this an official talk, or social?" Trev gestured for Charlotte to come around the counter to his desk.

She settled in the chair, crossing her legs. "Bit of both."

"Coffee?"

"I'm coffee-d out, thanks though."

"Water? Orange juice?"

"Trevor. I'm fine."

He nodded, leaning back in his chair to give her time to speak. She glanced around, her eyes showing none of their earlier amusement. They were cautious and it bothered Trev no end.

"I have a... a friend. With a question. If it's okay to ask something?"

"It's always fine to ask questions. For a friend or otherwise."

"Maybe this was a mistake."

"Charlotte. Ask. I'm approachable."

She hinted at a smile. "Okay. My friend has a concern about a third party. A person who might have some... intentions that are not the best. No proof or anything except a feeling. What would you do?"

"You're not giving me much to go on. Does your friend have some relationship with the third party? History that makes them feel this way?"

"No relationship! Of course not." Charlotte must have realised how sharp her response was, taking a couple of fast, shallow breaths. "I mean, not a personal relationship. But some previous knowledge of this person."

"Are you talking about intentions to cause harm to your friend?"

Charlotte opened her mouth and shut it again. Her fingers were interlaced tightly and when she saw Trev glance at her hands, she separated them and dropped them out of his sight. "I don't believe so. Not to anyone as such. Perhaps financial or property."

"I'd be suggesting your friend have a chat to me. Or someone like me." Trev kept his voice even. "Preferably me."

"What if my friend can't do that?"

"Why?"

"Because doing so might compromise a binding arrangement."

Trev leaned forward to reach for a pen. He found a piece of clean paper underneath a pile of files. "Humour me. Person one – let's call them 'Good Guy' – knows person two. Who we'll call 'Bad Guy', okay?" He drew two stick figures and named them, not willing to look at Charlotte in case she was laughing at him. "So, Good Guy has some sort of knowledge about Bad Guy." He drew a line to connect them. "Bad Guy might be planning something... bad."

Now, he glanced at Charlotte. She watched his hand, her face so worried he longed to reach over and smooth the lines away. Instead, he wrote 'Danger' under Bad Guy.

"Good Guy wants to do something. She has good instincts but something stops her from doing what they tell her to. Let's call it 'Ethics'". Trev sensed Charlotte tensing up. "A good person with good ethics who is worried."

"What are you doing?"

Trev raised his eyes to Charlotte's. "Nothing is ever as simple as it looks on the surface, I know better than most. These silly stick figures mean nothing. The point is if there is any risk of Bad Guy harming someone, or something, then Good Guy needs to find a way to tell someone who can help. Someone like me, Charlie."

"I said it is a friend." Her eyes never left his and there it was, the unspoken plea in them.

"Let me help."

In a sudden movement, Charlotte stood. "I'm sorry. This was a mistake. I shouldn't have come here."

"Why?" He stayed sitting although he wanted to pull her into his arms and hold her close. Calm her until she trusted him enough to talk openly. "I won't betray your confidence."

Her eyes filled with tears. "But that's the problem." It was more a whisper and as soon as she said it, Charlotte put her hand to her mouth.

"Hey, don't cry." As Trev stood, Charlotte shook her head and turned, taking off through the gate beside the counter. "Charlie, wait!"

The front door shut behind her. He should have listened, not drawn pictures. His earlier gut feeling was right and whether she liked it or not, he was going to make sure Charlotte Dean stayed safe.

# 25

# TOO CLOSE TO THE TRUTH

*I*n the same spot on the cliff he'd sat in days earlier, Bernie watched a yacht cruise by. So many luxury boats around here and he'd seen where they moored – in the next harbour across, Willow Bay. Elizabeth said their owners were mostly weekenders who kept a house in one of the new estates. Fine for some, money to throw away, whilst others struggled for every dollar.

He'd come better prepared this time. Hours spent on his laptop, viewing all the photographs and local maps, helped him plan. A trip to an equipment shop in Warrnambool kitted him out with a harness and proper boots. Afraid to interact with the over-friendly assistants, he'd guessed at the type of ropes and descenders, grabbing a selection along with climbing gloves. He didn't bother with a helmet. It wasn't a long descent.

Bernie's heart raced in excitement. The rope was secured around one of the big bushes and all he needed was the yacht to pass by. And another drink. He pulled a bottle of water out and sucked it thirstily. Water and a touch of vodka. First drink in the morning and last one at night. Just taking the edge off.

The water drained, he tossed the lid into the backpack on the ground at his side and crushed the bottle before throwing it into the bushes further along the cliff face. Below, the ocean foamed against the base of the cliff. From this high, with the sun overhead, he saw rocks barely below the surface. One would not want to fall.

He slid the gloves on.

Deep breath in. And out. He turned onto his stomach and lowered himself bit by bit. His feet kicked around at first, instinctively seeking a foothold. Then he relaxed and let his arms do the work. He was strong and lowered himself five, ten metres. Then, as if caught on something, the rope refused to give any more length. And he heard a sound above. A bark.

He grabbed a rock and hung on. No more barking, only seagulls and the ocean itself. He listened to its power. Waves pounding the cliff wall, sending spray streaming upwards.

He pushed himself out and looked down. Just visible in the rock face was an opening, perhaps another ten metres down. But the rope wouldn't come with him and with a groan, he remembered the length he'd purchased. Not nearly long enough.

*A*s soon as she was clear of the shopping precinct, Charlotte began running. Somehow she'd stayed at a brisk walk since leaving the police station but now she gave in to the panic. Footpaths became dirt tracks beside houses on the outskirts of town, then nothing but grass verge. Her heartbeat filled her ears and tears blinded her eyes but on she flew, desperate to leave River's End behind. To leave Bernie and his evil intentions behind. And Trevor. With his stick figures and uncanny insight.

A side road came up and she turned into it, away from the traffic to and from town. It stretched before her, long and straight. The road she'd got lost down when she first met Trevor. Out of breath, Charlotte stumbled to a walk, then stopped and dropped onto the grass. She lay on her back, brushing the tears away and gulping in air. The sky was clear blue with no clouds.

*One breath. Two.*

Deep and slow. Start over.

*One breath. Two.*

Charlotte focused on the rise and fall of her chest. She opened each hand and laid the palms flat on the grass, imagining them becoming part of the earth. Sink into the ground, be at one with nature.

*One breath. Two.*

The mantra and routine always worked.

Her body and mind under control again, Charlotte sat up. A lone cow watched her from the other side of the fence through placid brown eyes. "Silly human, huh?" She stood, her legs shaky from the running. The cow was friendly and she scratched her velvet forehead before sitting against the fence.

What was she to do? Bernie was nosing around the property but was it with bad intent? His obsession with the diary his mother gave him as a kid was unhealthy but hardly dangerous. As her patient he'd shown no indicators of potential violence, just a belief he was owed something based on events from more than a century ago. Now he was here – because she was. She'd stopped seeing him professionally a year ago so his decision to visit her mother was bizarre. In fact, it was what distressed her most. A line he shouldn't have crossed, but it didn't mean she could cross her own line.

Ethics, Trevor said as he drew his ridiculous stick figures. Confidentiality was what he wanted to say, she'd felt it. Without a genuine belief Bernie was here to cause harm, she couldn't break his confidence. And now Trevor would be watching her, if not investigating her. Well, she'd find a way to redirect his interest because her private life was too complicated and uncertain to let him any closer. No matter how much he made her pulse race.

---

"*R*andall, leave the bunnies alone!" Christie called from the deck of Martin's house as she dug in the pocket of her jeans for the key. As soon as they'd crossed the meadow he'd taken off down the cliff path. She'd heard him bark, the same woof of excitement from finding something he liked. If he didn't hurry up she'd go and get him because she didn't have time to bath him if he decided to dig after a rabbit.

She opened the sliding door and left it open, stepping into the cool and dark living area. Martin had closed the curtains before leaving almost a week ago, and now Christie drew them to let the sunlight in. He'd be home tomorrow, although his timing, according to the last text, was vague.

As she crossed to the kitchen, Randall trotted in, his ears up expectantly. "Sorry, doggie. He'll be back soon though." Unconvinced, Randall disappeared to the other end of the house. Christie checked the fridge, pulling out old milk, seafood, and fruit. She should have done this much earlier instead of wasting it now. The milk went down the drain and she tossed the rest into the bin, which smelt pretty bad already.

After emptying the bin and replacing the liner, she left the rubbish outside the door for when she left. Going back to the kitchen, she checked the cupboards and made a quick shopping list. In the morning she'd come back up with fresh produce. And some flowers. She smiled. When she became Mrs Christie Blake, she'd grow lots of flowers and fill the house. She'd need them for the salon anyway, bringing the beauty of outdoors inside for the ladies of River's End.

Christie found Randall in Martin's bedroom, sitting beside the bed with his head resting on the covers. "Come on, you've still got me. And Thomas and Martha. Let's go find them."

Randall followed her out with less enthusiasm than when he'd come inside and her heart went out to him. Martin might joke about Randall adoring Thomas and even Christie above himself, but it wasn't true. The bond between dog and master was extraordinary and Randall missed him.

*So do I.*

She locked the front door behind them, collected the rubbish bag and headed to the studio.

In there, the rubbish bin was almost filled with empty paint tubes.

She took a few moments to plump the cushions on the sofa, check the small fridge for supplies, and do a quick sweep of the tiled floor. In the middle of the studio, beneath the biggest skylight, a sheet hung lopsided off an easel. Rubbish bag in one hand, Christie attempted to straighten the sheet but instead, the whole thing fell to the ground. With a sigh, she put the bag down to retrieve it.

Martin was private with unfinished paintings, unless he wanted an opinion. It would never occur to Christie to look under a sheet or steal a glance if she happened upon Martin as he worked. But, holding the corners of the sheet ready to place over the top of the easel, she was unable to look away from the work in progress.

In his customary oils, it was a self-portrait. Martin, black hair plastered to his skull, knelt in the shallows of the ocean. In his arms like a baby was Christie, her own long hair trailing back into the sea as her head lay against his chest. Her eyes were closed... or were they just open? Head on Christie's lap, Randall also was soaked to the skin. His eyes were on Christie's face, as were Martin's. They were in the middle of a storm, the sky purple-black with lightning behind Martin.

The sheet slipped from Christie's fingers and she stepped back, hand flying to her mouth to stifle a small, unbidden cry. It was as beautiful as it was terrible.

Since the night of the storm, the night *Jasmine Sea* almost sank and the ocean nearly claimed her life along with Randall's, flashes of fear had haunted Christie. Never once had it occurred to her Martin might very well be experiencing the same thing.

*It was all my fault!*

She'd led Derek to this town, refused to reconcile or sell him the cottage, and his subsequent rage might have destroyed everything. The pain on Martin's face in the painting was more than Christie could bear.

# 26

# A TRUNK AND A CLOCK

*M*artha ran her hands over the trunk, now on the dining room table. She remembered every inch of its old surface, even the smell of oak. Back when Dorothy was the big sister she loved to distraction, Martha was allowed to play with the dolls kept inside. Dorothy played less with them every year, although Martha knew she sang to them sometimes.

If only Dorothy had been permitted to pursue her dream of becoming a singer, how different both their lives would be. Mother hadn't seem to notice what Martha did with her time – often spent with the local girls – but Dorothy had potential. Her role in the family was taken seriously and the expectation she'd become a business-woman kept her attention on her studies. Mother ran the family and wanted Dorothy home with an education to take their timber business to new heights.

"Hello? Christie?"

"Oh. Charlotte!" Martha hurried to the open front door, its screen door locked. Charlotte stood on the top step.

"Hello, Martha."

Martha opened the door for Charlotte to come through.

"Christie's out I'm afraid. She's walked up to Martin's house with Randall."

"Is Martin home?"

"Tomorrow I believe. She said something about checking the fridge but I think she feels closer to him by being up there."

"Ah. Okay. Would you mind letting her know I have some information about the..." Charlotte trailed off.

"The trunk?" Martha led Charlotte to the dining room and gestured inside. "Christie mentioned you'd helped her retrieve it from the attic. I thank you for doing so."

"Not a problem. I take it she feels better if she's walked to Martin's."

"Better?" Martha titled her head. "What happened? Don't give me that look please."

"Nothing awful, just a slip on the steps going to the attic."

"And?"

"Bit of a bump when she landed. Winded, probably a bruise down her side but she wasn't concussed. Just embarrassed."

"All for this." Martha turned to the trunk. "And you have information about it? Are you an antiques enthusiast?"

Charlotte took out her phone. "Not me. A friend at home is though. She owns a rather successful business and was excited by the photos I sent. Umm, Christie said it would be okay, but if you would rather—"

"Child, stop fretting." Martha put a hand on Charlotte's arm. "Come and sit with me. I'm interested in what your friend has to say."

They sat at the other end of the table and Charlotte read the text message aloud. "Beautifully crafted and unusual as I think it is ahead of its time. The rounded top came into vogue only in the late 1800s but the base is in keeping with English pieces from the first half of the century. Possibly a one-off for a wealthy family. A gift or commission."

"She's good. It is dated 1840 and made in London."

"Oh. So, do you know its history?" Charlotte put her phone away.

"It belonged to my sister, Dorothy. When we were children, of course, living in Palmerston House."

"Then, how did it get here? I mean… I'm sorry, it's none of my business."

"It is a mystery all of its own, isn't it? Thomas wants to pursue it but I worry the answers might hurt him. You see, my one time best friend got together with Dorothy and created a situation that looked bad. Very bad. And made sure I saw it. After Tom and I went our separate ways, there was a time when we would have reunited. He even waited for me every morning for months, at the end of the jetty on the beach."

"He did? What stopped you reconciling?"

"All the letters he wrote and posted to me were intercepted by Dorothy. I never saw them and nor did he again, not until Christie discovered them hidden in a shoebox in this trunk. Frannie lied to him, Dorothy lied to me, and they won. We let them take almost fifty years away."

*Lost forever.*

"You are so brave, Martha," Charlotte whispered, her eyes wide.

Martha laughed. "No, child. Not brave. Lucky. I'm very lucky to have gone full circle and be back where I belong, with the man I belong with."

*I*n companionable silence, Thomas and George sat either side of the long glass counter in the jewellery shop. Each held an almost empty glass of whiskey from George's small but exceptionally well selected bar. Behind George on the wall, all manner of clocks ticked and tocked slightly out of rhythm.

In the corner, the grandfather clock slowly chimed four times, rousing Thomas from his thoughts. "The bride will be expecting me home soon."

"Did you come to see me, or is there a shopping list somewhere in your pockets?" George's eyes sparkled. "Like once or twice before."

"My bride doesn't need another sparkly gift until Christmas. Of course I came to see you. And this particular whiskey." He stared into the glass.

"Perhaps I should have given you a bottle on your wedding day. Would save you having to endure my company to drink it."

"Actually, I was thinking about a gift for the children."

Without being asked, George refilled both their glasses. "Something for their home?"

"Martha is keen to buy them a honeymoon." Thomas sipped his drink. "Thanks."

"A worthy idea."

"It is. We're thinking of Sydney, just for a few days. Art galleries, Opera House. Time somewhere a bit luxurious, where they can simply enjoy their own company without being away too long, given both are busy people."

"But."

Thomas smiled. "You know me too well. I want them to have something tangible as well. Something for their kids. Grandkids. An heirloom." He glanced at the grandfather clock and George followed his gaze.

"You want to give them a grandfather clock?"

"Maybe."

"Martin has a modern house."

"An eclectic house. Both of them love old things. Look at Martha and me." He chuckled and George joined in.

Thomas stood, and taking his glass, wandered to the clock in the corner.

"Still not for sale?"

"Ah, Tom. I can't." George joined him. "As long as a descendant of the Brown family lives, it can't be sold."

Thomas looked at his lifelong friend. "Sold?"

"You and I are the only ones who know the real history. Unless some fragment of the past is out there. But the Temples are long gone, Tom, not one of them in this whole region for a hundred years or more."

"It still matters though. To you, George Campbell, it matters. You have honour."

"It's what I was trusted with." George touched the face of the clock. "But I have no children to pass it on to. Perhaps the time has come."

"George? What are you thinking?"

"We'll see, Tom. We'll see."

───────────

*C*harlotte paddled through the lagoon, then stopped, sandals in one hand as she gazed at the jetty. Did Thomas really wait there every day for Martha for months? What an incredible story Martha told.

Ahead, a dog barked and Charlotte held her hand against the glare of the lowering sun. Randall ran toward her. Christie wandered behind at a distance, head down. Her steps were heavy and Charlotte hurried to meet her. Randall got to her first and she paused to greet him with a pat.

"Christie? Are you okay?"

Christie raised her head as if jolted out of deep thought. Her face was serious, drawn. She shrugged her shoulders and to Charlotte's dismay, began to cry. By the time Charlotte reached her, she'd brushed the tears away and regained some control, taking deep breaths. "Silly tears."

"Oh. Do you miss Martin so much?"

"Yes. No. Oh, I don't know. I might sit for a bit."

"I'll join you." Charlotte's tone was no-nonsense in case Christie wanted to argue. "I just saw you wince."

On the sand, legs stretched out, Christie managed a smile. "There's a lovely colourful bruise still, down my hip and leg."

Randall flopped down beside them.

"Why were you crying?"

"I saw something I wasn't meant to. I mean, he'd probably show it to me once it's finished but it isn't and being what it is he might not."

"Start at the beginning please. You lost me about halfway through."

"Sorry." Christie picked up a handful of sand and watched it trickle out of her fingers. "I accidentally saw a painting in the studio. Part finished, which means no looking unless I'm asked for an opinion. Martin is firm about it. It depicts that night. In the storm."

"The yacht?"

"No. But I shouldn't tell you."

"Let's call this an informal counselling session. One where I'm bound by confidentiality." A little jolt of guilt jabbed Charlotte.

*You nearly gave Bernie away.*

"You and me only."

Christie bit her bottom lip. "I think I've really hurt him. It's a self-portrait and he's on the beach... almost right here actually. I'm in his arms as if he's carried me out of the depths, and Randall has his head on my lap."

"How did you feel seeing it?"

"It broke my heart. He really thought I would die." Her lips quivered.

"It was traumatic. For everyone and of course for the man who loves you. He found you and got you to safety but then saw Randall on his side and imagined the worst. I've never heard such grief in a man's voice."

"What do you mean?"

"Him in the shallows in the painting? Mirrors what he did when he saw Randall. Dropped to his knees and cried out the dog's name."

Christie turned startled eyes to Charlotte.

"Listen, the painting is his way of dealing with the demons. Martin with you safe in his arms and Randall safe at your side. It helps him put the chaos of that night into an order his mind can accept. Whether he ever shows it to you, or destroys it, or keeps it locked away? Doesn't matter. He loves you so much and needs an outlet for what happened. It's normal. Very normal in fact."

For a few moments the women sat in silence. Charlotte watched Christie's face, powerful emotions crossing it until she nodded to herself. "Okay. Thanks."

"Anytime. Anyway you won't thank me once you get home."

"Why?"

"Sort of mentioned your fall. Sorry, just wanted to know you were okay."

"In that case I'd better go and explain myself." Christie got to her feet and Charlotte joined her. "I'm glad you've stayed in River's End. Even if you do give my secrets away."

# 27

## LOVING ARMS AND STARS

*P*almerston House was unusually quiet. Elizabeth sat outside on the verandah indulging in a glass of sherry, watching the sun set.

A car turned slowly into the driveway and, at first, Elizabeth thought it must be Bernie's SUV. But as it got closer, she saw it was a lot bigger and her heart raced. She stood, leaving her glass on the seat and arriving at the top of the steps as the Range Rover pulled up. The passenger window silently wound down and from inside, a man's voice called. "I know it's late notice, but would you have a room for the night?"

Elizabeth let out an uncustomary squeal, quickly restrained by covering her mouth. She rushed down the steps and around the vehicle just as Angus got out. He grinned and held his arms out and without hesitation she went to him. His arms folded around her and she snuggled into his tweed jacket, inhaling the familiar scent she'd missed so much.

"You don't ever need a booking." Her voice was muffled against him and he released her.

"I think you said Palmerston House is booked out?"

She smiled. "Silly man. Whatever are you doing here? I mean, had I known I'd have prepared dinner."

"Would you accompany me to dinner then? Perhaps the pub bistro, or we could go further afield?"

"The bistro would be lovely. We can call Christie and—"

Angus took her hand. "Much as I want to see her, I'd like to have dinner with you. Just you."

A delicious tingle of excitement filled Elizabeth and she squeezed his hand. "Your room is empty, so bring in your luggage and I'll make myself presentable."

"You go ahead, dear lady. I'll be right behind."

Elizabeth left the front door open and went up the staircase to make sure everything was right in Angus's room. As she passed a mirror she realised she was smiling. A wide, delighted smile going all the way to her eyes.

---

"*D*ear, would you find the old man please and tell him dinner is almost ready?" Martha glanced up from stirring a pot of her world famous chili, as she called it. Christie agreed it was about the best chili she'd ever eaten and once expressed surprise at an Irish Australian girl perfecting it. With a private smile, Martha had muttered something about spending time in South America and refused to elaborate.

"Garage?" Christie sniffed with deep appreciation, her stomach responding with a rumble.

"Most likely."

"Coming, Randall?" Christie opened the back door. Randall didn't move from where he sat near the door to the hallway, his eyes not leaving Martha. "Fair enough." She closed the door behind herself and stepped into the almost dark of early evening. The garage light was on, so she headed there first.

"Looking for me?" Thomas called from the front of the driveway.

As Christie reached him, he pointed to the sky. "Too much cloud about."

"For what?"

"Hmm."

"Okay. Dinner's about to be served."

"I like the stars."

"Me too." Christie glanced up. There were stars about but it was early and the light cloud covering made constellation spotting difficult. "Later it will be clearer."

"Hmm."

"What's wrong?"

"Stars aren't as bright down here."

"You miss the mountains."

"Don't tell the bride."

"So hard isn't it." Christie joined Thomas by leaning on the fence. "Different passions. Someone always compromises."

"She's worth it."

"No doubt she feels the same about you. You still own the cabin up there so why not visit?"

"Maybe. It needs checking anyway. Yes. Maybe."

The clouds parted, revealing a half-moon rising. "Thomas?"

"Christie."

"You're an artist."

Thomas straightened to look at her fully. "On occasion. Why?"

"When you paint, where does the inspiration come from?"

"Depends. Landscapes and the like are just there. Ready for my interpretation. The one I painted of Martha... after she left? From memory of a wonderful summer day when we were innocent of what lay ahead."

"It's a beautiful painting. I see the love for Martha every time I look at it. What about the seascape... but don't answer if you prefer not to."

"I'll tell you, but then you'll tell me why you're interested. Losing Martha was the worst night of my young life. Worse than the problems with my father or anything else. She was, is, my world. My soul mate. Out of sheer pain and desperation I brought the storm to life again. I poured my grief into it and as I painted, something happened. I began to find hope. You'll see it isn't exact. The jetty is different, not much, but enough to change what happened. And we were in the water on the other side, so in my painting, it might not have occurred."

"As if you rewrote the events to have a better outcome."

"Yes. It didn't change the fact she was gone nor how close she came to drowning, but on canvas, those little differences spoke volumes. Which is why I sent it to her. At least, I thought I had." He frowned, creases filling his forehead.

Christie put her hand on his. "I'm sorry. I shouldn't have asked. We should go inside."

"First, tell me why you did ask."

"I... I guess I wondered if art was a means of dealing with distressing events. Martin's painting, *Sole Survivor*, was kind of autobiographical although he won't admit it."

"Martin is a lot more expressive in his painting than I. If he paints something, there's a reason. Always. I'm hungry and even from out here I smell chili." Thomas started back to the cottage. "I'll close up the garage and be right in."

Behind him, Christie mulled over his words. It made sense to use your talent to change something. To give hope. And Charlotte pretty much said the same thing. Dealing with demons. The question was, how would she manage her own fears?

*Bury them.*

They'll disappear over time. She hoped.

## 28

# DINNER FOR TWO

*L*ance, who'd owned the pub for years, made a big fuss of Elizabeth and Angus when they arrived. He whisked them into the quietest corner of the busy bistro that was part of River's End Hotel. Before they'd had time to begin their conversation, he returned with menus, bread, and a bottle of wine. "I hope this one suits. On the house."

After he left again, Angus grinned at Elizabeth. "He likes you."

"Don't be silly. This is all because of a dinner I had here not long ago."

"Oh?"

"Yes, unfortunately I may have been a fraction tipsy toward the end of the evening."

"I think you should fill me in." Angus offered the plate of bread to Elizabeth. "Little details such as the company you were with. Surely Christie would not allow such a thing."

"It was the fabulous four." She laughed at Angus' expression. "Daphne, Sylvia, Martha."

"And you."

"And me."

"And you are. Fabulous. Now, a glass of this... oh, rather decent red." Intent on the label he missed the stunned look on she knew must be on her face. By the time he glanced up, she'd turned it into a soft smile. He poured two glasses. "Now, for a toast."

They held their glasses aloft, staring at each other as if not knowing what to say. Lance walked past and came back. "Earth to customers. How about to the best restaurant this side of Melbourne? If not in the whole world?" He held a thumb up as they turned amused eyes to him, then continued to the kitchen.

"To the warmest welcome I always receive at Palmerston House. And to the beautiful lady who makes it happen."

"Angus."

Angus tapped his glass on hers. "Cheers." He sipped his wine with his eyes twinkling. "Very nice. Try it."

Elizabeth did, her eyes never leaving his. She liked the creases around his eyes when he smiled. "Very nice."

*Oh dear, I'm copying him.*

She almost giggled and wondered what on earth was wrong with herself.

"What shall we order? Are you still partial to the gnocchi?"

"What a good memory you have."

"I haven't been gone that long, have I?" Angus reached over the table, his palm open in invitation. Elizabeth put her hand in his. This felt right. Perfect. Natural.

"You're here now."

"As if I'd miss the wedding. How are preparations?"

"There's so much to tell you! Before I do though... is everything alright with you, Angus?" Elizabeth had to ask. He'd left in something of a hurry, not saying much other than he had some business to attend to.

"There was a small issue with the final details of Miss Dorothy's estate. Actually, a claim against it from a person quite unknown to me, and I suspect, any of the family. Quite a mystery really and one I'd like to discuss more with the appropriate paperwork in front of me, and Christie present."

"Of course. I didn't mean to pry."

Angus squeezed her hand and leaned forward a little. "I expect you to be present also."

"Me?"

"The party named Palmerston House as part of their claim, so yes, you."

Elizabeth opened her mouth in surprise, but the arrival of Lance interrupted. As Angus ordered for them both, still holding her hand, she wondered how on earth anyone connected to the Ryan family would think they had some claim on her property. It was ridiculous.

# 29

# MOUNTAINS, CLOCKS, TEA

*I*nland from River's End, the Otway Ranges formed part of Trev's territory, dotted with remote properties and a handful of tiny villages. As the sun rose, he'd been on the road for a while and was ready for coffee at the first road stop.

He took his coffee outside and leaned against the patrol car so he could enjoy the view across a dramatic valley. He loved it up here, as much as the coast. Maybe he could persuade Charlotte to come hiking. Lots of nice trails and he could put a picnic together. They could talk about what was bothering her.

The familiar rumble of Martin's motorcycle interrupted Trev's musings and he lifted a hand in greeting as it turned into the driveway. Martin stopped near the patrol car and turned the motor off.

"How was the camp?" Trev shook Martin's hand.

"Great kids. Always are."

"I'm about to get one for the road." Trev nodded at his coffee cup. "Like one?"

"Thanks. No. Quite happy to wait to get home first. Thought I'd take a minute to stretch when I saw your car."

"Fair enough. I saw Christie out and about earlier."

Martin glanced at his watch. "Was it even light?"

"Nope. She was letting herself into the salon."

"Everyone been behaving?"

The muscles in Trev's cheek tightened. "Mostly."

"Trev?"

"Dunno, mate. Charlotte's upset about something but can't bring herself to ask for help. And Thomas went all secret agent on me."

"Spill it."

"Someone put him off-side. A guest staying at Palmerston House was lost up past the cottage and it spooked him a bit."

"Who?"

"Just a photographer. I ran his licence and he looks okay. Besides, Elizabeth wouldn't put up with any nonsense."

"Right."

"No right about it. Go see your girl."

Martin started the engine. "Are you heading up near Thomas' cabin?" He raised his voice over the rumble.

"I'll drop by and check on it. Safe travels."

Trev watched Martin accelerate back onto the road with a tinge of envy. No longer the semi-recluse he'd known for years, Martin's life changed the minute Christie came along. Her warmth and optimism lit up his darker side. There was a darker side to Charlotte... at least, there was a hidden, secret part she kept buried. If only she'd let him be her light.

---

*B*ehind the cottage, a wrought iron gate was flanked by wisteria on one side and a passionfruit vine on the other. From there, a path led to the orchard and vegetable garden. Trailed by Randall, Martha and Thomas wandered between the beds, each with a cup of coffee. It was a favourite morning ritual before breakfast to see what vegetables were ripening and plan the next planting.

"We should decide what to do with the trunk," Thomas said.

"I was thinking the same thing. Perhaps Elizabeth would like it. Return it to its original home."

"If that's the case, the grandfather clock should go back."

"George's clock? Did it come from Palmerston House?"

"It did. And rather a scandalous story attached."

Martha blinked at Thomas. "Dear, since when do you know the intimate history of a grandfather clock?"

"Always. I thought everyone knew, until George told me to keep it all to myself. Must have been about fifteen then. About the time the clock was in the cottage. My mother was distraught when the clock arrived and she had to put two chairs in the garage to make room."

"I always wondered why there were two chairs left in the dining room when Christie inherited it."

"When my parents moved out, somehow those chairs in the garage were forgotten. I found them after they'd left and put them back inside. It was possibly the final thing I did here. Until recently." Thomas stopped to pull a weed out from the lettuce.

"But if George's family owned the clock, why on earth did it come here?"

Thomas grinned as he straightened. "Probably shouldn't tell you, being a Ryan."

"I don't understand."

"You might insist on taking it back." He laughed at Martha's increasingly confused expression. "Let's sit."

She followed him to a bench Christie had put under one of the old trees. Randall trotted off, sniffing the track of a rabbit or some other small creature, his tail wagging.

"Originally, George's family were sworn to secrecy but when they found themselves in trouble, George's father told my father. If you remember, they were good friends."

Martha nodded, hanging on every word.

"You know George's great-grandfather established the jewellery shop? The grandfather clock was its first resident, in the corner where it is now. It became part of the background, just another clock amongst many, outshone by the sparkly stuff. But one day, your mother spotted it there."

"My mother?"

"She asked George's father if it was the clock originally owned by the Temples."

"Who built Palmerston? Is it?"

"Don't tell George you know... but yes. And before you ask, there's little I can tell about the how's and why's but some deal was done around the time Eoin Ryan took the ownership of the place. My guess is Henry Temple gave it away rather than leave it for the Ryans. Sorry." He put his hand on Martha's leg.

Her eyes wide, she leaned forward. "No, go on. This is fascinating!"

Thomas chuckled. "I can see where Christie gets her love of mystery. Anyway, Lilian must have found some evidence about the history of the clock and George's father got wind of her intentions to reclaim it. My Dad cooked up this plan to keep it here, knowing your family never visited. Well, until you did." He kissed Martha's lips.

"Behave, Tom. Tell me the story." Her smile earned her another kiss first.

"So it stayed here for a few months whilst the Campbell family finished building their new house. Once done, it went back to them and they never allowed anyone inside who they didn't trust."

"I imagine once Mother and Father moved to Ireland it was safe to return to the store."

Randall flopped beside them.

"Whatever the clock means to the Campbell family, George has nobody to leave it to and there was a pledge for it to never be sold. Perfect gift for our youngsters if you ask me." Thomas put his arm around Martha and they leaned back against the tree trunk. "Something to remind them of the past and how, no matter what, time makes things better."

---

*E*lizabeth had taken particular care with her appearance this morning. In front of the mirror, she'd applied make-up with a light hand, preferring the natural look Christie had taught her one day. Her hair refused to quite stay in place, one strand insisting on coming away from the others, so she reinforced it with hair spray. Then, a touch of her favourite perfume. In the many years since Keith passed on she'd not considered feeling this way again. Flutters in her stomach, tingles on her skin.

*Angus is here.*

Her eyes smiled back at her.

The house was quiet when she tiptoed downstairs, deliberately avoiding the creaky spots. He'd had a long drive yesterday and their dinner lasted a long time. In fact, they were the only patrons left when Lance finally left the bill with Angus. She'd pulled it to her side of the table and giggled like a schoolgirl when he'd shaken his finger and swept it away.

From the moment she'd met Angus, the connection was perfect. They laughed at the same things, and shared a love of old-fashioned cooking and English traditions. He was a gentleman who brought out the lady in her. When Christie was lost at sea she'd seen the distress in his soul and her heart hurt for him. In their conversations she'd learnt about his past, the young wife he'd tragically lost and his unwavering focus on his career afterwards. His commitment to Dorothy Ryan – a difficult and sometimes dreadful employer – was him at his best. He saw and accepted people for who they really were, faults and all.

Elizabeth put the kettle on the stove to boil, then laid out two breakfast trays for the guests and two places at the table.

"Something smells wonderful!" Angus appeared in the doorway, sniffing the air in appreciation.

"Perfect timing, Angus. Would you care for some tea?"

"What kind of question is that, dear lady?" Angus wandered to her side and leaned down to kiss her cheek, ever so gently. "I always care for tea. And I shall make us a pot whilst you continue creating your gourmet offering."

He turned away to collect the teapot and Elizabeth remembered to breathe again. Her legs were just a little bit shaky, in a good way.

*Now, what was I doing?*

The kettle whistled. Perhaps there was time to sit together and enjoy some tea before cooking. Perfect.

# 30

# IN THE GRASP OF HISTORY

George swept the pavement outside with the same broom he'd used for ten years

This shop had outlasted all of its jewellers except George and each one was a Campbell. His father, grandfather and great-grandfather – the man who'd started the business more than a century ago. A tradition he would one day end and this saddened him. But jewellery from a master such as himself held less value these days than in his youth, certainly out here away from the city. Martin spoke of setting him up to sell online but he had little use for computers. Give him a yacht and a fair wind and he was happy. Not so much with technology. And he did sometimes miss *Jasmine Sea*, although she'd had a different name all the years he owned her. *Free One*.

George realised he'd stopped sweeping and was leaning on the broom, staring rather blankly down the road. Someone walked toward him and he recognised the young man from the other day. The photographer. He nodded to the other man as he drew closer. "Good morning, lovely day for a walk."

"Good morning. I'm pleased to see you… Mr Campbell?" Bernie stopped a few feet away, head tilted slightly.

"Please, just George. I'm afraid I've forgotten your name."

"Bernie Cooper. I don't think I introduced myself last time. Would you have a few moments to speak with me? I'm photographing Palmerston House for a new book and would love to ask you a couple of questions."

"Come inside, Bernie. I don't know how much help I'll be though, Elizabeth is very knowledgeable." George led the way inside, shuffling around the counter to place the broom against a wall. Bernie went straight to the grandfather clock. "I see this still fascinates you."

"What a journey it would have had from England. It's a wonder it arrived intact and working!" Bernie wandered back to join George, who perched himself on the stool and put his glasses on. "And then it was moved yet again, and more than once."

"What makes you say that?"

Bernie gazed around. "How old is this lovely shop, George?"

With a small smile, George shook his head. "The date is above the door outside – 1902. One hundred and sixteen years old." For a photographer, Bernie lacked some powers of observation.

"So, given its age, the clock must have been somewhere before arriving here. In a local home, perhaps? So at least one other move." Bernie's smile didn't make it to his eyes and George narrowed his own eyes. "Where was it kept in those years?"

"A bit before my time, I'm afraid. You are most welcome to take some photographs, if you wish."

"Thanks. I'll drop back a bit later with the right camera." Bernie leaned against the counter and lowered his voice. "You can tell me, George. I'll keep your secret."

"I have no secrets to tell." George levelled a stern gaze over his glasses.

With a quick intake of breath, Bernie straightened. "Look, this is important and I don't want to have to resort to—"

"Morning, George!" Daphne's bright greeting coincided with the jangling of the door. She stopped abruptly. "Oh, sorry to interrupt."

"Not at all, Daphne. We'd finished our conversation, I believe. Good day to you, Mr Cooper." Whatever the young man had been about to say sounded like a threat of sorts. George saw something like anger or disappointment flash in the other man's eyes then it was gone. Without a word, Bernie turned and stalked out, brushing past Daphne, who jumped aside as if stung.

utside the jewellery shop, Bernie got as far as the kerb before turning around.

*Damned old man. Stupid woman.*

She'd butted in just as he'd begun to make himself clear to George Campbell.

Bernie glared at the shop. There, above the door, the words 'Est. 1902'. Where was the clock all those missing years? Through the window he saw the woman – Daphne – at the counter with George. They looked back to him. Judging him. Pointing their fingers just like everyone did. He tapped his jacket and felt the comforting shape of a water bottle.

He crossed the road and walked to the bakery, its outside tables and chairs empty. He sank onto one and took the bottle out, sucking on it until the vodka warmed his guts.

*Calm down and focus.*

Much as he longed to take back the grandfather clock, there was no way to do it. Yet.

"Sir? Excuse me?"

A teenage girl stood a few feet away, wearing an apron. There was a birthmark on one side of her face and he stared at it.

"Er… would you like a coffee? I can bring one out."

"Why would I want coffee?"

"Sir, any food or drink at the tables must be purchased here. Sorry." She looked at the bottle in his hand.

"I don't see a sign anywhere."

"You are most welcome to sit here as long as you purchase something. Unless of course you are unwell?"

"Yeah. I'm sick."

"Shall I call someone for you?"

"Yup. Sick of people like you, sweetie pie." Bernie took another swig from the bottle. "Oh, look. You've got a name badge. Jess. Aren't you too young to be working? Do you sell cocktails? A nice shot of vodka on ice?"

"This is a bakery, sir, not a bar."

"But if you don't sell what I want to order, whose fault is that? See, I'm a taxpayer and this is the pavement. Side of the road. Okay?" He burst into laughter at the confusion on Jess's face. Small town people were so easy to trick. Now she was looking in the direction of the jewellers. Bernie followed her line of sight and scowled. Daphne. Headed their way.

"You win, sweetie pie. I'll give up my seat for your crowd who wait to taste your wares." Bernie finished the bottle, crushed it, and tossed it on the ground. He slipped the lid into his pocket.

"Please pick that up." Jess stepped back when he stood. Daphne was halfway down the road.

"See you round." He turned his back on her and Daphne and walked away.

*Stuff you all.*

He'd find the answers himself.

---

*D*eep in thought, Christie climbed the stone steps leading to the graveyard. Martin was home at last, but exhausted. She'd made him a belated breakfast, kissed him not nearly enough, and left him to get some sleep. Once he woke and phoned, she'd bring Randall home.

Near the very edge of the cliff, where the oldest graves were, Christie was surprised to see Charlotte. She was intent on a headstone, peering at the inscription. Not wanting to startle her, Christie cleared her throat, then smiled widely when Charlotte glanced up.

"Oh, Christie. I didn't know anyone was there."

"Just on my way home."

"Home, from Martin's? He's back?"

Christie wove past a couple of graves to where Charlotte stood. "He is."

"He must have been happy to see you there."

"Yes. No. Maybe."

"Oh dear. Everything okay?"

"He spotted the remains of the bruise on my hip so I've been resoundingly scolded for taking risks."

Charlotte failed to hide a grin.

"Thanks. You don't know what he's like when I do something he deems dangerous."

"He loves you. Maybe stop doing dangerous things."

"So whose grave is this?" Enough talk of Martin and danger.

"This? Henry John Temple."

"Temple. Didn't he built Palmerston House? What's he doing buried here I wonder."

"Apparently he drowned."

Christie stared at the headstone. A simple monument with only his name and date of birth and death, the edges were crumbled and the inscription hard to read. "1853. But didn't he lose Palmerston that year?"

"He did. And he should have left to find his wife and children. At least, that's what I heard."

"I didn't know you were so interested in the history."

With a shake of her head, Charlotte turned to look out over the sea. "Someone I know is. Too interested."

Her tone of voice, more than the words, caught Christie's interest and she joined Charlotte. "Come on, tell me the story. And don't say there isn't one, I'm known for my detective skills and insatiable interest in mysteries."

Charlotte's face change, the muscles of her jaw tightening and forehead creasing. Without meaning to, Christie took Charlotte's hand, who jumped, but didn't pull away.

"I'm really good with secrets, Charlotte. You've helped me. Let me be a friend for you."

For the longest moment, Charlotte stared at Christie, then she closed her eyes briefly and sighed. "You have no idea how much I want to talk to someone. I can't, Christie."

"You know, I'm feeling overwhelmed by the new salon, and the wedding, and dealing with… well, some memories. I'd love a distraction." She let go of Charlotte's hand with a warm smile. "And I'm really good at hypotheticals so don't even need to know names."

"Do you draw stick figures?"

"Umm, mind maps. But not stick figures."

"Good. Trevor does and it kind of freaked me out."

Christie decided she didn't need to know about Trev drawing stick figures. And why. "So, in fifty words or less, tell me about this person with an unhealthy interest in the past of our little town."

# 31

# ALL ROADS LEAD TO ONE COTTAGE

*B*ernie stood in the long hallway leading to the kitchen, studying the photograph of Eoin Ryan hanging on the wall.

*Thief.*

He'd loved to have met him face-to-face. Sorted him out for the damage he'd done to Harry.

*And his descendants.*

"Hello, Bernie. Would you like the light on?" Elizabeth had her arms full with a large basket of washing.

"Let me help."

"No, dear, I'm fine, really. Though if you'd open the back door, it would be wonderful."

"Here, you open the door," he said, taking the basket. "I'll bring it out."

"Thank you. For some reason the outside door of the laundry is sticking." Elizabeth ushered Bernie into the backyard. "Over there, please."

Bernie nodded and crossed the lawn to the clothes line tucked near the corner of the house. "I can take a look at the laundry door for you."

"Goodness, Bernie. You are my guest! What a sweet man you are, but no, it will be taken care of. Just pop the basket onto the little stand if you will."

Sure, why not?

*Mother would be amazed.*

As soon as he put it down, Bernie reached into a peg bag and started hanging washing. "I've been to the library in Green Bay. I was actually a bit disappointed."

"Why?"

"There is some information about Palmerston House and the foundation families of River's End, but lots missing."

Elizabeth rehung a shirt Bernie had pegged. He scowled, then picked up another and hung it the way she had. "A few tantalising little details but when I searched, a dead end. And I wanted so much to get copies of old photographs for my book."

"Have you spoken to George? His family had a lot to do with the library, particularly with his knowledge of local trade. He's been on local council for as long as I've been here. Probably has all sorts of things tucked away in his house."

"Doesn't he live behind the shop?"

"No. His father built a nice house on the next block over back in the 1950s... or was it 60s?"

Bernie sighed. "I have spoken to him but he's a bit defensive about the old grandfather clock. Almost as though he thinks I'll steal it."

"I'm sure he doesn't, dear. He loves talking about the past and has such a good memory. Would you like me to let him know you are my guest, and quite genuine?"

"He did say I could photograph the clock, so maybe I'll visit the bakery first and take him something nice as a peace offering."

"You are a sweet young man."

*You won't think so for long.*

"Elizabeth, something intrigued me from the library. There was mention of a timber trunk here in Palmerston House that arrived with Henry Temple and his family. Would it still be here?" Bernie stopped pegging and stared at Elizabeth, willing her to say yes.

She finished hanging the last of the washing, brow furrowed. Then, after picking up the empty basket, she started back toward the house. Bernie walked with her. "A trunk. Most likely Lilian and Patrick Ryan took it with them when they moved to Ireland. Or their eldest daughter, Dorothy, may have taken it when she moved to Melbourne."

Bernie dropped his head. If it was in Ireland he had no hope of finding the key. He already knew it wasn't in Dorothy Ryan's estate.

"Unless—" At the back door, Elizabeth hesitated.

"Unless what?"

"Now, I am probably completely wrong, but there was a trunk with a tie to Palmerston House. It is in the old stationmaster's cottage. Somebody hid Thomas Blake's letters to Martha in it sometime in the 1960s and it was only discovered last year. But I'm sure it won't be the same one."

She disappeared inside. Bernie followed, his mind elsewhere. Time to pay the cottage a proper visit.

---

*A*s Christie turned into her street she spotted the Range Rover on the far side of the railway line, parked outside the cottage. *Angus!*

She sprinted the rest of the way. The front door was closed so she let herself into the kitchen. Laughter led her down the hallway, where Randall met her.

"Where are they hiding?"

"Is that you, dear?" Martha called from the lounge room.

Angus stood just in time to open his arms as Christie flew into them. She leaned her head against his shoulder. "I'm so happy you're home."

He released her with a wide smile. "So am I."

"Morning, Christie."

"Oh, Thomas, I'm sorry. Good morning to you both." Christie grinned and flopped onto the sofa. "I didn't disturb you when I left?"

"Yes. Old men need their sleep."

"Take no notice of Thomas, dear. I'm going to make some coffee so you two catch up and we'll be right back." Martha stood, tapping Thomas on the shoulder as she did. He joined her with a sigh, but winked at Christie on his way to the kitchen.

Angus settled himself next to Christie. "You look well."

"So do you. When did you arrive?"

"Early last evening. I am sorry I didn't call but the opportunity presented itself to take Elizabeth out for dinner."

"And?"

"A gentleman doesn't give secrets away."

From the sparkle in his eyes, Christie didn't need him to say a word. "You both deserve every happiness."

"Still early days. Now, I believe Martin returned early this morning from a trip away. How is he?"

"Tired, which is hardly surprising considering he spent almost a week managing a group of disadvantaged teens. He's getting some sleep then we're talking about the wedding."

"Ah. Which reminds me. Elizabeth extends an invitation to you both, as well as Thomas and Martha, to join us at Palmerston House for dinner tonight. Apart from allowing us to catch up, there is a matter I need to discuss with you all."

"Are you alright?" Christie grabbed his hand.

"I am. It is about Miss Dorothy's estate, and whilst it hasn't changed anything, I'd like to apprise you all of a rather odd claim made – the reason, in fact, for my absence."

"A claim? I thought Gran's will was already finalised? Is there another relative I don't know about?"

Angus laughed. "So many questions. I will answer them all. So, seven o'clock tonight?"

"What's happening then? Sounds like my dinner time." Thomas carried a tray in, followed by Martha with a plate of cupcakes. "And I do insist on having a decent dinner. At my age—"

"You sound as though I don't feed you, old man." Martha offered Angus a cupcake. "I know it's almost lunchtime—"

"Another of my favourite meals of the day."

"But this recipe is a little bit indulgent and really goes well with the coffee." Martha shook her head at Thomas who had put the tray on the coffee table. "And we would love to come along tonight. Shall I bring anything?"

"Me." Thomas tried to take a cupcake but Martha whisked the plate away. "Tell me again why I waited for you at the jetty?"

"Because I was worth the wait."

Thomas nodded, managing to get a cupcake as Martha began pouring coffee. "These are worth the wait."

"Thomas, do you know anything about Henry Temple's grave?" Christie watched as Thomas bit into the cupcake and closed his eyes in pleasure.

"Mmm. The bride was worth waiting for. It's a grave. What's to know?"

"How did he end up buried in River's End?"

"You know, I'll be pleased when you marry Martin and move out." Thomas raised his eyebrows and took another bite of cupcake. Martha looked at him in horror. Christie burst into laughter.

"This cottage is a bad influence. Every time you come up with some new mystery to solve, you're here."

"Except this time I was at Henry's grave, Thomas. With Charlotte."

"Oh dear. Now there's two of you. May I have another cupcake, beloved?"

# 32

## HIDING THE UNRIDEABLE

*T*rev arrived back in River's End after lunchtime and headed straight to the car park at the top of the cliff. Whenever his mind was worrying about something, he'd go there, to the top of the stone steps. The view was every bit as good as the one from Martin's house, though for him nothing beat the rugged scenery in the mountains. Up there though, the air was rich with the scent of gum trees and ash, cooler high-altitude smells. Here, his senses would fill with the sea.

He parked the patrol car and got out, stretching after the drive. The chance meeting with Martin stirred him up. His friend was a man in love, a man whose protective instincts were at the fore wherever Christie was concerned. And there was a deep contentment in him. Since Martin rode off, Trev's mind had spent way too long on Charlotte Dean.

The ocean was a reflection of the sky. Perfect blue.

*Unlike the night of the storm.*

He'd run down the steps and along the beach at break-neck speed to join in the rescue effort. He'd never forget Charlotte appearing from nowhere as Randall lay on the sand, soaking wet and barely moving. She'd told Trev what to do and how to do it. And with such authority he'd never questioned it. She saved the dog and as she did so, a part of him was lost.

Behind him, he heard a sob. His heart went out to whoever was distressed by their grave side visit.

*How much we love and hard we take their loss.*

The sob came again and he turned his back on the sea. There was nobody in sight, so he wandered around the graveyard until he followed the sound to the oldest part. Where the founders of River's End were buried.

Charlotte sat cross-legged near a grave, head in her hands.

With a deep sigh, she wiped her face and looked up. Straight at Trev. Her eyes filled with confusion, or conflict. He couldn't tell. Then she scrambled to her feet.

"Hey, Charlie. I didn't mean to startle you."

"You didn't. What are you doing here?"

"I came here to think. To the top of the steps, actually."

"Oh."

"I heard a sob or two and wanted to be sure nobody was hurt. Or too upset. It's a high cliff."

Charlotte raised her chin. "I'm not about to throw myself off."

"I didn't know it was you." Trev read the headstone. "Henry Temple. Okay, now I'm curious. You're not his relative by chance?"

"Of course not! I just... happened to stop here."

"Right."

"What were you thinking about? On the steps?"

"The storm. Town being down there all helping rescue Christie. You."

"Me?"

"Bossing me around as you worked on Randall."

"Sorry." Charlotte smiled a little. "Not sorry."

"Funny."

"But you said you came here to think. Surely not about that?"

"No. Now, why were you crying? Has someone upset you?"

Charlotte looked away.

"I'm here for you." Trev moved a step closer and Charlotte looked up. "I'm your friend."

"I can't."

Trev was certain there was hesitation in her voice. Time to change tactics. "I've been on the road for hours, to the mountains and back. Have you eaten?"

She shook her head.

"Cool. Pies on me at the bakery, or whatever you want. No more questions, okay? Two friends having lunch." Trev watched her, expecting her usual refusal.

Instead, she smiled. "Friends having lunch. I'd like to."

"Come on then." Not willing to let her change her mind, Trev started walking to his patrol car. She joined him.

"In that?"

"In that. I'll let you turn the lights and siren on if you like."

---

*C*harlotte was fascinated by the equipment inside the patrol car. Radios, a small computer, lots of interesting dials and switches. Not to mention the man driving it. She snuck a sideways look at Trev. His shirt fitted well around a strong chest and abs. As he turned the steering wheel, his triceps caught her attention. Being so close to him made his physical presence obvious. He kept his body in good shape.

*Great shape.*

He glanced at her, and she was sure he smiled ever so slightly at catching her checking him out.

"You must have been in one of these before?"

"No, actually never. Although I once wanted to go into forensic psychology."

"Work with criminals? What stopped you?"

"Stuff. I still might, particularly if I could be away from an office a bit more."

Trev drove over the bridge into River's End. "Happy to put you in touch with someone. We need more people like you."

"Perhaps. Thanks." She wasn't going back to her practice, Charlotte knew with sudden clarity. This might be worth exploring, a change of direction and being able to be more hands-on with people who needed it.

*More than Bernie Cooper did.*

Being in this little town suited her soul more than Brisbane. Although a beautiful city, she'd craved space and quiet. And a chance to reinvent herself, for what it was worth.

Trev pulled into a parking spot close to the bakery. "I had breakfast before the sun made an appearance and now all I want is one of Sylvia's pies and even more coffee."

Out of the patrol car, Charlotte and Trev strolled to the bakery. They'd never done this before, hung out together. It was… nice. Two friends getting lunch together. Like with Christie. Except this was a red hot police officer who knew a bit too much about her soft spots. And had just seen her crying at the grave of a stranger. Charlotte slowed as they reached the door. Maybe not such a good idea.

With a push, Trev opened the door and held it for Charlotte. Too late now. It would be rude to back out.

"Hi, Sylvia, got anything left for a couple of starving people?"

"What's your fancy?"

Trev tilted his head to look at Charlotte. "You first."

"Oh, those pies look nice. Any flavour is fine thanks."

"And same for me. But I'll have two. And coffees. Flat whites."

"Inside or out?"

"Outside, if you're happy?" he asked Charlotte and she nodded.

"You find a table and I'll have lunch out in a jiffy." Sylvia reached for plates. "But later, would you mind if I tell you about an odd incident earlier?"

"Tell me now if you like. Charlie, do you want to grab a spot?"

Charlotte found a table and sat looking toward the intersection. From here she could see the real estate agency and George's shop. She liked George.

She gazed into the bakery, watching Trev lean on the counter as Sylvia waved her arms around. Upset. How could anyone stay agitated around Trev? His nature was so calm and solid... he resonated strength and compassion.

"Hello, Charlotte!" Daphne hurried toward her.

"Would you like to join us? I mean, me at the moment."

Daphne glanced into the bakery. "Oh, are you with Trev? How lovely. He's such a nice boy."

"We're getting lunch. I mean, we ran into each other at the grave-yard and realised we'd not eaten. So. Here we are."

*What is wrong with you?*

"Well. At least she's telling him what happened. I told her to make a complaint.

"What happened?"

"Oh." Daphne sank onto a seat, her eyes now on Charlotte. "There was the nastiest man here earlier. So rude to Jess and I think he'd upset George beforehand."

A sense of dread crept through Charlotte. "To Jess? What man?"

"The photographer staying at Palmerston House with you. He even threw an empty bottle on the ground and waltzed off as though he was outside the law!"

"Where's the bottle now?"

"What? I think Sylvia threw it away. Why do you ask?"

"Did you see him?"

"Did I see him! I saw him slam the door of his car a few times and drive off like a madman the other day. He reminded me..."

Charlotte's dread turned to concern as something close to fear crossed Daphne's face. "Reminded you of Rupert, yes?"

With a small nod, Daphne gave away the emotions she'd bottled for so long. Her eyes glistened.

"Listen, you're safe. And I'm going to come and see you later. Okay? We'll have a chat, girl to girl, and I'll give you some tricks to deal with all of those feelings."

"You are so sweet. I can see why Trev adores you." Daphne stood.

"I'd better get John his lunch. And I think your young man is heading out now."

***

"*O*ne pepper beef pie, and sauce on the side. Didn't know if you wanted it." Trev put a plate in front of Charlotte, pulling her out of her thoughts.

"Thanks. Yes."

Trev sat opposite. "Coffee's on its way. Once we've eaten, I can drop you home if you like."

"Oh, I'm fine to walk." Charlotte sliced into the pie and sniffed the steam as it rose. Her stomach growled.

"No trouble though 'cos I'll be going to Palmerston House anyway."

Fork halfway to her mouth, Charlotte stared at Trev. "Why?" She knew why.

Intent on his own pies, Trev didn't look up. "Have you had much to do with Elizabeth's guest, Bernie Cooper?"

"Why?"

"I'm interested in your take on him."

"Why?"

*Run away. Stop this now.*

When Trev lifted his eyes to hers, serious and kind and curious, she was overwhelmed by a need to tell him everything.

"Stop saying why. Because I value your opinion. I trust it." He took a bite of pie, eyes never leaving Charlotte's. The need to flee dissipated under his unwavering gaze and warmth worked its way from her toes up. To give herself time to think, she put pie in her mouth, hardly tasting it as she chewed. The corners of Trev's mouth turned up as though he was quite aware of what she was doing.

"Do you want my professional opinion or personal?"

"Whatever you're comfortable giving."

"My observation of him at Palmerston House is that he is very respectful... of Elizabeth. I have little to do with him."

*Is that enough?*

"Okay. See, he was pretty rude to Jess this morning. She's a kid. Sat himself out here with his own bottle of water, which he tossed onto the ground mind you. She offered him coffee and he got nasty."

"Do you know where the bottle is now?"

"Probably in the bin. Why?"

Charlotte smiled. "Now you're saying it. He didn't hurt her though?"

"I wouldn't still be here if he had. Have you seen any sign of this sort of behaviour?"

"As I said, I've not had much to do with him at Palmerston House. He's out with his cameras most of the time. Apparently doing some sort of coffee table book on the region. Elizabeth is quite excited."

The way Trev stared at Charlotte unsettled her. As if he could read between her carefully constructed lines. See past her literal responses. Any more of his level gaze and she'd cave. Spill everything and then ask him to forgive her for not being honest earlier. Would he? Or were his ethics so strong he'd lose any respect he had for her?

"Charlie? Why so sad?"

"I'm not. I'm okay. I have to go."

"Finish lunch. No more talk of Bernie, okay?" As if it were agreed, he took a bite of pie. Charlotte forced her muscles to relax, to regulate her breathing until the slight tremble in her hands abated. He'd be more suspicious if she ran. Again.

# 33

# ALMOST TAKEN BY THE SEA

*M*artin let himself into the studio. One by one he opened the windows, then the skylights, relishing the warmth flooding in. Enough to air the place and bring the temperature up a bit. Christie must have come in to do her thing. The bin was empty and the small fridge was freshly stocked with bottled water. He smiled at her need to look after him, something that once would have driven him away. Now the little touches pleased him.

He only had one painting underway at the moment and it needed finishing before the wedding. He stood before the sheet-covered easel, frowning.

The sheet was straight. He had a way of covering paintings. Left side slightly longer. This was even. Perfect. But Christie respected his insistence on keeping his paintings to himself until he was ready to share. She'd never lift a sheet. With one motion he pulled the sheet away, dropping it onto the floor.

If Christie had seen this she would have told him. The subject matter was intense and personal to them both. This would have distressed her, the things she didn't know from that night.

*I thought I'd lost you both.*

Martin dropped his head, hands clenched as gut-wrenching

anguish tore at him. She blamed herself enough for nearly losing Randall so how could she ever know how devastated he'd been in the shallows? His dog. His sweetheart. So nearly taken by the sea.

*Except they weren't.*

Martin steadied his thoughts. The purpose of this painting was to expel the demons. And it was doing that, bit by bit as he mixed colours and turned them into powerful images. But what was meant for him, as a kind of therapy, was not for her eyes in this unfinished state. If it ever was.

"You in there, son?"

Before Thomas stepped through the door, Martin scooped the sheet up and tossed it over the easel. Randall raced in, tail wagging furiously. With a delighted whimper, he threw himself at Martin, who sank into a squat to pull the dog against himself. He held Randall's head with both hands, smiling into his soft eyes. "I missed you too, dog."

"What about me?" Thomas held his hand out and Martin stood and gave him a hug instead.

"What about you. I'm surprised you returned my dog."

"Martha made me."

Martin released Thomas. "He wasn't a burden, was he?"

"The opposite. She's concerned one day I'll forget to give him back. Not that she'd mind, considering she's the one insisting he share the bedroom with us."

"Not in with Christie? Would you like some water?"

"Please. Well, he starts in there and gravitates to our room during the night. Probably because she gets up so early and he likes his sleep." Thomas followed Martin to the fridge and accepted the offered bottle. "Thanks." He lowered himself to the sofa and opened the lid. "She missed you."

Martin perched on the arm of the sofa, opening his own bottle. "She fell out of the attic, Thomas."

"Thought she might keep that to herself."

"There's a bruise all the way down her hip and leg. Why would she keep it from me?"

"In case you got cross."

"I don't get cross. I did tell her it was dangerous and could have been a lot worse."

"Like I said. Anyway, Charlotte sorted her out and between them they got the trunk down."

"Beside the point. She should have waited for me. Why would you encourage it, Thomas?"

"Son, I was in Green Bay and had no idea she'd decide to surprise me. Didn't know she'd fallen either, not until after Charlotte visited days later."

"Meaning?"

"Charlotte came to check on her. She assumed Martha would know. Drop it. Now, Angus requests our presence at Palmerston House tonight. Elizabeth is doing dinner and he'd like to discuss the reason for his return to Melbourne. Something about Dorothy's estate."

"This isn't going to affect Christie?"

"Dunno. Angus says not, but something's not right. Not right in town and now this."

"Granddad?"

"Don't granddad me. Just have a feeling."

Randall tore out through the door and a moment later, Martin and Thomas laughed as a rabbit streaked past the window with the dog in pursuit, losing ground in seconds. He stopped, the tip of his tail wagging a little as he watched the rabbit disappear into a burrow. Despite the light moment, Thomas' words repeated in Martin's head.

## 34

# A CHALLENGE

*a* bit before seven, the four wheel drive backed out of the cottage driveway, spluttered a bit, then rattled across the railway line, its headlights missing the SUV parked down the siding on the far side of the abandoned station.

Bernie waited a few moments in the dark, then started the motor and pulled back onto the road. He drove past the cottage to the spot he'd parked in last time, hidden from the road by dense bushes.

Backpack on, he cut across the paddock to the back garden of the cottage. He slipped through a gap in the fence, and pulled a torch from the backpack.

Tonight he'd find the key to the door and then, as everyone slept, he'd make his way down to the cellar. His heart lifted.

*Soon, Harry, soon your legacy will be with its rightful owner.*

For now though, he needed to get inside.

Bernie circled the cottage, testing each window. All locked and with stupid old-fashioned clasps he couldn't open without breaking. The doors weren't much better, so he helped himself to a ladder from the unlocked garage. He opened it to its full length and leaned it against the wall. A moment later he'd opened the attic window.

Inside the attic was an old chair. Workbench. Nothing else. He opened the access hatch, pushed the sliding ladder down and lowered himself into the hallway.

The trunk was on the dining room table, its curved top closed. And no key. But it was unlocked so he opened it and read the carved words in its base. *London 1840.* What now? This was the trunk from the diary and there should be a key with it.

By the back door was the customary rack for keys and other items. But only a letterbox key on it. He wanted to scream. Set fire to the place and let the whole damn thing go up in smoke. In a minute his head would explode. Except Harry left clues behind. Clues in the diary and one he must have missed. Bernie retraced his steps, ensuring he left the cottage the way he'd found it.

On his way through the paddock to his car, Bernie remembered. There was one more place the key might be. Harry only made a brief reference in the diary to the pond and he needed to reread it in context. Things might still be salvageable.

---

*D*inner at Palmerston House was finished, and now everyone sat in the front living room as coffee and tea was poured. Angus settled onto a comfortable armchair with a grin. "My goodness, you all look so expectant, and I really don't have much to tell."

"You've kept us in suspense for hours!"

"And you are still such an impatient young woman, Christie."

Christie glanced at Martin for backup but he was quiet. As he'd been all evening. He briefly met her eyes and squeezed her hand.

"You mentioned there'd been some sort of challenge to Dorothy's will?" Elizabeth prompted from her spot beside Martha and Thomas on the sofa.

"Jacob Bright – her solicitor, you might recall meeting him, Christie – received a letter from a person suggesting they were a member of the Temple family."

Thomas straightened. "There's none left. Not according to George anyway."

"This person claimed otherwise. Stated they are the direct descendant of Henry and Eleanor Temple through their daughter. It's a fairly convoluted ancestry with a couple of gaps in the records along the way, but this person certainly believes themselves to represent the line."

"But even if they are a Temple, what would it have to do with Dorothy?" Martha frowned. "She had no relationship to the Temples."

"No, but your family once owned this beautiful home. This challenge concerned the exchange of ownership of Palmerston House from Harry Temple to Eoin Ryan."

"Oh, do you mean the poker game?" Christie leaned forward.

"Yes. The person asserts Eoin Ryan illegally and immorally tricked Harry Temple into wagering the family home." Angus stopped to sip his tea.

"Even if so, what does any of this have to do with Dorothy's estate?" Martha wound her fingers around each other until Thomas put his hand over them. "Palmerston House was sold many years ago. It formed no part of her will."

Martin picked up his cup of coffee. "Presumably, if this person is correct and able to prove Palmerston House was unlawfully obtained, they expect to claim to be its true owners."

"Exactly. They didn't care at all about the money or Miss Dorothy's Toorak home or the cars. They wanted Palmerston House."

Elizabeth gasped.

"They presented no proof. Not one shred of evidence other than some photocopied extracts from a diary allegedly kept by Harry Temple. When Jacob requested access to the entire diary to verify its authenticity, the claim was withdrawn."

"But who'd come up with such a thing? And if it were true, would they really have the right to take... take..." Elizabeth's face paled and Angus reached across to pat her leg.

"I didn't wish to alarm you. Jacob thinks not and besides, whoever is behind this has backed down."

"Who is this person? Maybe Martin and I should pay them a visit."

"No need, Thomas. We never met with him, but he signed everything as William Temple. Jacob's enquiries into him led nowhere. Quite an odd situation, but not one you need worry about, Elizabeth."

"Where do things stand, Angus?" Martin asked.

"There's been no contact from this man for more than a week, despite Jacob making several attempts to finalise things. He thinks it was a fanciful exercise and expects nothing more to come of it."

"Too many odd things going in River's End." Thomas squeezed Martha's hand. "I suggest we all keep our wits about us and treat strangers with suspicion."

*A*nnoyed to see the four wheel drive, Bernie walked around the outside of Palmerston House and let himself in through the back door. Even from here, laughter and chatter reached him and he scowled.

*They're in my house.*

Sitting on his furniture. Enjoying their privileged lives as if nobody else mattered.

Was Lottie with them? He inched closer, thinking up excuses if anyone found him listening.

"Did I see Trev here earlier?" The speaker must be the new guest.

"You did, Angus. He was looking for one of my guests."

"The one with the SUV?" Another voice he didn't know. One with an edge to it.

"Bernie. The photographer."

"Humph."

"What's wrong, Thomas?" Another male voice, younger.

"Like I said earlier. Treat newcomers with suspicion."

"But he's a nice young man. Tidy, quiet. Likes to talk about Palmerston House."

*Good on you, Elizabeth. Maybe I'll let you stay in one of the guest rooms.*

"Then why'd Trev want to talk to him?"

"What are you doing?"

Bernie jumped, then glared at Charlotte who stood partway down the staircase, arms crossed. "Are you eavesdropping?"

All hope of hearing Elizabeth's answer disappeared and Bernie stalked to the foot of the stairs. "What the hell are you doing?" he hissed.

"Getting coffee. Why are you listening to their conversation? If they wanted to include you, they would."

"Are you planning on running over and telling them? Maybe you're the one who set the copper on me."

"Oh, what did he have to say?"

"It *was* you." Bernie advanced up the steps until eye level with Charlotte, grinning when she flinched.

"It was not. You're responsible for any police visits so don't blame me. And stop lurking around."

"I'd be very careful, Lottie." He joined her on the same step, intruding on her personal space and, although she didn't move, he relished the fear in her eyes. "Little girls shouldn't mess with things they don't understand."

"Are you threatening me?"

"Take whatever you want from it. But stay away from me."

He brushed past her and ran up the stairs. Once in his room, he locked the door and threw his bag on the floor. Now he'd never know what Elizabeth said. Bernie dragged the diary out and, not bothering to remove his shoes, lay on the bed and opened it.

# 35

## A KEY IS LOST

*1* *853*
  Harry hid behind the stables, waiting for dusk. The Ryan family themselves had yet to arrive but, all day, drays filled with furniture had come up the driveway. He recognised Eoin Ryan's timber workers, pulled off their normal duties for the apparently more important job of wiping all traces of the Temple family from Palmerston House.

The last dray left and Harry climbed up to the second floor, finding hand and footholds in the limestone and dragging himself upwards. The furthest bedroom window was unlocked as he'd prayed it would be and in moments he was inside.

The trunk wasn't in his daughter's bedroom and new furniture filled the room he and Eleanor once decorated together. No more laughter. No soft footsteps running from here to the master bedroom for a little girl with a big smile.

"Damn you." He slammed the door behind himself, not sure who he was damning. He sat at the top of the staircase, built to his specifications from Eoin Ryan's timber. Below, the foyer mocked him with memories. Music from the string quartet he'd brought all the way from Melbourne. Women in billowing gowns danced with suited men. His friends, all here for the house warming of the century, barely two years ago.

Where were those friends now? All turned their backs on him the moment he asked for help. And one of them probably housed his wife and child with no word to let him know they were safe. His life was a failure.

After a few moments feeling sorry for himself, Harry lit a lantern and went searching. The trunk was in the front parlour. He slid the key into a pocket with a satisfied sigh, but there was no time to enjoy the moment, for the distinctive sound of more drays filtered through the window.

He hurried out of the parlour and toward the back of Palmerston House, startled by the sound of a key in the front door.

Before he reached the end of the hallway, light from Eoin's lantern flooded into the foyer. "Who is it? Stop!"

Harry ran until he reached the back door. Cool air met his face as he burst outside. Heavy footsteps followed and he dropped the lantern and sprinted down the rough path into the night.

"Come back here!"

Harry threw himself behind a tree. As lights approached, he wrenched the key out of the pocket. He couldn't be found. Not with this on him. Jail was not an option and he'd be heading there if Eoin or his men got hold of him.

"Boss, think he went this way." A voice called from the other direction and Harry held his breath until he heard Eoin tramp back along the path and out of earshot. He stepped from behind the tree. Almost straight into the back of one of Eoin's men.

"Where'd you think you be going?" The man spun around and grabbed for Harry, who ducked and scampered past. Fear drove Harry toward the pond then around it but his pursuer was catching him.

With a flick of his wrist he tossed the key into the shallows. He'd come back for it. His feet slipped on the softer ground around the edge of the pond and he scrambled for higher ground. Straight into Eoin Ryan's fist.

*J*n bed, Bernie crossed his arms behind his head, eyes on the ceiling. Was the key still in the pond, or had Harry come back for it? The diary mentioned Eoin Ryan warning him to stay off the property or face prosecution. Then some self-pitying speech about his bad luck. The final entry a week later referred to obtaining rope long enough to climb down to the cave entrance.

*And then you died.*

Or gave up. He'd probably taken his final breath as an old, lonely and bitter man somewhere miles from River's End. Beaten by the Ryan family and his own lack of pride. No guts. First he wagered the family home and then he simply walked away.

Bernie closed his eyes. Tomorrow would be busy. First, a visit to Senior Constable Sibbritt to sort out his good name. Then, another visit to the cliff. And once it was dark, his search for the key would continue.

# 36

# NOTHING I WOULDN'T DO FOR YOU

*H*and in hand, Martin and Christie wandered across the meadow to the house, pausing for a kiss, or a moment to look at the sea. The air was cool but still pleasant in spite of the hour. They'd walked up the hill talking about the revelations after dinner.

"Have you met this Bernie Cooper?" Martin asked.

"Nope. I've seen him from a distance on the beach. Taking photos."

"Of the sea?"

"Actually, no. Of the cliff face. He was at the far end of the jetty with some huge lens pointing to this end of the beach."

"Hmm."

"Now you sound like Thomas."

"Thomas has formed an opinion of him."

"And Trev wants to speak with him. Wonder what about?"

"None of our business, sweetheart."

"But—"

"Christie."

"Okay, okay."

Martin unlocked and opened the sliding door. Randall rushed out, tail plumed high in excitement. He followed them inside, then dashed out again. Christie went to the kitchen. "Coffee? Water? Wine?"

"Water, thanks."

By the time Christie brought two glasses of water to where Martin sat in the living room, Randall was at his side. She put the glasses down and closed the sliding door, locking it.

"Thanks. I think today has caught up with me."

Christie sat beside Martin and handed him a glass. "You didn't sleep, did you?"

"No. Did I tell you I ran into Trev at the roadhouse? He was drinking some excuse for coffee and enjoying the view."

"Oh, that's where he was going so early."

"He mentioned he saw you in town." Martin stared at Christie over the rim of his glass as he sipped.

"River's End is safe. Again."

"I'm not comfortable with you wandering around in the dark."

"It was almost light. Stop worrying about me." Christie kissed his cheek with a smile.

"Never going to happen." Martin put his glass down. "You'd better enjoy these last days of single life." He took Christie's glass from her and put it beside his. "My wife won't roam the streets before dawn." He wrapped his arms around her. "Nor will she take risks such as lifting heavy objects from attics."

"It wasn't heavy."

"She won't forget to charge her phone and tell people where she's going. And definitely she won't ignore her husband when it comes to looking after herself."

Christie tilted her head, eyes sparkling. "This wife of yours has a lot of don'ts. What if she refuses such archaic control over her free will?"

"It is her free will to change her ways." Martin brushed his lips over hers. "I'm not forcing her to do anything."

"So, what is she allowed to do... with her free will." Christie's fingers played with the buttons on Martin's shirt.

"She can laugh a lot. And create her beautiful new salon. Spend every night with her handsome husband. Raise their children with him." He kissed Christie deeply, crushing her against him. When he raised his head, his eyes were dark as the night. "Does that outweigh the small changes she'll make about her own safety?"

"I love you so much." It was barely a whisper. "There's nothing I won't do for you, Martin."

***

*M*uch later, Martin sat before the easel in the studio, one spotlight creating a narrow workspace around him. He dabbed at the painting, unsettled. He'd slept but only briefly. Christie's words bothered him.

"There's nothing I won't do for you, Martin."

Yet she was keeping secrets again. Not to hurt him or be deliberately deceptive, of this he had no doubt. She was an honest person. But also a deeply caring one who never liked burdening those in her life. Coupled with how her grandmother taught her to put up barriers to protect herself, Christie's default was to say nothing, share nothing, unless it was positive.

He put down the paintbrush and stared at the canvas. What must have gone on in her head out there? In the painting she was safe in his arms, along with Randall at his side. The end result. But for Christie, when did she feel safe? When did she know the ordeal was over?

*Does she know?*

And what would happen when *Jasmine Sea* returned?

Exhaustion overwhelmed him. Too tired to even clean his brush, he stood and picked up the sheet. This was the other problem. His gut instinct was she'd seen the painting. It bothered him on so many levels, but mostly because she'd said nothing. He didn't want to ask outright. *Give it some time.* His usual approach.

Martin turned off the light and locked the studio door. The grass was damp from a low mist. He left his shoes on the deck and quietly closed and locked the sliding door. All was peaceful in here, although Randall raised his head with sleepy eyes.

Christie was asleep on her side, the covers pushed down. He touched her shoulder and it was cold, so he pulled the covers up. She stirred as he slipped into bed, but didn't wake, so he watched her until his eyes were too heavy. Soon, this would be their reality. Every day and night together. Perfection.

37
---

# AN OPEN WINDOW

*O*n her way home the next morning, Christie dropped in to see Elizabeth, finding her in the kitchen having tea with Angus.

"Did you even leave?" Angus hugged her, then drew out a chair as Elizabeth found another cup.

"Only as far as Martin's house. He shooed me out after breakfast, something about secret bridegroom's business. Do you two know what he's up to?" Christie sat and smiled her thanks as Elizabeth handed her a coffee.

"Not a thing, and you shouldn't be worrying about it either. A man needs time to prepare for such an important day." Angus took his seat again.

"So, is he meeting with Thomas?"

"Christie."

"Now you sound like Martin. Don't ask questions. Don't worry about what other people are doing. He refuses to speculate about why…" Christie looked at the doorway, then lowered her voice, "Trev came to see your guest."

"And here is not the place to discuss it." Elizabeth smiled slightly but her tone was firm.

"I'm sorry. You're right. So, I did wonder if you know any of the history of the trunk."

"The one you found at the cottage?"

"Yes. Thomas and I talked about it the other night for a while. He said he was surprised I wasn't curious about why those letters and rings were locked inside it and hidden in the attic of an empty cottage. And it kind of shocked me, because I'd imagined he lived there with Frannie and she'd kept her secrets close by."

"But he didn't. As long as I've owned Palmerston House, until he married Martha, I've only known him to live at his little cabin in the mountains. Of course, by then he was raising Martin on his own."

"I wonder where Thomas and Frannie lived. Or was it in his mountain house?"

"No, he bought it after the tragedy happened. I remember Daphne mentioning it once. John handled the sale of his family home and found him the other place. Going back to the trunk though, you're not the first person to ask me about it." Elizabeth played with her cup. "Bernie Cooper asked me the other day."

"He did?"

"He said he'd come across a mention of a timber trunk in some old papers at Green Bay library and was curious about it. I did mention there was one in the cottage. Oh dear, have I done the wrong thing?"

Angus put his hand over Elizabeth's. "The young man was just interested in history. It's not as though he's a thief, dear lady."

"Exactly. No harm done, Elizabeth. I'm sure if he's as nice as you say he's simply curious about anything to do with your home. But I had no idea Green Bay library kept any records. Might be worth a drive over."

"And don't forget George knows just about everything about our town. I'd be asking him."

"*Whatever* are you doing, old man?" Martha hurried down the hallway from the kitchen, having heard the ladder drop from the attic.

Thomas stood underneath the open access door, staring upwards and tapping the hooked tool on the ground. "The window's open."

"Open? How would that happen? More to the point, Thomas, how do you know?" She took the tool from him and hung it on the ring Christie had added on the hallway wall.

"Heard it in the night. Creaking back and forth. Thought it was a tree on the roof but I've been around outside to have a look and it's open."

"I'm sure it can wait until Christie gets home."

"Martin already blames me for her falling off the ladder last time, so I'm not about to let her back up there. Here, you can hold it and I'll be right back." Thomas raised a hand to grasp a rung.

"I'm not happy about this." Nevertheless, Martha gripped the upright.

"Used to shimmy up and down here every day." He grunted as he lifted himself onto the first rung.

"You're not a teenager anymore."

He grinned and aimed a kiss at her cheek, missing as the ladder swayed. "Feel like one around you, bride."

"Watch your footing. I'm not at all happy about the idea of having to call an ambulance. Perhaps I should do it now. Just in case."

Rung by rung, Thomas hauled himself upwards. At the top he stopped. "See. All good. Put the kettle on. I'll be ready for some coffee in a couple of minutes."

"I'm not moving until you're back on solid ground!"

He grinned and rotated his body to sit on the edge of the hatch. Then his smile faded. Almost five decades since he'd last been up here.

Thomas got to his feet and turned on the light. Everything was the same. His workbench still covered with splatter upon splatter of colour. Once, hard earned paints lined the top of it, punctuated with his favourite brushes. Hours working at the pub would pay for just one, but he demanded quality and every cent was worth it. He'd kept three easels. One with a blank canvas, one part finished, and one ready to sell. Not that he'd sold many at first. Only after Martha left and he'd poured his heart into his work had the buyers come. One then another until he expanded to four and five easels. Money he'd raised a family on.

"Tom? Are you okay?"

"Just checking for mice."

"Mice?"

With a laugh, Thomas went to the window. It swung back and forth in the breeze and he reached out and caught it. He closed and locked it. Then pressed against the timber frame. It didn't yield. He frowned. How had it got open?

A long time ago, rain thundering on the metal roof, he'd stood here for hours, staring sightlessly at the storm. The storm that took Martha from him. Changed his life and hers forever. Broke his heart yet made him the man he was today.

Outside, brilliant sunlight filled a garden rich with greenery and emerging flowers. Thanks to Christie, the other woman in his life. Frannie was no longer a love of his. She'd ruined that with her deception. All she was now was the mother of his beloved son, and grandmother of Martin, the light of his life.

"Hi. Need a hand?" Christie appeared through the hatch.

"Did the bride send you? Doesn't trust me."

"She's making coffee and she does trust you. Just doesn't want to lose you."

"Not gonna happen." Thomas had been there long enough. "Glad you're here though. Not sure how to get back down again."

## 38

# CAT AND MOUSE

"*I* believe you want to see me?" Bernie leaned on the counter in the police station as Trev headed his way from a back room. He glanced around. Small for a cop shop. One office with two desks. The doorway Trevor Sibbritt just came through – probably to his residence out the back. Another door with heavy locks. Cells?

"Thanks for dropping by. Bernie, isn't it? Or do you prefer Bernard?"

"Bernie."

"Enjoying our town, Bernie?"

"Love it. Elizabeth is a wonderful hostess and Palmerston House feels like… home."

"And how long are you planning on staying?"

Bernie stared at Trevor, forcing the smile to stay on his face. The copper's arms were crossed and he stood back a bit from the counter. As if he was sizing Bernie up.

"Dunno. I'm putting together photographs and some information on the town, particularly its history. For a book, you know."

"So, what kind of information are you after?"

"The usual. Early settlers. Who built the town. Where did the resi-

dents come from? Where did people go to gamble? Ha ha, just joking
about that. Why?"

The copper leaned his hip against his side of the counter and
uncrossed his arms, placing a hand on the timber top. "This is a nice
town. Nice folk live here. Families, older people. Teenagers. All nice."

*This is leading us where?*

"Sure are."

"So it bothers me when one of these nice people has an unpleasant
experience with a... visitor."

"Before this gets out of hand, I need to apologise." Bernie dropped
his gaze and softened his tone. "Yesterday morning, early, I got a call
about my uncle. Real close to him, almost like a dad to me." He looked
up at Trev, eyes glistening. "He'd had a heart attack. Died in his sleep
and no warning anything was even wrong."

"I'm sorry for your loss."

"Thanks. Hit me hard, have to say. Went for a walk in a bit of a
daze and ended up sitting outside the bakery. No idea the seats
belonged to them and was pretty upset when the young girl there told
me to move on. As if I was a vagrant or something."

"Why don't you talk me through what happened?" Trevor put his
other hand on the counter and stood with his legs apart.

Strong body language and a stare he probably imagined was
authoritative. Bit comical really.

"With the girl? I sat down and drank some of my water. Always
carry a water bottle. Sorry to say I was having a small cry to myself.
Feeling alone now he's gone. My uncle." He gave a big sigh. "She came
out and said unless I ordered something to eat, well, I had to go. I said
I just needed a moment to compose myself. Had some more water and
realised I couldn't stand the thought of food. Told her that but it kind
of came out wrong. Think she misunderstood me."

"And then what happened?"

"Took my bottle of water and left. Felt like the world was against
me. Still pretty sad."

"Right. Bernie, your account is quite different from Jess's. Who is a
teenager helping her mother out at work."

"Oh. I didn't realise. Perhaps I was more distressed than I realised and said stuff out of grief. I'm going to go and offer a sincere apology right now. If you think that's okay?"

*Come on. Let it go.*

"I won't upset anyone else. Never planned to and I don't know why I let my uncle's death affect me so badly."

"I'll speak to Sylvia and if she and Jess are comfortable with it I'll set up a time and attend. As I said before, I'm sorry for your loss. But we're a tight-knit town, mate. Someone messes up and we all hear about it. Okay?"

"Understood." Bernie offered his hand and Trev shook it. "Thanks for the chat." Not waiting for Trevor to ask any more stupid questions, Bernie turned and let himself out. He had no intention of apologising to anyone.

rom across the road from the police station, it was clear to Charlotte how angry Bernie was, storming to the gate and slamming it in his wake. Something was going terribly wrong in Bernie's head and she'd missed the early signs. His obsession with Palmerston House was escalating and his ability to control his behaviour diminishing. Not a good combination.

He stalked along the footpath. She took a few steps along her side of the road, coming to a halt when he stopped and looked at his watch. He stared at it for a while.

*He remembers!*

At one of his first sessions with Charlotte she'd taught him a calming technique, using a watch to time his breaths until what then was anxiety came under control.

When he started walking again it was less hurried. The tension was gone. He crossed to the opposite corner where George sat on the bench outside his shop in the sunshine. Bernie dropped beside him, out of her sight. She ran over the road to get a better view.

Trev leaned on the gate, eyes on her.

Her heart jumped. "Oh. I didn't see you. Nice day."

"Morning, Charlie. It is."

"Not off on some patrol today? Visit to the mountains?"

"Nope."

"Okay."

"Coffee?"

Charlotte couldn't help herself. She shot a quick look at the jewellers. Bernie was talking, but George looked straight ahead, not giving him any attention. "Thanks but no. I've got to go."

"Are you planning on following him all day?"

"What?"

"He's in my sights now. So relax. Let me worry about Bernard Cooper."

"I don't know what you mean." She forced herself to look at Trev and wished she hadn't. His expression was intense and serious as his eyes moved from hers to the scene playing out up the road, then back to her face again.

"Sure you do. And you'd make my job a whole lot easier if you'd trust me enough to be honest about him."

"I do trust you."

"Then what's the issue? And before you run off or lie to me again, I saw you watching Bernie all the way down the road. Ready to take off after him." Trev reached over the gate and took one of Charlotte's hands in his.

The warmth of his skin was so nice. His hands were large and hard but he held hers gently. The warmth spread up her arm and through her body.

"Was he a patient? You feel you can't break some doctor-patient confidence?"

Anything she said would be wrong. But she couldn't talk about Bernie.

Trev looked past her and his face hardened. "Now what."

Daphne headed toward the jewellery shop at a fast walk. George and Bernie were on their feet. "George is upset." Charlotte said.

"And so is Daphne. There goes Bernie."

Before Daphne was halfway over the road, Bernie stomped off in the direction of Palmerston House.

Trev opened the gate with his free hand. "We'll continue this later."

"I'll come with you."

"Charlotte, if you won't help me, then no." He released her hand and a chill replaced the warmth. "This is police business and unless you intend to assist me when I ask you to, then you're better off being somewhere else."

The finality of Trev's words sunk in as he strode away. One minute his hand was there to steady her, then he'd left her in no doubt of his expectations.

*Help me or stay out of the way.*

"I can't help you." She whispered, tears pricking. With a few blinks and a couple of deep breaths, she regained control.

*Better off alone.*

Always better alone.

## 39

# A TRUNK OF IMPORTANCE

*O*ver a lunch of salad rolls in the cottage kitchen, Christie updated Martha and Thomas about her visit with Angus and Elizabeth.

"So, do you know what Martin's up to?" Christie bit into her roll, not missing the look passed between the other two. "I saw that."

"Don't talk with your mouth full, dear." Martha poured tea.

"Besides, the poor man is about to lose his freedom. At least let him have a day to himself." Thomas grinned as Christie almost choked on lettuce. "In other words, whatever Martin is doing is not for you to know about. Not yet."

"Do you and Angus rehearse your answers?" Christie grumbled. "How does Martha put up with you?"

"Surprises me every day to wake up and find her there." Thomas reached his hand out and Martha put hers into it. "Reminds me I have one or two redeeming features."

"More than one or two, old man." Martha squeezed his hand.

"Anyway, why were you up in the attic? There's not much there now."

"Window was open."

About to take a bite, Christie stopped. "The attic window?"

Thomas nodded, picking a piece of tomato from his roll and tossing it in his mouth.

"I will admit I have never checked whether it was locked. How did you even know?"

"Could hear the creak of it swinging around all night. It opens outwards, not up and down like the others. It wouldn't have been opened in decades, not since the attic was my work space."

"It probably just worked loose over time. Bit of wind and it opened." Martha played with her own food, not really eating anything. "Stop worrying."

"We were out last night. You didn't hear it before then?" Christie asked.

"Nope."

"You have a theory, Thomas?" Christie glanced at Martha, who was pulling bits of lettuce out of her roll, then stuffing them back in. "Auntie, it's just speculation."

"We've had quite enough upsets here."

"And if something else is going on, then it's better to know."

Martha nodded and picked up her roll. "Just don't let the old man go off on some tangent."

"I'm here, you do know I can hear you?"

"So, what is your theory?" Christie winked at Martha then turned to Thomas. "Is it a giant possum?"

"More like the driver of an SUV."

Christie put the remains of her roll on her plate, eyes never leaving Thomas'. His face was grim. Did he mean Elizabeth's guest? Her mind raced back to the conversation with Elizabeth. Why was Bernie Cooper interested in a timber trunk?

"Thomas."

"Yes, Christie?"

"What old records does Green Bay library keep on Palmerston House?"

"You're not making sense. What does this have to do with the attic? Unless…"

"The trunk."

Martha pushed her plate away, finished at last. "Neither of you are making sense. I'm putting the kettle back on."

"Thanks, Auntie. I'd love another. Sorry to upset you."

"Ireland seems very peaceful and non-eventful." Martha got to her feet and began clearing plates.

"Explain." Thomas leaned forward.

"Okay. This morning, Elizabeth told me Bernie Cooper asked if she knew of a timber trunk. He'd apparently been to Green Bay library to research the region for his book, and came across some reference of interest."

"Allegedly."

"Sorry?"

You said apparently. Sounds like allegedly to me. There's old pictures and newspapers, some mention of my paintings, a record of the decline of the local timber industry, and the change in the railway gauge. Go and look, Christie. Actually I'll come with you. I've read a lot there because it helped with my work, but I never saw a word about the trunk." Thomas sat back.

"Elizabeth suggested I should speak with George."

"Yes. Not much he doesn't know about River's End."

"Maybe she told Bernie to talk to him as well."

"Then we'd better go talk to George."

The kettle whistled and Martha picked it up to fill the teapot. "All of this is interesting, but what makes you suspect this Bernie person isn't above board?"

Thomas tapped the table a few times with his fingers. "Didn't want to say anything, but the night you were out with the ladies, he was up the road. Randall got all security dog on me and I had to stop him chasing after the SUV. Went hurtling past me in the dark."

"What! Where?"

"I was at the end of the driveway, Christie, and Randall went stiff. Growled in fact. Then this vehicle hurtled past, stones flying everywhere. Trev reckons he stopped him a few minutes later speeding down the hill. Warned him and let him go."

"You've not said a word!" Martha carried the teapot over and put it down with a bang. "Why not tell me?"

Thomas stood and wrapped both arms around Martha. "Sorry. Thought I was imagining things after all the troubles with Derek and Rupert."

Christie's stomach churned. Surely there wasn't another problem in town? Years of peace and then she moved in and all these wonderful people were subject to endless issues. She put her head in her hands. Then she felt Thomas' hand on her shoulder.

"Talk to us."

"Elizabeth mentioned something to Bernie."

"Mentioned what?"

Christie lifted her head. "She told him there was a trunk in the cottage."

"What is so important about the trunk?" Martha lowered herself onto her seat, eyes troubled. "And what does it have to do with the attic window?"

Thomas and Christie stared at each other.

"Somebody speak please."

"Sorry, Auntie. I have no idea why the trunk matters to this man, but assuming it does, would he really go to the trouble of climb—"

"Anyway, it might be better to go for a drive to Green Bay library. In case he's telling the truth." Thomas shook his head at Christie.

"Thomas Blake, I am not some child to protect! You think he was in the cottage, don't you both?" Martha turned to Christie. "Finish what you were saying."

"Martha—"

"No, I'm quite able to understand this may be some kind of problem and would much rather know than have an unpleasant surprise. Did he climb up to the attic, through the window, and come down through the hatch?"

Christie shrugged. "If he did, he certainly didn't touch anything that I am aware of. The trunk is still in the dining room. Do you remember anything else about it? Is it valuable?"

"It is old and unique. But why wouldn't he take it, dear?"

*Why indeed?*

None of this made any sense to Christie.

"What are you thinking?" Thomas poured tea whilst Martha watched him, still looking upset.

"I might go and see George. Find out if this man has asked him about the trunk and what George knows about it. Afterwards, I'm not sure. Let's see what comes of it first."

"I'll come with you." Thomas started to stand.

"No, why don't you stay and spend some time with Martha? I don't like it when you two are at odds."

"We're not. You two go together and I'll clean up here. Then take a walk in the garden." Martha reached for Thomas' hand with a smile. "Go on."

Thomas leaned over and kissed Martha on the lips. "Whatever you say, bride."

# 40

# CREATING HAVOC

*B*ernie peered over the edge of the cliff at the sea swirling at its base. The wind was picking up and he braced himself against its buffeting. His rope remained tied to one of the bushes, neatly coiled in the undergrowth.

*Like a snake waiting to strike.*

Not long now and he'd be the snake. Unnoticed by his prey until it was too late.

He laughed.

From somewhere above him, the wretched dog barked. Bernie slipped back through the bushes and leaned against the rock face. Why couldn't it stay away? For that matter, the whole damned town should leave him alone. He clenched his hands into fists. The only one who'd shown him any friendship was Elizabeth, but now this Angus person was here, even she was less accommodating. Time was against him.

There were no more sounds from the top of the cliff, so Bernie went back through the bushes. From here he could just see the top of the cave. How much easier to access by boat, if only the tides would cooperate. High tide at dusk or dawn would be perfect, times when fewer people would notice a small boat than midday. And the middle of the night was asking for trouble. Even if one managed to get a boat close enough to climb up to the cave, tying it up and filling it with treasure in the dark was beyond possible.

So, two options. Up and down this cliff, dragging load after load of the precious collection once he worked out the logistics of hauling stuff back up. Or through the tunnel. Bernie groaned. Why couldn't the key have been in the trunk? Now he had to paddle around in a pond in the cold of night.

---

*T*he grandfather clock was as beautiful now as the day it was made. Perhaps more so, with the ageing of the timber and small signs of its long life. George ran a hand down its smooth surface. It almost breathed.

*What a story you would tell, had you words.*

"George? Everything okay?"

Martin let the door close behind him with a jangle of the bells at its top.

George patted Martin's shoulder as he made his way around the counter. "I'm going to close up early. No shoppers around."

"Trev called me."

"Did he now?" George opened the cash register to count his takings.

"Should I be having a talk to this Bernard Cooper fellow?"

"Such a confused young man."

"Stop being so generous. Trev told me he upset you."

George glanced up at Martin. "Not the correct word." He went back to counting.

"What does he want?"

"Seventy-two. He rather likes the grandfather clock, and Palmerston House. Now, he's asking about a key."

Martin leaned on the counter. "What key?"

Not speaking again he finished tallying his takings, George

nodded at the front door.

Martin locked it and returned. "You mentioned Bernie Cooper asking about a key."

"Ah." George placed his takings into a calico bag and rolled it up. "He asked about a trunk. One with a key. Told me it is the property of the Temple family."

"The Temples? What world does he live in?"

"Quite. He was, however, insistent."

"I think I'll pay him a visit."

"Trev has things under control. And Daphne is keeping watch over me."

Martin laughed shortly. "So I heard. I wonder what she's done to make Cooper afraid of her."

"She has taken a dislike to him."

"Do you know what he's going on about?"

"I didn't say one word to him. Would you like a drink?"

"Thanks. No, I might go to the cottage. Check in."

"Give my love to Christie."

"I will, George. Are you sure you're okay?" Martin watched George closely. "I can stay."

"Not necessary, son. I'll let you out."

---

*D*aphne locked the front door of the real estate agency, checked it twice, then turned the Open sign to Closed. It was exactly five o'clock and she wasn't waiting a minute later to finish for the day. John was showing a house up in River's End Heights to a potential buyer, and she had to run to the supermarket and find something for their dinner.

She stared across the road to the jewellery shop. Already closed, which was not at all like George. He was normally sweeping the pavement outside his shop when she arrived, and closing up as she left. During the day, if not working on a piece of jewellery or taking care of a customer, he was often on the bench outside the shop, chatting with someone he knew, or watching the world go by.

With a heavy sigh, Daphne turned off the lights and went to the kitchen to collect her handbag. Somebody needed to do something about Bernard Cooper! Yet again he'd been bothering a valued member of River's End, and although George assured her nothing bad happened, the hairs on her arms went up the minute she spotted the man sitting beside George on his bench earlier. By the time she'd got there, Bernie was long gone. Coward. As if a small, older woman like herself would be threatening.

The office phone rang just as Daphne had her hand on the back door. She hesitated, but then hurried back to the reception counter to answer.

"River's End Real Estate. Daphne speaking."

"Mrs Jones?"

"It is she."

"Is your husband John Jones?"

Daphne sat. Something about the tone of the male caller's voice was unsettling. "Yes. He's not here at present but I'm able to help you."

"I'm calling to let you know he's on his way to the hospital."

"What!" Daphne jumped up. "Why? Is he okay?"

"There was an accident. You might want to meet the ambulance there."

"At Green Bay hospital?"

"Yes."

Daphne's hand snaked around inside her handbag for keys. "What accident?"

"Not sure. I was asked to ring."

There was only her house and office keys. She rarely used their car and the keys were at home. But John had the car anyway.

"Please, wait a moment. I haven't got a car."

The caller was gone.

"Hello? Oh, no. John." She hadn't even heard an ambulance, which would have come from Green Bay. But John only left twenty minutes ago, perhaps thirty. This didn't make any sense. Hands shaking, she dialled the police station.

"River's End Police. Senior Constable Sibbritt."

"It's Daphne. Oh, Trev, John's had an accident."

"Tell me what's happened."

"I don't know. I mean, someone just rang and said he was on his way to Green Bay hospital and I haven't got the car and I don't know if he is okay and—"

"Hey, hey, deep breath. Give me a sec and I'll check, because I've had no alerts."

Daphne's legs gave way and she landed on the chair with a plonk. There was photograph of their wedding day near the phone. John smiled at Daphne. Such a handsome young man. Her heart might have stopped because she couldn't feel anything.

"You there, Daph?"

"Yes." Her voice was tiny.

"I can't find anything. No ambulance call out, no accident report. Nothing. Where was John?"

"At River's End Heights. Showing a house to someone."

"Okay. Why don't you hang up and phone him. Where are you?

"At the office."

"I'll be there in two minutes. Okay?"

"Okay." Was it even possible the caller was mistaken? But who would mistake John for anyone else?

"Hang up, Daph."

"Yes. Okay." Daphne disconnected the call and dialled John's mobile. She heard it ring three, four times, then go to voicemail.

"You've reached John Jones but I'm not at my phone, so please leave a message and I'll return your call as soon as I can."

"John, John call me. Please. Please, love. It's Daph."

*Of course it's Daph. Phone me back.*

John was the love of her life and if someone happened to him… what would she do? They were going to retire soon and travel. She picked up the photo and kissed his picture. She wanted to ring him again but what if he was trying to call at the same time?

*What if it is true?*

It couldn't be.

The phone rang and Daphne almost dropped it. "John?"

"Hi, Daphne. No, it's Christie."

"I can't talk." Daphne hung up and burst into tears.

# 41

## DAPHNE'S DREAD

"*H*ow strange." Christie frowned as she put her phone onto the kitchen table.

Martin looked up from his coffee. "That was short."

"She hung up on me."

"Did the phone drop out?"

"No. She said she couldn't talk and hung up. Sounded so upset."

"Probably just had a client there."

Christie shook her head. "Even so, there was something in her voice... I might drive down and make sure she's alright."

"You worry so much about everyone." Martin took Christie's hand. "Let's go check on Daphne."

"Thank you. I'll let the others know whilst you finish your coffee." Christie leaned across and kissed Martin's cheek, then stood. "I think they're outside still."

Since arriving back from their trip to Green Bay library, Thomas had been outside with Martha. Christie saw them walking around the vegetable garden before Martin arrived, taking her attention with his concerns about George. Now she hurried out, her thoughts with Daphne rather than the curious information she and Thomas came home with. Somehow she felt it was all connected, though she didn't know how. Not yet.

Martha and Thomas sat on the bench near the orchard. Intent on their own conversation, Christie politely coughed as she got close to alert them.

"Did I hear Martin's voice, dear?" Martha smiled.

Christie noted how tightly Martha gripped Thomas' hand and knew he must have shared his worries with her.

"Yes, you did. Are you okay, Auntie?"

"Course she is. Just loves holding my hand."

"I'm so sorry. I really, truly am."

"Whatever you are talking about, you're being quite silly." Martha shook her head at Christie. "You are not responsible for the actions of other people. Never have been, so get over yourself."

Thomas and Christie stared at Martha, mouths open. Then, she laughed. "Heard the term on the radio and always wanted to use it."

"Well, I will think about getting over myself, but in the interim, Martin and I are going to check in with Daphne."

"Daphne?"

"I called her to see if we could get together to have a talk about... umm—"

"Bernard Cooper. I already talked to Martha about our suspicions."

"Oh. Daphne has had a bit to do with him, so I called to see if Martin and I can drop by to talk about it all. She was really upset and said she couldn't talk to me. Hung up in fact. So, we're going to see if she's okay."

"Shall we come along?" Martha got to her feet.

"Not yet. I'll update you once we see if she's okay. What if I ask her and John to join us for dinner? I'll grab some takeaway so no need to cook or anything."

"Rubbish. I have a basket full of winter vegetables and will whip something up in no time." Martha held her arms out and Christie hugged her. "Take care, darling."

"I will. You are a rock star. Seeing as you like modern terms."

Christie grinned. "I'll phone. So, go inside before it cools down too much."

"Best time of the year." Thomas picked up Martha's basket.

"You say that no matter what the season." Christie reminded him.

"As long as there is food, it is the best time of the year."

---

*T*he digital clock on Daphne's desk counted every second as though it were an hour. No phone call.

*Where are you, John?*

She checked the landline was working, then her mobile. Had it really only been two minutes since she'd left the message? A pile of wet tissues filled the rubbish bin near her feet. For some reason, the tears refused to stop. Her hands still shook so hard it was difficult to dial the phone, but she had to try again.

"You've reached John Jones but I'm not at my phone, so please leave a message and I'll return your call as soon as I can."

Beep.

"Love, please call me the minute you get this. Please, please be okay. I love you. It's Daph."

She hung up.

*He knows it's you.*

Now her head was thumping so hard she couldn't think straight. Bang. Bang. Bang.

"Daphne! Are you in there?"

It wasn't her head, it was Trev at the front door. She flew to unlock it. "Have you—"

"There's nothing, Daph. Come and sit down, you look ready to fall down." Trev took Daphne's arm and guided her behind the counter to her seat. "I'll get you some water."

"Don't leave me, please."

"Okay." Trev squatted beside her. "You've tried calling John?"

Daphne nodded, her throat suddenly constricting too much to speak.

"He didn't answer? You said earlier he was with a client so probably wouldn't answer the phone. Right?"

She nodded again and grabbed Trev's hand. "Find him." It was barely a whisper.

"I will, but I'm not happy about leaving you alone."

"Trev? Is everything okay?" Christie, followed by Martin, burst through the front door. Daphne looked up, fresh tears pouring down her face. Christie ran to her side and threw her arms around her. "What's happened?"

Trev straightened to make room for Christie. "Someone phoned Daphne a few minutes ago and told her John's been in an accident."

"No!" Christie squeezed Daphne tightly.

"Thing is, there's been no reports, no call outs, nothing at all. I reckon it's a mistake."

Martin pulled his phone from a pocket and dialled. He listened and then hung up. "John's voicemail. How long since you've spoken to him?"

"Half... half an hour."

"I'll get you some water." Christie sped into the kitchen.

"He went to River's End Heights to show someone a house. If you can stay with Daphne, I'll go for a drive now."

Christie came back with a glass of water. Daphne sipped at it, spilling some over herself. She reached for more tissues but the box was empty.

Martin handed her a clean handkerchief. "I'll come with you, Trev."

"We'll be fine. You two go and we'll ring when we hear from John." Christie took the handkerchief and dabbed the wet spot on Daphne's top. "Which will be any second now."

With a nod, Trev stepped around the counter. "Appreciate the company." He led the way out and in a moment it was just Christie and Daphne. The patrol car, lights flashing, did a U-turn and disappeared up the road.

Daphne checked her mobile phone. Nothing. "I'm sorry I couldn't talk when you called."

"You should have told me. I knew something was wrong, not that anything is, but you know what I mean."

"He'll be alright. He will."

"Of course. But what did the caller say? Who was it?" Christie perched on the edge of the desk.

"I don't know, although the voice was a bit familiar. He didn't say. Except John was in an ambulance and I should go to the hospital."

"Doesn't make sense. It would take at least twenty minutes for the ambulance to get here, let alone turn around with a patient and head back. I didn't hear any sirens, did you?"

"No, and that's the only thing giving me some hope. But why would anyone say that?"

"Mistaken identity, although Trev said there's been no reports of anything. Oh, look! There's John now."

Daphne's heart leapt and she pushed herself onto her feet, peering through the window. It was his car. And... John! Somehow she got to the front door and flung it open and there he was. John. Not hurt at all.

"I got your messages, doll. Whatever is wrong? You've been cry—"

The rest of his sentence was buried as Daphne launched herself at him.

---

From the window in his room, Bernie watched the police car – lights flashing – speed past in the direction of River's End Heights. He chuckled, quite pleased to see the police officer busy worrying about someone else for a change. His grin turned into a frown when it reappeared a moment later, lights off, following a car he recognised as belonging to John Jones. He sucked on the dregs of a water bottle, crumpled it and tossed it onto the floor.

On the bed were waterproof pants attached to braces, with built-in boots. A thick water repellent jumper. Beanie. Alongside these, a long tool with a net on one end and a hook on the other. Elbow length waterproof gloves completed the gear he would use in a few hours, once the house was quiet and pesky Charlotte asleep.

He needed to eat. Early as it was, he put on a coat and slid his wallet into a pocket. At the last moment he pulled the diary from under the mattress. He locked his door and went downstairs.

As he closed in on the main street, Bernie spotted the police car parked outside the real estate agency, along with John Jones' car and the Lotus. He slowed, tempted to wander past and see what was going on inside. The lights were blazing and there were a number of people around the counter, but that was all he could see. It wasn't worth the risk of being caught looking in.

He pushed the door of the pub open to music and laughter, the smell of hops and early dinners. His stomach growled. This was a good idea. Refuel for his watery nocturnal excursion. He'd been here before, usually having a meal at the counter where the conversations around him reminded Bernie of his mother. She'd always worked in bars and, even as a little kid, he'd learnt to do his homework at one end whilst half listening to adult subjects. A person learns a lot from listening.

Tonight there was no hurry so he dropped into an empty booth. From here he could see the police car. A movement caught his eye... was someone in the doorway watching the pub?

"Greetings, world renowned photographer." Lance stood beside the booth, eyebrow raised in readiness for an order.

"Lance. Dunno about world renowned. But thanks."

"Never undersell yourself. Or so my dear old mother always said. So, a beer? Or would you like some wine tonight? I can highly recommend either the award winning Chardonnay from the coastal winery up the road, or the equally wonderful warm climate red from the foothills."

"Not a big fan of white wine."

"You are missing out. Our very own Christie Ryan is a big lover of the vintage. But I respect a man who loves a red, so will return with one."

"Actually, if it is such a favourite, I'll give the white a try."

Lance beamed, then hurried away.

Keep your friends close and your enemies closer.

*Let's get inside her head.*

It was a whole lot more fun to see them implode than to just take everything they love away. Bernie took out the diary. Some wine, dinner, perhaps dessert. Plenty of time to reread Harry's notes and finalise his plan of action.

# 42

# FAMILY, FRIENDS, FEAR.

*T*he dining room in the cottage was ablaze with light and the table filled with food. Martin had brought in the extra chairs from the garage for Angus and Elizabeth. Daphne sat beside John, her face still pale despite Christie insisting on redoing her make-up. Trev was in the middle with Martha and Thomas at the end nearest the door.

"But shouldn't we have invited Charlotte and George?" Martha asked as she offered a plate of homemade bread rolls to Trev.

"George is better left out of it for now." Martin filled wine glasses. "We talked earlier."

"Do I need to visit him?"

"Tomorrow, Thomas. He was heading home for an early dinner and a good book. He's okay."

Elizabeth frowned. "I'm really not sure about this dinner. Not that it isn't lovely, Martha. And thank you for inviting us. But bringing us together to discuss one of my guests behind his back feels rather... odd. At the least."

Angus smiled at her. "I do love your integrity. But look at it this way... if there is something peculiar going on, wouldn't you rather know?"

"Well, yes. So perhaps Charlotte should be here, then."

"Charlotte won't discuss Bernard Cooper." Trev said.

Christie opened her mouth to speak, then closed it again, and he gave her a curious look.

"Thomas and Christie went to Green Bay library this afternoon to follow up on Bernie's conversation with Elizabeth about the trunk." Martin finally sat. "What did you discover?"

"More what we didn't discover!" Thomas put down his fork. "To bring everyone up to speed, we drove there today after an odd series of events. Last night whilst we were out, someone had a wander through the cottage."

There was a collective gasp.

"A break-in?"

"Not sure, Trev. The attic window was open but nothing was moved or taken."

"So what does this have to do with Green Bay library?" John slipped an arm around Daphne's shoulder. "I'm not following."

"We pondered why anyone would bother to climb up to the attic, through the window and down the ladder to the cottage but not take anything. Then I remembered Elizabeth mentioning a comment Bernie made. About the trunk." Christie smiled at Elizabeth. "It occurred to me the trunk might be of interest to him in some strange way."

Elizabeth's eyes widened. "He was quite specific actually. Said he'd found out about the trunk at the library, as part of the original furnishings brought from England to Palmerston House."

"And that," Thomas commented, "is what troubles me greatly. There is nothing there about it. Nothing at all."

"But a bit about Harry Temple, who built the house," Christie added. "Mostly rumours, but quite interesting. There's mention of him telling Eoin Ryan he'd kept a record of what he called the 'theft' of Palmerston House, in a diary. Although his family left town, he lingered, thrown off the estate more than once for trespass."

"But what on earth does this all have to do with Bernie?" Elizabeth turned to Angus. "He seems such a nice young man."

Up until now, Daphne hadn't spoken. But now, with tears brimming again, she couldn't contain herself. "There's something wrong with him. Something sinister and not at all good. And I'm a decent judge of character, aren't I John? I knew Derek Hobbs was bad news, and as for that Rupert man... don't get me started! Bernard Cooper upsets people. He upsets George and... and..."

"Look, there's a lot of speculation going on tonight." Trev looked around. "I'm not about to let anyone disrupt this town again and I've already got some investigation underway. At this point, there is no proof Bernard Cooper has done anything other than be offensive and disrespectful, but I'm watching him."

"As we all should be."

"No, Thomas, you shouldn't. What I'll do is ask each of you to drop by the station tomorrow and we'll have a chat about your concerns and anything you want to raise with me. But leave the police work to me. Please. Okay?" He stared directly at Christie.

She had no theories. Not yet. But although she smiled at Trev and nodded, her mind worked overtime and she longed to get her hands on a big piece of paper to create a mind-map.

---

"I've made some wonderful friends here, good people with kind hearts." Charlotte, wearing pyjamas, sat cross-legged on her bed, phone in hand. "You'd really like them, Mum."

"I am so happy, darling. Although I miss you so much."

*I miss you too. I miss the real you.*

"There's such a nice beach. Not a lot of people visit here so most days, you can walk its length with barely another footprint in the sand. There's an old jetty where you can sit and watch the fish swimming below amongst the seaweed."

"I like fish. What did you have for dinner?"

"Dinner? Oh, I made a toasted sandwich. Cheese and tomato."

"You made it? Darling, you should always get a grown up to use appliances like a toaster."

"Mum, I'm quite grown up now, remember? I moved out of home when I went to university."

"Why did you go?" The pitch of her mother's voice rose. "And why do I live here? All by myself!"

"You're not alone, Mum. There's lots of lovely people there with you. Maggie looks after you."

"Maggie? I need to find her. Maggie!"

"Mum, calm down. If you press the button beside your bed, Maggie or someone will be there in a minute. I didn't mean to upset you." Charlotte stood, then paced the room, heart racing as she calmed her own voice. "Did you press the button?"

"Maggie! Maggie, where are you?"

"Mum, I'm going to hang up and ring Maggie. She'll be there in a minute. I love you."

"No, don't go. Don't leave me here. I don't like it here. Charlotte, you must get Daddy to bring you here right away. He'll know what to do and I want to cuddle my little girl." Sobs followed the plea.

"Shh, Mummy, it's okay. You'll feel better in a minute, I promise. Sorry." Charlotte disconnected the call and dialled the clinic, stopping near the window as the phone rang.

"Lakeview Care. Maggie speaking."

"Maggie, I'm so sorry, it's Charlotte Dean."

"Hello, Doctor. How are you?"

"I've managed to upset Mum and she won't press the button to call you. Would you check her for me, please?"

"Hang on. Lee, pop in to see if Mrs Dean is okay. Thanks. Okay, I'm back, Lee is running up there right now. What happened?"

"The usual. Thinks I'm a child and Dad is still around. All about being abandoned."

*Sure, Mum, you were the one left alone.*

"Do you think she's deteriorating?"

"She's on some new medication and was going quite well. But... well, sometimes a familiar voice or face is enough to set them back."

"Will you message me once she's settled for the night? And send me through what she's on."

"Of course. Are you coming back to Queensland soon?"

Charlotte stared at her reflection in the window. "I'm a bit caught up right now but maybe later in the year. I'll let you know."

"Okay. Well, we'll look after your mum. Most of the time she is so sweet and we all want what's best for her. Perhaps if you don't call for a few days? Let her settle down again. I'll message you the information."

"Thanks. I mean it, Maggie. I appreciate you and the staff."

"Well, you take care."

The phone disconnected. Charlotte dropped the phone onto the table. With a deep, sad sigh, she crossed to the door, checked it was locked, and turned off the light. Then she wandered back to the window, leaning her forehead against it. Why? How cruel was life, to take more than the mind but also the personality.

*It won't happen to you.*

But only time would tell.

Someone was walking – or staggering – towards Palmerston House. Charlotte peered at the figure, then ducked down as she realised it was Bernie, and he was looking in her direction. Surely he couldn't see her up here? Yet in spite of his apparent inability to move in a straight line, his gaze was unwavering.

He closed in on the fountain and stopped there, both hands on it. Then he leaned closer and drank from one of the outlets.

"Are you serious?"

Bernie stayed there for a moment or two, then continued to the house. His stagger improved but clearly he'd been drinking. At least he'd be quiet tonight and, for that, Charlotte was grateful. Elizabeth and Angus were out and the last thing she needed was to babysit the man. Or deal with him trying to intimidate her.

Charlotte slipped into bed. Footsteps approached. Bernie was outside her door. She watched the light under her door shadowed by feet.

The door knob turned.

"Come out and play."

It was barely above a whisper but shivers rushed through Charlotte and she pulled the blankets higher. A moment later, he stumbled away.

This had to end. No more implied threats. Invading her personal space. Testing her integrity. She couldn't live like this anymore. Tomorrow, she'd visit Trev. Throw herself on his mercy and understanding of how she'd had to follow her sworn duty to keep confidentiality. Especially since the last time. Charlotte stared at the ceiling. She was done.

# 43

# CHANGES AND FINDS

*T*rev let himself into his house, not bothering to put on a light as he locked the door behind himself. Tonight had proved interesting and there was a lot to digest. Much as he appreciated his friends wanting to assist, the only person he actually needed some help from was Charlotte.

*If only.*

Trev sighed, opened the fridge and took out a beer. Charlotte was so clever and so intuitive. He knew in his gut if this situation was about anyone else, she'd be at his side helping. Instead, she spoke in riddles and refused to accept he would protect her, no matter what. Even if she had to break a confidence, nobody would ever know about it. Not from him.

The phone rang as he took his first sip. He glanced at the clock as he answered. "Trev Sibbritt."

"I should hope so!"

"Hi, Mum. You okay?"

"Yes, dear. I called a bit earlier but it went to your message machine."

Trev took the phone with him to the bedroom, piling pillows against the bed head. "Sorry. Was out tonight." He pulled off his boots.

"With a nice young lady?"

"Several. But none in the way you hope for." He leaned back and stretched his legs out on the bed, taking another sip of beer.

"Pity. Anyway, I've decided it's time."

"For you to stop worrying about my love life?"

"Never going to happen. No. Time to take a step back." Her voice suddenly changed tone. There was a tinge of sadness.

"Are you selling the bookshop?"

"I don't want to. Not yet. But young Braden finished his degree and has a wonderful job offer in Melbourne. Such a smart boy. And once he goes, well…"

"What about reducing the opening hours?"

"Not really viable. Saturday is such a big trade day here and Monday is perfect for ordering, so I really should stay open six days."

"So, hire someone new."

"I have an idea. And I'd like your opinion. In fact, I need it."

"I'm listening, Mum."

"What I want to do is bring in a person who will love the shop as much as I do. Someone with a bit of a quirky nature and eye for detail, a love of books and ability to talk to people. You know what I mean… understand them. But they need to be strong and tough inside. To find ways to increase business. I'd like to train them up and gradually let them take over. With view to selling to them when the time is right."

"Sounds good. Anyone in mind?"

"Nobody. I don't know where to find a person like this. There's the apartment upstairs vacant so if they aren't local, this might suit someone looking for a change. Someone who needs a fresh start."

Beer bottle almost at his lips, Trev paused.

*Someone who needs a fresh start.*

Was that what Charlotte tried to do by coming to River's End last year? She'd left Queensland where she'd practised as a psychiatrist. Walked away – he thought – from any family up there. Yet she'd not looked for a job here, or found herself a house. Most of the time, she wandered along the beach, helped Elizabeth, and... read books. Always a book in her hand or bag.

"Darling?"

"Sorry. I have a... a friend. She reads a lot. Was just thinking about books."

"I see." She chuckled. "Well, if she would like to move to my gorgeous little town and sell books, then bring her up for a visit. I promise not to match make."

"Wouldn't matter. Don't think she sees me that way."

"Sad to hear. Unless she has potential for me, in which case, that's life."

"Thanks, Mum."

"My pleasure. But seriously, would she be interested?"

*Why would I tell her? I want Charlotte here. Where I can see her and talk to her and take her to lunch sometimes.*

But would this make her happy? Unease settled in his chest.

"Maybe. I don't know."

"Well, ask her. See if she'd like to meet me. Okay?"

"I'll think about it. At the moment, I don't believe she likes me very much. Had to set some rules today about a case."

"A case? Is she a bit of a detective?" His mother laughed. "Exactly what this town needs, my darling."

"Fine. I'll ask her. But don't expect me to drive her to meet you."

"How else am I supposed to get you to visit?"

A few minutes later, the conversation ending on a pleasant note, Trev put his empty beer bottle onto the bedside table and stared upwards. Charlotte and his mother would love each other. Charlotte needed something, but whether it was a new start he didn't know. What he did know was the thought of her being three hours away almost broke his heart.

---

ance swept the floor of the bistro. He enjoyed this time of night, with the customers all gone, well fed and happy. Most of the lights were off and he hummed as he cleaned, stopping to straighten a chair or blow out a candle.

In the last booth he found a book wedged between the cushions. He dropped it onto the table and tidied the seat. Invariably something was left behind. Usually glasses, keys, or a phone. Not very often a book.

Actually, a diary. He picked it up and moved into the light for a better look. Leather bound, it was old and worn. The date 1853 was etched into it. Very old indeed. Lance frowned, working out who'd been in the booth tonight.

Earlier it was the photographer staying at Palmerston House. Bernie. But after dinner, he'd moved to the bar to keep drinking and talking to Lance. There'd been a group of four, who only stayed for mains. Then a couple. Out of them he only knew Bernie, but he hardly seemed like the diary type.

He opened the cover. The writing was old-fashioned, heavily slanted with loops and curls, but eventually he made out a dedication. "For my husband Harry. With love from Eleanor." He shrugged. Could be anyone. He'd drop it into Trev in the morning and let him sort it out.

## 44

# UPON A POND

*O*n her way to the salon, Christie stopped to let Trevor's patrol car exit his place. He wound down the window.

"Morning, off to the mountains again so soon?" Christie grinned.

"Palmerston House, actually."

"What!"

"Sounds as though Bernie Cooper fell into the pond overnight."

"Is he—"

"Unconscious. Got to go."

"Wait, I'll come with you." Before he could stop her, Christie climbed in the front seat. "I'll go to the salon later. Do you need sirens?"

Trev turned onto the road. "No. And don't touch anything."

"Oh. Not even the—"

"Do I need to arrest you?"

Within a couple of minutes they turned into the driveway of Palmerston House and Trev parked outside the front steps. "We can go around this way." Christie led Trev to one side of the house and though a rambling garden until they reached the path to the pond. They ran until the path opened up and then stopped. "Where are they? Angus!"

"Over here."

Trev forged ahead in the direction of Angus' voice, to the left side of the sprawling pond. Amongst heavy reeds, Angus and Elizabeth stood back as Charlotte monitored Bernie.

Trev squatted beside her. "How's he doing?"

"He'll live." Her voice was flat. "Came home drunk last night and must have decided to go for a swim. Or fish."

Christie joined them. "What on earth is he wearing?"

"Waterproof pants and boots. Goodness knows how long he's been here so they probably stopped him freezing."

"Who found him?"

"I did." Elizabeth stepped closer, hands tightly entwined. "Made an early morning cup of tea and came to sit under the tree. But I heard a sound... a moan. He was a bit further into the water and groaning so I helped him up to here but then he became unconscious."

"We thought it best to call an ambulance and you, Trev, rather than drag him out anymore. In case there's injuries." Angus touched Elizabeth's arm. "Why don't you go and change now? Get out of your wet clothes."

"I'm fine for a bit longer."

"Do you think he's hurt?" Christie leaned closer, wrinkling her nose at the alcohol fumes from Bernie's open mouth. "Or just inebriated?"

"His breathing is fine and pulse is a bit slow. Typical drunk response."

"Do you know where he was last night?" Trev glanced at Charlotte.

"Nope. And don't care. He staggered down the driveway after ten when I was about to go to bed. Heard him come upstairs and... and go to his room."

"And what? You hesitated."

"Don't, Trevor."

Christie dropped to her knees and put a hand on Charlotte's arm. "I'll sit with him. Your arms are freezing. Go and put something warm on."

Trev started taking off his jacket, but Charlotte jumped up and shook her head. "I'm fine. Thanks, but I'll get my own jacket." She ran off before he could answer, and he stared after her. Christie couldn't work out if it was frustration or sadness on his face, deciding it was both and almost time for her to have a good talk to Charlotte.

Bernie moaned and his eyes flickering open. "Not... there."

"Keep still, mate. There's an ambulance on its way." Trev squatted again. "Do you know where you are?"

"No sign of it. Searched everywhere."

"No sign of what?"

Trev helped Bernie as he struggled to sit, finally getting him right out of the water where he slumped against a tree, legs outstretched. Bernie gazed around, eyes focusing on Christie.

"Thief."

She thought she hadn't heard him right. "I'm sorry. What did you say?"

"You should be sorry." He snarled at her, his hands shooting out to grab her leg, but she jumped back, almost ending up in the pond herself.

Trev steadied her, then spun back to Bernie. "Watch yourself."

"Thief. You and your whole family. Thieves."

"Look, I don't know what you think you know, but once you are sober, we can have a chat."

Bernie rolled onto his hands and knees and forced himself up, leaning against the tree. Angus drew Elizabeth away, putting her behind him.

"I'm sober. Where is my key?"

"What key?"

"You or your kind stole it. None of you belong here and I'm going to prove it. Get you all evicted."

Elizabeth gasped and put a hand to her mouth.

"Might let you stay. You're nice." Bernie directed this to Elizabeth.

"Did you think the key was in the pond?" Christie inched toward Bernie. "What's so special about it?"

"Are you stupid? Or think I'm stupid? It belongs to me and once I have it, you won't know what's hit you. Thief." He lunged at Christie, arms outstretched and just as Trev charged between them, Bernie fell flat onto his face.

The wail of a siren cut through the stunned silence in the small group.

Charlotte jogged back wearing a thick jacket. "Did you kill him?"

"You sound hopeful." Christie found her voice. "He keeled over after accusing me of stealing a key from him."

"Oh."

"Oh, indeed." Trevor checked Bernie's pulse. "It is time to explain how you know him and what you know about him."

"Dear, what does he mean? Did you know him before Palmerston House?" Elizabeth pulled out of Angus' embrace. "He tried to attack Christie."

Charlotte went white and sank to the ground. Trev was at her side in seconds. "Breathe. We'll talk later, okay. But breathe." He reached his hand out and, without looking up, Charlotte grabbed it.

Angus and Elizabeth went to the bench under the oak tree.

Christie sat beside Bernie, close enough though to hear the conversation.

"I'm so sorry." Charlotte's words were whispered.

"Will you talk to me? Be straight with me?" Trev squeezed her hand and she turned wide eyes to him. "I'll need a statement, Charlotte. This is beyond keeping patient confidentiality now. He would have hurt Christie if I wasn't here and he wasn't so inebriated."

Charlotte held on to him like a lifeline. "I'll tell you everything I know. He shouldn't be like this. Aggressive."

"Yet you know he was extremely unpleasant to Jess, and George. Daphne cannot stand him."

"I… I'm sorry."

Voices approached along the path. Trev leaned closer to Charlotte. "We'll talk soon, okay?"

She nodded as he released her hand and stood to greet the paramedics.

Christie got up to make way for them. "He's been checked by a doctor. Just needs a good dose of reality." She pulled a face at her humour and went to Charlotte, reaching out for her. "Come on, let's get you inside and have some coffee."

In the kitchen, Christie filled the kettle whilst Charlotte stood behind a chair. "Sit." Christie glanced over her shoulder. "Pull the chair out and sit in it. I'll have a coffee ready in a min."

By the time Christie carried two cups to the table, Charlotte was in the chair, arms wrapped around herself in spite of still wearing the jacket. "Come on, hands on the cup and sip slowly."

"I should be looking after you." Charlotte slowly did as Christie suggested. "Are you okay?"

"Me?" Christie joined her and took a quick sip of coffee. "It takes more than a drunk and very confused man to worry me. And I moved a whole lot faster than he did. But I would like to know what he was going on about. Do you know?"

"He thinks he is the descendant of Harry Temple."

"Ah. But I don't have a key to Palmerston House. And what does the trunk have to do with it?"

"Trunk?"

"Is that why you were at Harry's grave?"

"Oh. Elizabeth mentioned something about it. My understanding was Harry left River's End a short time after losing Palmerston House. The story I know is about him following his family and going on to lead a life somewhere in far north New South Wales. Which is where Bernie grew up, believing the story his mother told him."

"You knew who he was?" Elizabeth walked into the kitchen and around the table to face Charlotte. Her eyes were red and puffy. "All this time, you knew a madman was in my home and you said nothing?" Her hands shook and her face was white.

Christie jumped up and put an arm around her shoulders. "We've all had a bit of a shock this morning, Elizabeth. Where's Angus?"

"He's with Trev. I'll make some tea. I need to be doing something." She smiled very faintly at Christie "I'm upset."

"I am terribly sorry, Elizabeth." Charlotte played with her cup, eyes down. "It's my fault completely."

"But how do you even know Bernie? Why on earth wouldn't you be honest with me from the beginning?"

Charlotte pushed her chair back as she got to her feet. "I'm... I'm so sorry." She ran out of the kitchen door. Straight into Trev.

"Hang on. Where are you going?" He stared at her face. "Don't cry." His voice softened.

"Everyone's just a bit on edge, Trev," Christie said. "Come back in, Charlotte. Elizabeth is okay, she's not angry. Coffee, Trev?"

Trev's eyes hadn't left Charlotte's. "Thanks, but I might take Charlie to the station for a chat. Okay?"

Charlotte nodded.

"Be nice to her, Trev. She had a job to do."

"I'm always nice, Christie."

*Better be.*

Christie returned to the kitchen where Elizabeth hadn't got any further with making tea. "I seem to be telling people to sit down a lot today, so don't argue and I'll make a pot of tea."

"But I am angry." Elizabeth sat, her fingers drumming on the table. "I heard what you said to Charlotte, but I am so upset with her. Is Bernie some sort of criminal?"

"Probably not. But if Charlotte used to treat him, she'd be bound by some confidentiality thing. I'm sure she didn't think he'd get drunk and lose his inhibitions."

"Be that as it may, I'm not sure I can trust her. And if I can't trust her, then I'm not sure I'm comfortable having her here."

Christie stopped near the stove, teapot in one hand and kettle in the other. "But this is her home. You wouldn't make her leave?"

"Make who leave?" Angus came in. "Bernie's on his way to hospital. No real damage done but he'll have a mighty headache in a few hours. Now, who is leaving?"

The phone in the foyer began to ring.

## 45

## SHAPE OF THINGS TO COME

George was on his bench outside the jewellery shop when the ambulance drove through town with lights flashing and sirens on. He watched it take the road leading to Martin's house, and something tightened around his chest. About to go inside and phone the boy to check on him, he sighed with relief as Martin come out of the bakery with a full shopping bag. He raised a hand in greeting as Martin crossed the road.

"Where did it go?" Martin sat beside George.

"Actually, up your way. Thought… well, anyway, you're here."

"Stop worrying about me. It's also the road to River's End Heights and several towns."

"And Palmerston House."

Martin pulled his phone out. "Let's check on them, then." He dialled and listened. It rang out. "I'll try again shortly. Probably all outside enjoying this lovely weather. Did you have a good night?"

"I played solitaire. Read a few more chapters of a book Charlotte recommended. She knows her books."

"Sounds relaxing."

*Shape of things to come.*

"What's in the bag?"

"Part of the dinner I'm making for Christie."

"You should both have dinner with me one night. I still make a decent casserole."

"Would love to. Let us know when and we'll be there. And we'll bring dessert."

"Would you call again?"

"Sure." This time the phone only rang a few times before Christie answered. Martin put the phone onto speaker. "Sweetheart, George is with me and you're on speaker."

"Hi George. I was going to call. Bernie Cooper fell into the pond and passed out."

"Hence the ambulance."

"Yes. And Trev. But he's heading back to the station with Charlotte now."

"Why?"

"Turns out she knew Bernie in the past. I don't have many details but he seems to believe he is somehow—"

"Entitled to Palmerston House." George interrupted. "Sorry, Christie, to cut you off. I've had more than one uncomfortable conversation with the young man and this is my conclusion."

"Well, you are correct. He thinks he's the last descendant of Harry Temple or something. Though how this would entitle him to Palmerston House doesn't make sense."

The police car cruised past, Charlotte in the front seat, staring straight ahead.

"Is Charlotte alright? Trev just drove past with her and she looks rather unhappy."

"She's blaming herself for not saying anything, but it was patient confidentiality. Elizabeth is pretty upset with her. Martin, would you come to Palmerston House?"

"I'll be there shortly."

"Goodbye, Christie. Look after yourself." George leaned toward the phone as if to be heard. "Come and see me when you can."

"I will. Bye."

Martin put his phone away and reached for the bags. "I'll let you know what's going on. Don't worry, okay?"

"I'm perfectly fine, thank you. I think Daphne is coming over, so will update her."

"Ask her to make you a coffee and sit with you for a bit. Enjoy the sunshine." He stood, smiled at Daphne as she stepped off the pavement across the road, then strode away toward Palmerston House.

George watched him go. How much he loved his godson. The sun was warm today and nobody was in harm's way. So why did he feel a shiver down his spine?

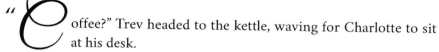

"Coffee?" Trev headed to the kettle, waving for Charlotte to sit at his desk.

"No." A whisper.

"Well, I need one. Didn't even get a coffee before Angus called."

Trev made two coffees and put one in front of Charlotte anyway. He sat opposite. "He was your patient?"

With a deep, almost shuddering sigh, she nodded. "I'd already decided last night to talk to you. After... well anyway, I treated him for a while in Brisbane."

"After what?"

"Nothing."

Her eyes pleaded with him not to pursue it so he let it drop. For now. "How long ago?"

"I stopped seeing him almost a year ago."

"You stopped? Or he stopped coming to you?"

"Does it matter?"

"Why were you treating him?"

"He was referred to me for anxiety. Some trouble sleeping and moving forward after the death of his mother."

"And then?"

She picked up her coffee, but stared at it, biting her bottom lip. "Charlie?"

"Once he accepted his mother was gone, he decided he needed to prove her theory about his bloodline, as he called it. As a child she'd told him stories of their rightful inheritance of a vast estate in Victoria. A homestead and its land."

"Palmerston House."

"Apparently."

"Where did this belief originate? I mean, what did his mother know?"

"She gave him a diary. He showed it to me once, at least, the outside, but he kept the contents to himself. After a few visits, he told me his mother was an alcoholic who moved from place to place. Was always picking up objects from where they lived or street markets."

"So it might not even have belonged to his family?"

"I suggested he go through proper channels to find out and then..." she finally sipped her coffee, eyes down.

*Then, what? Why is this so hard for you?*

"Then?"

"Nothing."

"Charlie, why did you stop treating Bernie?"

Her eyes flew to his. "It was nothing to do with him. Personal reasons, Trevor. I stopped seeing all my patients. Okay?"

Trev leaned back in his seat. "I'm here for you, Charlie."

She pushed her seat back and abruptly stood. "We can't do this."

"Why?"

"Some things just aren't meant to be. Some people aren't meant... aren't allowed to be... happy." She moved to the back of the chair, her hands gripping its top. "May I go?"

"Thanks for your honesty. I'll be in touch if I need a formal statement." He kept his tone even and hoped his expression matched, but in his chest, his heart hammered painfully.

Charlotte hesitated, her lips opening. Then, with a quick turn she was gone. Through the first door and then the second, closing them behind her and leaving the police station silent.

# 46

# A FUTURE IN DOUBT

*W*ith no thought to where she was going, Charlotte followed her feet to the river. She couldn't go back to Palmerston House – not yet – and needed to put distance between herself and the police station. The panicked escape left her close to tears and even closer to despair. Turmoil racked her body and it wasn't until she'd followed the river to the lagoon that she felt herself breathe.

She kicked off her shoes and stood in the water, its coldness helping control emotions threatening to overtake her.

*One breath. Two.*

She curled her toes into the sand beneath the water.

*One breath. Two. Slower, Charlie.*

Sea air filled her lungs as she inhaled, held, then exhaled. Around her, seagulls swirled then landed, hopeful of some food. She timed her mantra with their deliberate steps.

*One breath.*

Better.

*Two.*

She waded toward the sea, now encouraging her breathing to glide in and out like the waves. All imagery with purpose. As the river met the waves, Charlotte stepped out onto the beach, and then to the jetty. Here, at its end, the breeze strengthened, turning her hair into a jumbled mess. She sat, dropping her shoes at her side and stretching her toes toward the water.

The seagulls followed her, one stepping along the timber boards until almost within arm's reach. "Want to swap lives?" The seagull rested on one leg. Charlotte closed her eyes.

Footsteps on the jetty intruded. Surely Trev hadn't followed her? She couldn't, wouldn't let herself give in to these confusing needs. She gathered her words, ready to ask him to leave.

A joyful yip made her turn, just as Randall rushed to her side. Behind him, Thomas wandered toward her. With a grunt, Randall settled beside Charlotte, his head on her lap and his tail wagging hard enough to scare off the seagull. His gentle eyes melted her heart and, deep inside, the well overflowed. Silent tears slipped down her face, onto her arms, where Randall licked them.

"He doesn't normally have such an effect on people." Thomas lowered himself onto the jetty, then felt around in a pocket. "Think this is clean." He offered Charlotte a perfectly ironed handkerchief.

"Thanks." The tears weren't stopping so she gave up trying to dry her face and let them fall.

Thomas sat with her, occasionally patting her shoulder, Randall between them. The dog rolled onto on his back, demanding a chest rub. Scratching his coat made her feel better, a lot better. Dogs were great like that. The tears dried up.

"Thanks. I'll wash and return this."

"Got plenty. No rush. Feeling better?"

"A bit. I don't normally cry. Sorry."

"You were here first. Cry as much as you need."

Charlotte stared at the handkerchief. "May I ask you a question?"

"As long as it's not about mathematics. Never was good at it."

"How about people?"

"Know a bit about them."

"Okay. So, if you let someone live in your house, trusted them and stuff, but they kept a secret. One they believed they couldn't share.

And then another person does something bad and the secret comes out. Would you lose your trust in them?"

"I'm hoping this isn't a roundabout way of telling me Christie or Martha are up to no good?"

Her eyes shot to Thomas', to see he was obviously teasing.

"Charlotte, I've had my share of secrets being kept from me and it does hurt when the truth comes out. Dents the trust, if not destroys it. Is this about Bernard Cooper?"

She nodded.

"You afraid you'll upset Elizabeth by saying something?"

"A lot happened earlier. Elizabeth knows, so does Angus and Christie. And Trev. Everyone's upset with me, except Christie."

"Then you've got to make it right."

"I don't understand."

"And nor do they. My suggestion, seeing as you asked, is to lay all your cards on the table. Hold your head up high about your ethical choices but let them know how you feel about hurting them. Tell them what you want and find out if there's a way to make it happen." Thomas got to his feet. "They care about you. We all do. Don't under-estimate it."

"You're very wise."

"I know. I'll send you my bill. Come on, Randall, time to get you home to Martin."

With a quick lick of Charlotte's hand, Randall stood, shook, then tore after Thomas.

*What do you want?*

It might just be easier to pack and quietly leave.

---

*E*lizabeth and Angus stood in the foyer of Palmerston House with Trev. Headlights of an approaching taxi shone through the windows, and Elizabeth reached for Angus' hand, her face set.

"I am happy to do the talking, dear lady, should you prefer it."

"Thank you, Angus. But I need to be the one to tell him my decision. And I'm thankful you are here. Both of you."

"No news from your friend in Brisbane, Trev?" Angus asked.

"Short of hiring a private investigator there's not much to do. He's squeaky clean. I'll be doing an interview with him tomorrow and be assured I'll drive home a few truths."

The front door opened as the taxi drove away. Bernie closed the door behind himself. His skin was pale and his feet were bare. "I'm okay. But thank you for being here to greet me. Means a lot." He took a few steps forward then stopped again. "Pretty ashamed of myself and got a lot of apologising to do. Particularly to you, Elizabeth."

"I'm glad you are feeling better. I really am, Bernie."

"All I could think about today was a cup of your tea and being able to say sorry. Went for a quiet dinner at the pub and Lance encouraged me to try some local wines. Don't normally drink and before I knew it, I was waking up in the pond. So, any chance of a cuppa?"

Elizabeth took a deep breath. "I'm afraid not. Whilst I do understand you are sorry, it's my responsibility to consider the comfort and safety of my other guests, as well as myself. What happened this morning was dreadfully upsetting and quite frightening. I can't risk it happening again."

"It won't. I promise it won't." Bernie smiled widely. "Made a real fool of myself, didn't I?"

"Bernie, I'd like you to leave, please."

"I just got here."

"Elizabeth means permanently." Angus took over. "We've made arrangements with River's End Motel for you to have a room there for the night, so if you would, please attend to packing your things."

As though the words made no sense, Bernie kept smiling. He looked from one to the other, then back to Elizabeth. "This is my home."

"No, dear. It is my home and you were a paying guest."

"But I like being here. And I'm not feeling the best so can we leave this 'til tomorrow?"

"Would you like me to assist you up the stairs, if you are feeling unwell? Or should we call the ambulance back?" Trev stepped forward. "It shouldn't take you long to pack."

Anger and disbelief flashed across Bernie's face. He stared at Trev, who didn't blink. Then, with a dramatic sigh, he dropped his head. "I made a mistake. If this is your final word, Elizabeth, then I'll go."

"It is. Thank you."

"Do you need a hand?" Trev gestured to the staircase.

"Of course not. I won't be long." Head still down, Bernie slowly climbed the stairs.

Once he was out of sight, Trev turned to Elizabeth and Angus. "I'll drive him to the motel. Does he owe you anything?"

"No, in fact I need to get some cash to give him because he paid in advance. Thank you." Elizabeth disappeared in the direction of the kitchen.

"Thanks, Trev. You being here made it easier on her. She hates doing this."

"Can't have him here. Is Charlotte back yet?"

"Haven't seen her since this morning. I thought she was with you."

"She was. Give me a call when she arrives, would you? Getting a bit worried about her."

"Of course. Regardless of how Elizabeth might feel, she won't make her leave tonight. Hopefully, not at all."

"Keep me updated. If she needs somewhere to stay, I'll find a place."

The sound of Elizabeth's footsteps stopped the conversation. "I suddenly thought about his car?"

"I'll bring him up in the morning before the interview and he can collect it under my supervision."

Trev had no intention of allowing the man back inside Palmerston House. Bernie might be co-operating now, but he'd seen the streak of violence in him this morning and his gut told him there was more going on with him than anyone knew.

# 47

# FORGIVENESS AND FURY

*A* few minutes after Trev and Bernie drove away from Palmerston House, Daphne and John arrived, John carrying a foil-covered platter.

Angus opened the door. "Oh my! Whatever do you have here?"

"Elizabeth needs to rest, not be cooking, so we've brought over a little spread. To help, you know."

Elizabeth crossed the foyer with open arms. "How sweet you are, Daphne."

The women kissed and then Daphne slid her arm through Elizabeth's. "Now, I want you to come to the kitchen so I can reheat this, but you will be sitting down with a glass of something nice."

"You really didn't need to. I'm fine. We're all fine in fact."

"Is everything okay now?" John asked quietly as he and Angus followed the ladies.

"Improving. Trev just relocated Bernie Cooper to the motel in town. I can already see Elizabeth relaxing. For the first time today, I might add. Been somewhat stressful."

"Daph hasn't liked him from the beginning. She's good at judging a person." John adjusted the platter in his hands. "Don't know why we need to reheat this, it's pretty darned hot already."

"And very appreciated. We haven't really eaten today. You will stay?"

"Of course we will!" Daphne called over her shoulder. "I've got some good news to share."

A few moments later, around the kitchen table, the little group sat with a bottle of wine and the platter of freshly cooked chicken drumsticks, roasted vegetables, and garlic bread.

Daphne was unable to contain her news. "It's about the wedding."

"You look ready to burst with excitement, Daphne. Do tell us." Elizabeth finally was smiling again.

"So, this is something I've been working on for a while, but didn't think I'd have the chance so soon." Daphne said. "Well, with Christie and Martin's celebrant retiring and all."

"Sorry? When did this happen? Christie hasn't said anything."

"Only happened today, Elizabeth, and she's going to ring all her booked clients in the morning. They finally sold their business and want to move closer to their grandchildren as soon as possible."

"Well, I'm pleased for them, such nice people, but what about the wedding?"

"She did say she'd come back to officiate for them, but I mentioned it wouldn't be necessary." Daphne beamed. "This thing I've been working on? I've become a celebrant!"

"You have? Oh, Daphne!" Elizabeth's eyes lit up. "You will be perfect for the job. And who better to marry Christie and Martin?"

"Yes! I was there the very day they met. The moment they laid eyes upon each other for the first time! Of course, it was at poor Dorothy's funeral, but it was obvious even then those two were made for each other." Daphne grabbed a drumstick and took a bite.

A movement in the doorway caught everyone's attention. It was Charlotte.

"Come in, dear," Elizabeth said quietly.

Charlotte took just one step inside. Her hair was messy and her eyes were red and sad. She sniffed the air and almost sighed in pleasure. "I won't disturb you."

"Don't be silly. There's lots for everyone." Daphne got up to find another wine glass and plate.

Elizabeth tilted her head at Charlotte. She looked so lost. "Charlotte?"

Charlotte finally looked at Elizabeth with something akin to a plea in her eyes.

"Daphne's right. There's lots here. Please join us."

Angus stood and pulled out a chair for Charlotte, then leaned down and kissed Elizabeth on the lips. In front of everyone. "I quite adore you, dear lady."

Tears sparkled in Elizabeth's eyes, and Daphne whispered to John, "I see another wedding in my future."

---

*C*racks in the walls, a lumpy bed. A scarred benchtop holding thick, ugly mugs and a barely serviceable kettle. Bernie had stayed in plenty of motels like this one without considering their appearance, but after weeks at Palmerston House, the differences were stark.

*I shouldn't be here.*

Yet, here he was. Checked in under police supervision as though he were a criminal. The police officer even carried his bags to the room and offered to arrange a meal. All the time, Bernie stayed polite. Compliant. Regretful. And he should have accepted the meal because his stomach refused to stop grumbling after twenty-four hours without food.

He moved the thin curtain to one side. The patrol car was gone. There were no cars in the car park and why would there be? Who in their right mind would stay in this dump? It looked as though someone had died in it.

The terrible turn of events this evening threw all his plans into disarray and now he had to rethink some things. With a curse, he crossed to the bed and opened one bag. If he reread the diary, there might be a clue he'd missed. Some other way to fulfil his dreams.

*Mother's dreams.*

One day he would take a piece of Eleanor's jewellery to leave on her grave. A tribute to her.

He found his phone at the bottom of the bag, its battery depleted. Piece by piece he piled up his clothing on the bed until the bag was empty. No diary. He repacked the bag, checking every pocket as he went.

His camera bag was next. Three cameras, seven lenses. Smaller bags with accessories. A tripod bag. No diary.

Bernie checked the clothes he was in. Nothing. When did he last read it? A few days ago in his bedroom. But he'd checked under the mattress when he packed and, not finding it, assumed it was in amongst his clothing.

Someone must have stolen it. Broken into his room and found it and now must know his secrets. Was it Lottie? Or Elizabeth? Yes, she had a key and would excuse herself as being in there to clean. Yet she'd stood there tonight with a stony expression as she'd evicted him from his own house.

"Well, of course she did. Couldn't reach my treasure with me still there."

It was clear now. Elizabeth had the diary and planned to conspire with Christie – the keeper of the key – to steal Harry's treasures.

*My treasures.*

Bernie picked up one of his cameras. He had to find a way back in. Call the police. Except the local police were in collusion with Elizabeth. The whole town wanted him gone so they could get their dirty hands on the little left of his inheritance.

Blood rushed to Bernie's head and stars danced in his eyes. He'd burn the place down before he let them take everything he'd worked so hard to get. He'd burn the whole town down. With all his might, he threw the camera against a wall.

# 48

# BOTTLES AND KEYS

ollowing a night of fitful sleep, half-dreaming of Charlie leaving town without a word, Trev turned his patrol car into the motel car park. Bernie emerged from his room and, with little more than a grunt, climbed in.

"Get any sleep?" Trev asked more cheerily than he felt. Better to keep things pleasant.

"Some."

"Me, I slept like a baby." One who stayed awake most of the night. "Got your car keys?"

"Yup."

They drove through town. George sat outside his shop and Bernie stared at him. "Oh, there's George," Trev said. "He took my advice and got a whole new security set-up. Cameras, alarm going direct to me, both here and at his house. Can't be too careful these days."

"He has some nice pieces. Pays to protect them." Bernie smiled.

*Being nice now?*

A few moments later, Trev nosed into the driveway of Palmerston House. "So, grab your car and follow me back to the station for that chat. Then we're done."

"Mate, I think I dropped something in my room last night. Wasn't feeling too steady and think it might have gone under the bed. Any chance I can ask Elizabeth to let me run up and retrieve it?"

Trev parked behind the SUV. "No chance. But I'll ask her if she's found it. You get behind your wheel and I'll be right back. What did you drop?"

"A… a leather bound book. But I can—"

Trev strode to the front door and tapped.

Elizabeth answered, glancing past Trev as Bernie opened the door to his SUV. He stood there, watching. "Ignore him, Elizabeth. He's got a date at the station next so pretend he's not there."

She dragged her eyes back to Trev. "You don't think he'll try and come back?"

"I'm going to make it very clear what will happen if he does. I'm only bothering you because Bernie reckons he dropped something in his old room. A book."

She shook her head. "Angus helped me clean the room right out this morning. It was rather a shock to find a whole lot of empty water bottles under the bed. All crushed. But no books or any other personal items."

*Water bottles?*

"Sorry to hear about the mess."

"No trouble. Angus did most of the moving and cleaning." Her eyes lit up. Was everyone in River's End in love?

"Okay, well I'm going to get him off your property and I insist you have some fun today."

"Actually, Angus and I are going shopping in Warrnambool for a gift for the wedding. And lunch. So it will be fun."

Trev headed back to the cars. Bernie slowly climbed into his SUV. "Follow me. Okay?"

"Of course."

As Trev got into his patrol car he glanced at his side mirror. Charlotte was watching from her bedroom window.

"*J* don't know about the reception counter. Do you have any ideas?" Christie stood in the centre of the partly constructed salon, staring at an empty space with a frown. "It has to be right."

"In keeping with the feel of the whole business," Barry said, taking notes.

"Exactly. It's one of the first things clients will see and has to be perfect."

"I'll give it some thought. Now, I'm waiting for some bamboo to arrive for the screen outside."

"Did you just change the subject? I'm worried about the counter and you are the most creative builder I've met so far."

Barry laughed. "Are you sure?"

"Look at the cottage."

"Isn't Martin more creative?"

"Well, yes. But he's not really a builder. Oh, you're suggesting I ask him about it! Great idea."

"Sylvia mentioned you might employ Belinda."

"There's no might about it." Christie headed for the back of the shop and Barry followed. "The minute she graduates from her course she'll be coming here. Such a talent and the clients will love her sense of humour."

"Anyone else lined up? Can't imagine you can do it all yourself."

"I'm interviewing someone tomorrow and might rent part of the space out for specialists. There's been some interest from remedial masseurs and some natural therapy practitioners, so they'll use the private rooms on a booked basis." Christie stopped at where there was once the old back door. Now, natural light streamed through glass walls. "I love this. Windows that are doors."

"Summertime you can open everything right up if you want."

"Perfect for evening special events. Invitation only of course."

"Of course. Say, will you do gift vouchers?"

Christie turned to Barry with a grin. "Yes. And we will cater for men as well, Barry."

"No. Not for me. Quite happy with my level of beauty, thanks."

"I don't know. Have you waxed lately?"

Barry's eyes opened wider. "Enough of that. I'd like to arrange a gift voucher. Or a few."

"And I will make sure Sylvia has the most beautiful, relaxing visits ever."

"How did you… never mind."

"I keep telling people I'm good with secrets and mysteries. Will nobody ever believe me?"

"Everyone does. So what's your take on the secrets of Palmerston House?"

"Don't you start. It's bad enough Bernie Cooper thinks he is owns the place, and then Thomas is suspicious of everyone he doesn't know. Oh, and Daphne with her various theories."

"I'm serious." Barry leaned against a wall. "I've only heard bits and pieces so might be completely off base. But if Cooper was looking for a key in the pond, what does it unlock? Who put the key there anyway and what does it have to do with you?"

Christie bit her lip, thinking. "You know, we think he broke into the cottage and might have moved the trunk. Martha was sure it was further along on the dining room table when we left for dinner that night. But the trunk is empty."

"The one your Gran left?"

"Yes. Now, the trunk came from Palmerston House. Martha remembers it being in Gran's bedroom when they were children. It must have had the key then and Gran ended up with it. She left me the key, along with one to the cottage and one to her little tulip box. But the skeleton key only opens the trunk."

"Does it?" Barry checked his watch. "Locks can be duplicated so how do you know there isn't a door or cupboard somewhere your key will open? I've got to run some plans into Green Bay."

"Where should I start looking? For the appropriate keyhole?"

He shrugged. "I'd be checking the lock on the trunk for any details and work from there."

After Barry left, Christie wandered around the shop. So much still to do. Unfinished framework. Plumbing inside for sinks and outside for a hot tub. Wiring dangled from the ceiling and everywhere was dust and offcuts. Hard to imagine in a couple of months she'd be opening the doors.

Before then though, her wedding. Not long now and she'd be Martin's wife and begin her new life less than a year since coming here to River's End.

As she locked the front door behind herself, she took a closer look. A simple lock. Barry was right, she should see if it gave up any information and then look for clues. A little rush of excitement began in her stomach.

## 49

### ROAD TRIP

*W*hat were you thinking?

Charlotte gazed out of the window of Trev's car as the landscape changed from coast to hills. One moment of weakness and she was on a road trip.

An hour earlier, alone in Palmerston House after Elizabeth and Angus took the road to Warrnambool for their day out, an older sedan had drawn up out the front and Trev had climbed out.

She'd opened the door in surprise. Dressed in jeans and a T-shirt, his smile was infectious, encouraging her agreement when he'd made his invitation. "We won't get back here until early evening, so if you have other plans…" Of course she didn't.

"You'll love Mum."

Charlotte glanced at Trev. "Are you sure she's okay with me arriving on her doorstep unannounced?"

"I am. And it isn't her doorstep we're visiting. It's her bookshop."

"She owns a bookshop?" Now it was making sense. When Trev asked her to go with him to the Macedon Ranges on a day trip to check in on his mother, she'd worried he might be expecting more from her than the sort-of friendship they shared. "And you know I love books."

"Exactly. So even if you don't feel up to socialising, you'll have free run of the place whilst I do."

Relief had flooded through Charlotte. He'd mentioned his mother was thinking of selling up and needed a bit of his time to talk things through. With Bernie out of Palmerston House it was an opportunity for him to have a rare day off. And he liked company on the long drive. So she was here as company and could then immerse herself into the wonders of a small town bookshop.

"You're smiling."

"No I'm not."

"You are, Charlie. You know, they say food is the way to a man's heart, so are books the way to yours?" He chuckled. "Don't answer."

She hadn't intended to. Books were her escape. The world she could rely on when the real world fell apart. So perhaps a man who understood this, and bought her lots of books, might be… attractive. She sneaked a look at Trev. There was so much more to him than his muscular arms, six pack stomach, and good looks. But those were definitely the icing on the cake.

"I saw you earlier. With Bernie." Anything to redirect her silly thoughts.

"He thought he'd left a book in his room. All Elizabeth found was a pile of crushed water bottles."

"A book? It would be Harry Temple's diary, I imagine. Maybe he dropped it in the pond."

"Don't say that! Elizabeth won't tolerate anyone else in there, even if it's evidence."

"Probably in the bottom of a suitcase. Did you say crushed water bottles?"

Trev shot a look at Charlotte. "Why?"

"Habitual. His mother refused to allow him any bottled drinks growing up. No soft drink or even bottled water. Had some sort of phobia about the sound they make being crushed. He told me the day after she died he bought a twenty-four pack of bottled water, emptied them all and crushed them one by one."

"And now he can't stop."

Charlotte looked at her hands. "I thought water bottles were the focus of his anger. But the way he was with Christie..."

"Inhibitions disappear when alcohol's involved, you know it. Had he not drunk too much we'd not have known."

"I should have spoken up earlier."

"You should have trusted me to use your knowledge to evaluate the situation. But I admire your ethics, Charlie."

*You might not if you knew why. Really why.*

"Why do live so far from your mother?"

"Do you always change the subject if you don't like what you hear? 'Yes, Trev, I do' is the correct answer so don't screw up your face at me. Moving right along then, when I was looking for a post there was nothing closer to home. She and Dad always lived there. Knew everyone and will never leave the Ranges. I grew up playing local football and club cricket, went to the local schools, all that kind of stuff. Always hoped I'd find something close by."

"And you've stayed in River's End ever since?"

"Love it. Never a day I've regretted accepting the job there."

"Except you don't get to see your family so much."

"True. I do miss Mum. Dad's long gone but she's surrounded by friends and refuses my twice a year offer to bring her to River's End to live."

With a soft sigh, Charlotte turned her eyes back to the passing scenery. A coherent, loving mother. And father, once. One home growing up in a place where everyone knows everyone. A bit like River's End. How different Trev's upbringing was from hers. How perfect it sounded. And how completely out of her reach to ever experience.

## 50

## BEYOND THE CELLAR

*M*ore than an hour after hiding in bushes on the opposite side of the road, Bernie was certain Palmerston House was deserted.

First, Angus and Elizabeth drove off in his over-priced, showy Range Rover. They turned toward Warrnambool so hopefully would be out for the day. Then, something unexpected happened. Lottie got in Trevor Sibbritt's car and they drove off. She'd carried her handbag, a book, and a jacket. They'd even laughed as they walked to his car.

*Well well. Won't he be interested in what you really are?*

Bernie darted over the road and sprinted up the driveway. He let himself into Palmerston House through the back door, using a key Elizabeth kept hidden beneath a pot full of herbs. At least, she thought it was hidden but he'd made it his business to know about it. He replaced the key, careful to leave the pot exactly as he'd found it.

The keys to each room dangled from the hooks near the door to the cellar. He grabbed them with a laugh. Why bother locking anything?

Elizabeth's rooms were first. She had a bedroom with a walk in robe, a small sitting room, and ensuite. Quite elegant and most likely the room he would make his own when the time came. He wanted to linger over photographs lining the walls but knew time was against him. Lots of knick-knacks, old books, a diary of her own, but no evidence of his. Not even under the mattress.

Lottie was tidy. Her clothes were folded in drawers or hanging neatly and there wasn't a lot to go through. He held one of her jumpers against his cheek.

*So soft.*

Then looked under her bed, under the mattress, in the empty suitcase. No diary.

Room by room, Bernie searched the bottom floor. After no success in the kitchen – the final room – he hung the keys back in their place. Then he opened the door to the cellar.

Down here, the light was so bad he could miss the diary if it was against a wall or under a box. Another pointless search ended at the door to his treasure. So close. Before he had time to think it through, Bernie pulled the cupboard away from the small stone door.

He hurried back up the steps and across to the old stables where he collected a heavy hammer and small crowbar, excited about this unexpected opportunity.

For hours he worked, forcing the crowbar into the cracks around the door then hitting it with the hammer until it was deeply embedded. All his weight on the crowbar didn't move anything. Not even a bit. Over and over he tried until his arms were like jelly and plaster and timber shards littered the floor. In fury, he slammed the hammer into the centre of the door, chipping off a little stone, but the door held firm.

Bernie replaced the shelving and restacked the boxes. Kicked the mess to one side. Nobody would see it in this light anyway. Sweat poured down his body and every muscle ached. All for nothing. He needed the key.

He froze as a distinctive creak came from above.

Another creak. And a laugh. Elizabeth's laugh.

*T*he trip to Warrnambool was both productive and enjoyable, with Elizabeth and Angus choosing the perfect wedding gift and enjoying a delightful lunch overlooking the water. Back at Palmerston House, they'd gone straight to the kitchen, more than ready for a cup of tea. As the kettle boiled, Elizabeth prepared a teapot and Angus told her a story from his time in London, making her laugh. But then, when the kettle stopped whistling, there was an odd sound. A scrape, almost like a footstep from the other side of the door to the cellar.

"Did you hear that?" Elizabeth asked.

"Yes. Probably a mouse."

"A mouse! In my home?"

Angus grinned. "Or a rat."

Elizabeth put her hands on her hips.

There was a soft thud, further from the door.

"I'd better take a look." Angus headed for the door to the cellar. "Probably a misguided possum."

"Oh, perhaps we should call… now I'm being silly."

"Don't need the pest control person yet. Let me see if I can locate the culprit."

"Not what I meant, but be careful."

As he opened the door, Angus blew her a kiss. "No rodent is a match for me."

His footsteps faded and Elizabeth opened the drawer where she kept the torches. "I'll bring some light."

"What on earth?" Angus' words were muffled by distance.

Elizabeth stepped through the doorway. "Angus?"

"Why are you—" his words cut off with an oomph.

Footsteps approached, fast footsteps. Fear cut through Elizabeth. "Angus?" she cried, flashing the torch around at the top of the steps.

Bernie loomed into her vision, face red and clothes covered in a white substance. At the base of the steps he stopped, swaying. In one hand was a hammer, and a crowbar in the other. Elizabeth turned and ran.

She couldn't leave Angus. In the kitchen, her eyes darted around and as Bernie's heavy footsteps grew louder, she seized a knife from the sink and backed away.

---

*B*ernie burst through the doorway. He staggered to a stop near the kitchen table, blinking at the sun streaming through the window.

His eyes roamed the kitchen, coming to rest on Elizabeth who had squeezed herself between a counter and a tall cupboard.

"Are you holding a knife?"

"Don't come near me." Her voice was weak. Scared.

"I'd never hurt you. Elizabeth."

She glanced at the tools he still carried. He placed them, one at a time, on the table. "See?"

"Bernie, please go. I need to go to Angus."

"Angus? Oh, he's fine."

"Then where is he?" Elizabeth stepped forward, knife still in hand but lowered to her side. "What did you do to him?"

"Nothing."

"I don't believe you! I heard him."

"He was surprised to see me."

"Please. Please, Bernie. You've told me before you like me so please go now. Let me pass."

"I don't mind if you'd like to keep living here." He smiled "I'd like your room though, because I prefer all the space and such a pretty outlook, over the back garden. But you can have any other room you want."

"Thank you."

What on earth was he going on about? From the doorway to the cellar, a groan emanated and fear clutched her stomach.

"Bernie, I left the washing basket outside. Would you mind fetching it? Then we can have a cup of tea."

"I'm not crazy, you know. But I'll go. I've done all I can here."

"All you can?"

"I tried. With so little to go on, I've exhausted almost every avenue."

"I don't understand."

"And it is isn't your fault. Oh, dear Elizabeth, you simply purchased a property. How were you to know it was stolen?" He shrugged. "My poor great-great-grandfather Henry was left with nothing, thanks to Eoin Ryan. It is his family who will pay, not yours."

Elizabeth was desperate to go to Angus. But Bernie kept talking.

"I will have Palmerston House back. For Harry. He may have lived out his days poor. He and his family, driven to work like common folk but at least he had them."

"Bernie? Have you been to the graveyard?"

"In River's End?"

"Near the cliff are some interesting graves. From the early settlers. Perhaps you should stop there. To see who they are."

He tilted his head. "I might do so."

Then he was gone, and a moment later the back door closed with a click.

# 51

# A PLACE OF WELCOME

The scenery changed again as Trev rounded a long, slow curve, twisting downward into a valley. As if cast back in time, the first sight of the village always drew him back to his childhood. Long, lazy summer afternoons splashing through the creek on the other side of town, kicking a ball with his mates. Not a lot changed here over the years.

"Is this it?" Charlotte sat up straighter, keenly gazing around.

"Sure is. See the oval over there?" He gestured to a sports ground nestled beside a tree-covered hill. "Kicked my first goal there."

"Cool. How far are we from Hanging Rock?"

"Not far. Maybe fifteen minutes."

"I loved the movie. And the book."

"Mum carries copies. Pity we haven't got time to go there for a picnic." He laughed at his own joke.

"Funny. This is so like River's End."

"Except the ocean. But yeah, it is."

There was the shop. His spirits lifted. So many great memories helping Mum out as a kid, making extra money as a teen. Out of habit he drove into all-day parking over the road, so as to keep the spots in front of the shop free for her customers.

"And we are here."

"It was a nice drive. Thanks."

"Not too long for you?" He unbuckled his seatbelt.

"Not with a bookshop as the prize." Charlotte smiled and his heart flip-flopped. Then she was out of the car, waiting for him to join her.

"I thought spending the day with me was the prize." He locked the car.

"Nope. Bookshop."

"There's a train station not far away. Will only take you… maybe a day or so to get back to River's End."

"Nice."

"Or you could accept the fact you enjoy my company. Careful, no jaywalking or I'll arrest you." He steered them toward a pedestrian crossing.

"Is this even in your jurisdiction? Not as though the road is busy."

"Rules are there for a reason." The silly conversation continued as they crossed the road.

Outside the bookshop, Charlotte stopped with a little squeal of delight, something Trev had never heard from her. She peered at the window display, mouth slightly open and eyes wide. "There's so much detail. Look how perfectly placed the flowers are… even the petals across the plate to accentuate the cupcakes. And they are almost the same as the cover of the book being promoted! Does your mother do this on her own?"

"Come and ask her."

Trev held the door open for Charlotte to go through first. She brushed against his chest and the scent of her hair filled his senses. There was no way to remove the smile on his face.

His mother was at the back of the shop, rearranging books on a shelf. She glanced up with a smile as the door closed behind him then her eyes lit up with recognition.

"Darling! How wonderful."

"Hi, Mum. Thought I should visit." He met her halfway and reached down to put his arms around her. She squeezed him back but not with the strength he remembered. A little bit of his happiness disappeared. "New wheelchair? When did you get this?"

"At least six months ago."

"Oh." Was it really so long since he'd been up? He wanted to kick himself.

"Er. Hi. Lovely shop."

Trev straightened. "Charlie, come and meet Mum. Mrs Rose Sibbritt. Mum, this is my friend, Charlotte Dean."

"Do you prefer Charlie, or Charlotte, dear?"

"Either is fine. Just not Lottie."

"Never Lottie! And it's Rosie, please call me Rosie." Rosie held out her hand and Charlotte took it. "Long drive for a quick visit. Or are you staying?" She turned her head to Trev.

"Not this time, sorry. The opportunity came up this morning for a day off, so I took it. We did."

"Good. Shall we have coffee?"

"Why don't I go and get us all coffee so you two can talk?" Charlotte offered. "Who makes the best coffee in town?"

A couple of directions later, Charlotte slipped out through the door. Trev watched her go.

"I approve. She likes my shop."

He laughed. "Charlie always has a book in her hand it seems. Didn't know if she'd come with me but once I mentioned this place, she almost leapt into the car."

"Good taste."

"Thanks, Mum."

Rosie wheeled toward the counter. "Didn't mean you."

"I know." Trev followed. "Charlie will amuse herself in here for hours, so how about we have a talk about the shop? If you want to."

Rosie turned the wheelchair and backed it a bit to make room for Trev to pull a stool from under the counter. "You've driven all this way for me?"

"You needed me. Of course I did."

Tears welled up in Rosie's eyes and she grabbed Trev's hand. "There's a lot to talk about."

*A*fter coffee and casual conversation, Charlotte left Trev and Rosie to talk and immersed herself in the book shop. Bookshelves lined the walls but in the centre were reading nooks. Single comfy armchairs, complete with a side table and lamp. A coffee table between two sofas. What she loved most was a child-friendly area with a colourful mat, a pile of second-hand kids' books, and a table set up with pencils and paper.

With nobody else in the shop, and a quick glance to make sure Trev and Rosie weren't watching, she sat on the mat and soaked in the atmosphere. As a child, this set-up would have been a dream come true. Creativity everywhere and no angry adult telling her to clean the house or run to the shops for the third time in a day. This was for children to explore and learn in a fun way. And be kids.

Voices of incoming shoppers reminded her where she was. Charlotte jumped up and moved to the shelves where Rosie had been working.

*Might as well complete the job.*

Mysteries and thrillers filled these shelves and Charlotte touched the spines of those she'd read.

"Ah! Is that the new *J. G. Groggins* mystery?"

One of the shoppers appeared beside Charlotte, nodding toward where her hand was.

"It is."

"My friend told me I must buy it. Have you read it yet?" The lady looked over her glasses at Charlotte. "You look like a mystery buff."

"I do? Yes, I have."

"Then don't tell me a thing!"

"Never. Have you read the previous three?"

"Three? I thought this was the first in the series."

"You are in for a treat." Charlotte pulled out a total of four books, the newest one and its three predecessors. "Now, this is the first and it really sets up the whole series. I'd suggest reading them in order, so as not to miss a word."

"And they are good?"

"I love them. Devoured them one after another and cannot wait for the final three."

"Then I shall take them all."

"I'll pop them onto the counter and you keep browsing." Charlotte tapped another book on the next shelf. "If you like something a little bit... steamy, then perhaps you'd enjoy this as well. Maybe read the back blurb first."

Charlotte left the lady to look and took the four books to the counter. Rosie and Trev glanced up. "Not for me. The lady down the back wants them."

"Mrs Lane? She rarely buys anything. Looks here then goes to the library."

"I think she'll buy them. If not, I'll put them back."

With a grin at their surprised faces, Charlotte wandered off to look for books on the region. There were a few, mostly historical accounts of the founding of the village, its importance to the Macedon Ranges, an overview of its early industries, and some gorgeous photos.

*Photos like the kind Bernie said he'd take of River's End.*

She turned away, troubled he'd intruded. Why was she even thinking about him? He'd left Palmerston House. Earlier, Trev mentioned he'd strongly suggested to Bernie it was time to move on. So, by the time they got home tonight, Bernie might not even be in River's End. But why would he give up his lifelong dream?

"And your lovely new assistant was so helpful, Rose!"

Mrs Lane was at the counter, paying for her books. Five of them, as she'd also followed Charlotte's suggestion on the other one. A bit surprising, as it was indeed rather hot, but she wasn't one to judge people by appearances.

"My new... oh, Charlotte." Rosie smiled her way. "Yes, she is lovely."

Sudden warmth filled Charlotte. Rosie was so sweet and welcoming. Beside his mother, Trev gazed at Charlotte. He didn't smile; it was an odd expression almost of sadness. Was this to do with his mother?

Or was he thinking about Charlotte? Curious, she went closer as Mrs Lane left with her bag of books.

"Sorry to confuse Mrs Lane. About working here."

"I wish I had someone like you. I truly do."

"As a child I wanted to live in a bookshop. Perhaps, in another lifetime…"

Trev hadn't taken his eyes off Charlotte, but now he looked away, out of the front window. He blinked rapidly and she was certain something she'd said or done was behind it. But what?

# 52

# ANGUS

*H*eart pounding so fast Elizabeth could barely breathe, she took a few tentative steps forward. As far as the table, where the crowbar and hammer lay. She placed the knife beside them.

*What if he comes back?*

She ran to the back door and locked it, adding the security chain. Then, back through the kitchen, to the steps to the cellar.

"Angus? Where are you?"

He wasn't on the lower landing, nor in the cellar. The door to the storage room was ajar.

"I'm... here."

At first she couldn't see him. She'd dropped her torch in the kitchen. But then she saw him, on the floor, on his side. As Elizabeth dropped to her knees beside him, he reached out a hand. "You... you are okay?"

"I'm okay but what about you? What hurts? What happened? Are you bleeding?" The words tumbled out.

"Pushed me. Fell badly but if you can help me sit..." he moaned as he moved.

"I'm going to phone for help. I need you to stay still for a moment, okay?"

"Where... is he?"

"Gone. Stop talking for now. I have to run upstairs but I'll only be a moment."

Somehow, Elizabeth got back to the kitchen and grabbed the phone. The first call was for an ambulance and as soon as she hung up, she dialled Christie. She hurried to open the front door as Christie answered.

"Elizabeth! I was planning on dropping—"

"Christie. Sorry, but I need you here right now."

"What's wrong?"

"Bernie was here and he might have hurt Angus. He's in the room through the cellar and I can't move him."

"Angus is hurt? No! Elizabeth, call an ambulance!"

"I have, dear. Please come. Come soon."

With shaking hands, she unlocked the back door again. She dialled Trev. It went to voicemail.

*Leave a message.*

She left a message. Hung up and dialled emergency again. One way or another she'd have a police presence.

She ran into the laundry and took blankets from a cupboard.

When she reached Angus again, his eyes were closed. Elizabeth gently covered him with a blanket. "Angus. Help is coming. Wake up, darling. Angus?"

She sat beside him, afraid to touch him but desperate to know he was okay. Her fingers played with his hair. Brushed it to one side. His forehead was clammy. Elizabeth finally slid her hand under the blanket. Her fingers curled around his.

"I... Angus, I need you." The words echoed back at her. She was going to lose him. A small cry caught in her throat. "I love you. Stay with me, darling. Please stay."

*F*or the first time ever, Thomas drove the Lotus. One look at Christie's face and he'd taken the keys, grabbed her elbow, and hurried them to the car. He'd got her into the front seat and seat-belted as tears streamed down her face. Martha climbed into the 4WD to follow in case they needed a second car.

"He's tough as old nails. He'll be right."

As he backed the Lotus out of the driveway, Thomas' mind raced. How had Bernie got into Palmerston House, and why would he hurt Angus? He'd known the man was bad news from the moment Bernie had driven past him that night, showering stones across the grass verge.

Thomas stopped at the corner, checking the gears and adjusting the seat to allow for his longer legs. "Phone Martin. Pull yourself together, child. Angus needs strength, not tears."

Wide-eyed, Christie glanced at Thomas. "First gear is the other way." She pulled her phone from the bag Martha had thrown over her shoulder as she'd fumbled with the back door.

With Martha behind them, Thomas headed for Palmerston House, resisting the urge to plant his foot on the accelerator. Christie had several attempts at dialling.

"Deep breath. Relax your fingers. Darn it, doesn't your phone let you dial by voice?"

"No. Maybe." She got through and the panic in her voice as she spoke to Martin cut into Thomas.

He avoided town by taking the road closer to the beach, but Martha went the other way. He had no idea why, but had enough to worry about.

Christie dropped her phone into her bag. "He's going straight there."

"Good. Hold it together."

"What if…"

"What ifs don't matter."

"She sounded dreadful. As if—"

"As if she's had a terrible scare. We're almost there." He had to think about gears again as he slowed to turn. Sports cars were different. Rather nice to drive. But different. "And the ambulance is coming."

"Why was Bernie there? Didn't Trev tell him not to go there?"

"We'll find out."

"Where is Trev? I'll call him."

Anything to keep her occupied.

"Trev, when you get this please call me. It's Christie. There's been an… I mean, Bernie Cooper has hurt Angus." Her voice faltered and Thomas looked at her, shocked at how pale she was. "Please come to Palmerston." She finally managed.

"Christie, you need to stop thinking the worst. Where's my girl who's always positive?"

Thomas drove through the gates of Palmerston House and almost before he pulled up to one side of the driveway, Christie was clambering out.

"Go. I'm not far behind." Thomas turned off the engine and opened the door. "If I can get out." With his hand, he leveraged one leg out, then the other. Christie was almost at the front door of the house.

"Need help?" Martin appeared from nowhere, panting a bit and offering his hand to Thomas.

"These things are too low." Thomas grabbed on and let Martin help him. "Not as young as I once was."

"Why are you driving it?"

"Christie isn't coping. Go on, I'll straighten up and follow in a minute."

Martin followed Christie, bounding up the steps in her wake.

"Wish I could still do that."

# 53

## BE BRAVE

*C*hristie ran through the open front doorway of Palmerston House.

*Where are they?*

The foyer was empty. What had Elizabeth said... something about the cellar.

"Angus?" Her cry echoed back.

Christie ran to the kitchen. She almost slid through the kitchen doorway, grabbing the edge of the table as she saw the crowbar, hammer, and knife laid out. A torch was on the floor near the doorway to the cellar and she scooped it up.

"Elizabeth!"

"Down here."

Christie hurtled down the old steps. She remembered the storage room from the day Elizabeth took her there to recover a photograph of the cottage, taken when Thomas was only a child.

She'd only been a young child herself when Angus had appeared at her side on the worst day of her life, enclosing her small hand with a firm but gentle grasp and telling her to be brave. An anchor at her parents' funeral.

*Angus.*

Always the one to turn to, growing up in Gran's less than happy home. He'd taught her to cook. To dance. And how to laugh again.

Christie stopped inside the doorway, hand flying to cover her mouth.

Elizabeth sat on the stone floor, holding Angus' hand. He was covered with blankets, only the top of his head visible.

"No."

Mascara streaked down Elizabeth's face and Christie stifled a sob. Her legs buckled and she only made it to Angus' side before they gave way completely and she dropped to her knees.

His face was ashen. She stared at him, desperate for a sign he was breathing, and leaned close to whisper, "Be brave."

"Christie... I don't think he can't hear you."

"What do you mean?"

*Of course he can hear me. He's always heard me.*

Christie felt for his other hand under the blanket. It was so cold. "Angus, be brave. We're here for you. Elizabeth and me. We love you."

"And... I... love you both...dearly," he barely whispered, and weakly returned the pressure on Christie's hand.

"We heard you. Angus, there's an ambulance almost here." Christie reached out to Elizabeth and grasped her free hand, hanging onto it as though they were the lifeline for Angus. "Did you hit your head? Try to say yes or no."

It took a few seconds until he managed a weak, "Yes."

"Then you are probably concussed and need to keep awake. No more laying around sleeping the day away for you!" Christie squeezed both the hands she held. She glanced at Elizabeth. "Where's Charlotte?"

"I'm not sure. But not home. Do you really think he's concussed?"

"I guess it's possible. Still with us, Angus?"

"Mmm."

"Who is here with you?"

"You. Eliza...beth." His eyes flickered open. "Martin."

"Hi, Angus." Martin squatted beside Christie and ran his hand down her back. The fear and panic seeped away. She leaned into him but still held tightly onto Elizabeth and Angus' hands.

"So... tired."

"Do you remember what happened?"

"Christie, maybe not the time." Elizabeth let go of her hand to adjust her position.

"Surprised me. Thought a rat."

"Big rat." Martin frowned. "Bernie was down here? Did he have the hammer and crowbar and knife?"

"Oh... I had the knife."

Everyone looked at Elizabeth, even Angus managing to widen his eyes for a few seconds.

"I must remember to put it away."

"Perhaps everything should be left where it is. Until Trev says otherwise. Where is he?" Christie glanced over her shoulder at the doorway. "Can I hear the ambulance?"

Martin stood. "I'll go. Keep talking, Angus. Won't be much longer."

"Why... dear lady, did you have... a knife?"

Christie spoke for her. "To cut up some of your favourite pie, most likely. I definitely hear sirens."

# 54

# UNRAVELLING

*A*s sirens had approached the graveyard, Bernie stepped out of sight behind a tree. He'd peered through branches as an ambulance sped by in the direction of River's End. Once it disappeared, he'd lost interest and resumed his inspection of the headstones where Elizabeth suggested he look. She really was a nice lady, always considering his interest in Palmerston House.

Early settlers, she'd said.

Past the time of the theft of Palmerston House, he actually knew little about Eoin Ryan. Perhaps he'd lived a short and miserable life after throwing the rightful owners from their home. He put a hand to his pocket, expecting the diary to be there. It wasn't, reminding Bernie he needed to find out what happened the night he'd lost it.

The first few graves were names he didn't recognise. Old headstones with little to say. A number of Ryan graves followed. Generations of thieves.

Another siren cut through the quiet and he ducked, then snuck a look over the headstone, surprised to see a police car race past. First an ambulance, now this. Surely he hadn't actually harmed Angus? The man had appeared out of the gloom after Bernie picked up his tools, ready to go upstairs and tell Elizabeth he'd fixed a broken cupboard. He hadn't meant to knock Angus down, but he'd apologised and got a response, so expected him to get up and follow.

The police car gone, Bernie straightened. He turned to gaze out to sea. Blue-green and with a gentle swell, it was a perfect day to sail. Not nearly high enough tide to reach the cave though. He wanted the treasure. Needed the treasure.

*Mother wants me to find it.*

He missed her so much. She'd know what to do next, and how to finish this.

Bernie reached into his backpack for a bottle of water. The last one. He'd need to top up his supply as soon as he finished here. The water cooled him as it reached his gut, then the familiar, essential hit of vodka spread warmth through his whole being. These days it made up a quarter of each bottle.

He continued perusing the graves. Some cared for, most over-grown. And there... Eoin Patrick Ryan.

He read aloud. With growing anger. "Eoin Patrick Ryan. Eighteen-eighteen to eighteen... eighteen-ninety-three." This was no early demise. Seventy-five years to steal, bully and do whatever he wanted.

Three graves on, he stopped. Read. And reread.

Impossible.

It wasn't fair.

*Henry William Temple. Born 1820 in London, England. Died 1853.*

And nothing else. No elaborate headstone. Only a simple small plaque.

"Harry." Bernie sank to his knees beside the old grave. "How? Why?"

He put the bottle down, found his phone in a pocket, and switched it on. As it booted up, he stared again at the headstone. Why so small? Harry was the most significant man to come to River's End. The phone beeped and Bernie tapped in Harry's full name and asked where he died.

For a few moments he read the results, at first rejecting each but finally dropping his head in despair. Drowned. Assumed by his own hand. Found washed up on the beach, his body battered by the rocks at the base of the cliff.

"Not true. You must have fallen from the cave." Bernie turned off the phone, then returned it to his pocket. He reached for his half empty bottle of water and finished it in one long draught.

*So satisfying.*

The sound and feel of crushing the bottle.

*Sorry, Mother.*

He threw it toward the edge of the cliff, so she wouldn't know.

He stared at the grave of Harry Temple. His ancestor. The man who created Palmerston House, then lost it to a fraud, bully, and thief. If such a man as Harry was unable to retrieve the treasure, then how was he to do so?

Bernie sighed. A deep, despairing sigh. All was lost. It was time to leave River's End.

---

From the Macedon Ranges, Trev had headed through the quarry town of Bacchus Marsh and across country toward Geelong, sprawling beside the sea and second only to Melbourne in population in the state. These days, a bypass shortened the trip. From here, one could head for the beginning of the Great Ocean Road and wind along incredible ocean scenery, or take one of several inland options – as he was doing. It was almost dark as the car went through Colac.

"Another hour and a half or so. You still okay?" Trev glanced at Charlotte, deep in a book she'd bought from his mother. "Isn't it getting a bit too dark to read?"

"Oh, sorry. Maybe." Charlotte looked out of the passenger window. "When did it get so dark?"

Trev chuckled.

Charlotte closed the book and slipped it into her bag. "I really like your mother."

"She likes you back."

"Were you able to help her with the problem you'd mentioned? The reason we drove there today?"

"You were welcome to join us. None of it is a secret, but you seemed quite happy playing shopkeeper. Selling raunchy books to old ladies."

"Mrs Lane assumed I worked there so I went with it. Wouldn't want to embarrass a customer, would I?"

"Mum appreciated your help." Trev adjusted himself in the seat, feeling the complaints in his muscles from the long drive. "She's going to sell the shop. Not yet, but soon."

He had her attention. What did Dad used to say about impossible decisions?

*Plant a seed, let it grow into whatever it will be. Nurture it, because one day you'll want its shade and shelter.*

"Trevor? What's wrong?"

"Oh, thinking about growing trees. Never mind. Anyway, Mum is ready to stop working, but not quite ready to let go of the bookshop. She wanted me to tell her it's okay, I think."

"And is it? Okay?"

"She can't work forever. I grew up in the shop. Lots of memories there, but she's... she's not getting any younger."

"I think Rosie is incredible. Not only for the way she presents the shop and the fabulous range she carries, but to manage it alone... and with some limitations."

"The wheelchair? Injured her spine in a scuba diving accident almost twenty years ago."

"What?"

"She and Dad were right into it but now she won't even come to River's End to see me. Makes her sad to see the ocean, I guess." More than the accident. Probably brings back good memories as well. But even good memories hurt when the person you remember is gone.

*Miss you, Dad.*

"Trevor, she deserves to retire if it's what she really wants. But I see the love she has for her business. Wouldn't a partner be better? Let her take the back seat but still be involved as much as she wants."

*Plant the seed.*

"Funny you should suggest it." A little corner of Trev's heart cried out *no*. "She'd love someone to come on board and learn the business. With a view to taking over later on." There. It was said.

Charlotte was quiet for a while. He stole a look at her face, softly illuminated by the control panel of the car. She was thinking.

*Let it grow into whatever it will be.*

"Today she said money isn't even a consideration. Not at first. She'd rather have someone learn for a few months and then make some arrangement to suit both parties."

"She is very generous."

"And wise."

Charlotte smiled at Trev. "Yes. Does she have a Facebook page for the shop? I might leave a nice review." She pulled her phone from her bag. "Oh, I forgot this was off."

"So is mine. When you've turned yours on, would you mind doing the same for mine? Better see if anyone needs me."

"Sure. Can't have the town in a panic because you have a day off."

A beep from Charlotte's phone was followed by several more. She booted Trev's phone, then checked hers. "Text from Christie to see where I am. One from Elizabeth to see if I'm okay. Darn, I should have left her a note. Sweet of them to worry." She started replying to the messages.

Trev's phone beeped. And kept beeping. He laughed at how many messages came through. "Whose cat is in a tree? Would you take a look for me?"

"Trev, you might want to put those lights and sirens on." Charlotte scrolled through his messages. "There are twelve missed calls. From Elizabeth, Christie, Martin, Thomas..."

"Missed calls? Any voicemails? Just hit the phone icon on one."

"Okay. It's the first one from Christie." She put the call on speaker. "'Trev, when you get this please call me. It's Christie. There's been an... I mean, Bernie Cooper has hurt Angus. Please come to Palmerston.'"

With a loud and uncharacteristic curse, Trev sped up. "No lights and sirens on this. Can you call Green Bay station for me?"

# 55

# HOW DEEPLY WE CARE

*S*unrise at Palmerston House always filled Angus with a sense of peace, but soon, the quiet he'd enjoyed for the last few weeks – since coming home from hospital – would be broken as the property began its final preparations for the wedding tomorrow. Christie would be here most of the day, along with half of River's End. Later, everyone would meet at the pub for a dinner hosted by Martin and Christie.

Angus sat on the verandah at the front of the house. Here was where he'd first met Martin, dropping by to retrieve Randall after a day sailing with Christie. How surprised he'd been to learn of her new confidence on and in the ocean. But after a few moments with Martin, he'd understood. With a man such as Martin by her side, she'd rediscovered the part of herself hidden for years. Pushed down by her grandmother for so long. And now, the love he had for Martin was like the love of a father.

"You look deep in thought." Elizabeth came around the corner, carrying two cups. She handed one to Angus and kissed his forehead, then sat at his side. "Are you alright?"

"I am fine. Stop worrying about me."

She bit her lip and he put a hand over one of hers.

"I'm sorry, I know you care. But I'm quite recovered. Even the doctors agree I'm back to normal. So stop worrying so much." He smiled.

"It's only been a few weeks though."

"Time enough. No more headaches or odd vision. I'm cleared to drive and feel fine. Better than fine, in fact. Tomorrow, I have the honour of walking Christie along the path to meet her new husband."

Elizabeth smiled. "She will be the most beautiful bride."

"And thanks to you, dear lady, Palmerston House will be the perfect place for the wedding and reception."

"There's a lot to do." She frowned. "More food preparation for the reception. All the decorations. A final tidy around the pond and ensuring the space for the arch is cleared. And all in time for Daphne to have some practice runs because she is so nervous."

Angus lifted her hand to his lips and kissed it. "Let's put it in perspective. Food prep will be concentrated fun with you, me, Sylvia, and Martha all bustling around the kitchen. Yes?"

Once Elizabeth nodded, he continued. "Martin, John, and Barry – plus a couple of Barry's men – will sort the landscaping out and get the arch up. Christie, Thomas, and Charlotte will decorate and I believe Trev is providing assistance there as well. What have I left out?"

"Nothing. Everyone is being so wonderful."

"The town loves a wedding. So do I." He held Elizabeth's gaze for a moment, then released her hand to sip some tea.

With daylight, the ever-changing colours in the fountain lost their brightness. A kookaburra flew down from a tree to drink. Magpies sang to each other across the lawn.

"The world is stirring."

"I do enjoy watching the day begin. And with only the three of us to prepare breakfast for – today at least – I may sit here for a little longer than usual. I'll be busy enough with the guests staying for the wedding." Elizabeth laughed softly at Angus' surprised glance. "You are a good influence, my love."

"In that case, I shall sit with you. If I may." He slipped his arm around Elizabeth's shoulders and she shuffled over to lean against him.

———

*M*artin was awake before the first fingers of light crept into the bedroom. He lay on one side, Christie nestled in his arms, fast asleep. So warm, her body against his, and so deeply relaxed.

She needed her rest. Much as Christie believed she was unstoppable and invincible, she wasn't. Today would exhaust her, between the volume of work to be done and the emotional ride. He knew she'd keep going until she dropped.

One more night and then this wonderful woman would become his wife. He closed his eyes for a moment, inhaling her scent in time with her soft breaths.

Tonight, after their celebration dinner with their friends and family, he would kiss her goodnight, leave her at Palmerston House, and come home to Randall. They'd spend as long in the studio as it took to finish the painting, for he'd decided to give it to Christie. Heartbreaking and poignant it may be, but without doubt it stated his undying love for her in a way nothing else would.

Christie stirred, turning in Martin's arms to face him, her eyes flickering open, then closing again.

He kissed the tip of her nose. "Go back to sleep."

She shuffled a bit closer and settled against him.

These moments were etched in his memory. Christie safe here with him. Randall softly snoring in his bed near the window. His little family. A warm glow filled his heart. Peace. Love. Contentment. All the things he'd lost as a small child. Except for his life with Thomas.

"Why so sad?" Christie stared at him through sleepy eyes.

"No. The opposite. Aren't you supposed to be sleeping?"

"I want to be awake to enjoy every minute of today. And tomorrow." She wiggled to the side of the bed, laughing at Martin's expression. "Coffee! We need lots of coffee."

"I had something else in mind."

Christie swung her feet onto the floor as Martin followed her across the bed, missing her by a second as she stood. "Do you really want me to leave Elizabeth with so much to do?" She grabbed her dressing-gown and patted Randall as she passed him. "Good morning, doggie."

"Elizabeth will have plenty of help today."

"Well, yes she will, but there's lots to finish off. Fiddly stuff."

"Like making bows? Creating flower displays? All the things you thrive on?" She wasn't coming back to bed, so Martin threw on shorts and a t-shirt and followed her down the hallway to the kitchen.

Dressing-gown wrapped around her, no make-up, hair unbrushed, feet bare, Christie was the most beautiful woman he'd laid eyes on. She hummed as she made coffee, until noticing Martin leaning against the door frame, watching with a smile.

She grinned. "Get used to it."

"You making coffee?" He straightened and held out his arms. "Or how gorgeous you are?"

"Both." Christie put down cups and went to him, sliding her hands around the back of his neck. "Of course I mean making you coffee. I've not even showered."

"Yet you smell delightful." Her lips were irresistible and he touched them with his.

*Time to stop.*

Before he couldn't.

"I think you're smelling the coffee. Go have a shower and I'll start on breakfast. Most important meal of the day, so you keep reminding me."

"Behave." Martin gently turned her around and released her. "I love you."

Christie returned to the coffee machine. "I will never tire of hearing you say so. And I love you. Very much. Now, shower."

Randall wandered past Martin in the hallway. "Remind Christie to feed you." The dog wagged his tail and continued to the kitchen. What could be more perfect than his life now? From the moment Christie arrived in River's End, his life was changed. Their love was unbreakable and the future filled his heart.

————

*M*artha and Thomas sat at the kitchen table in the cottage, both deep in their own thoughts. A partly eaten breakfast was pushed back from each, and coffee went cold in forgotten cups near the kettle. Beside the sink, last night's dishes were piled up ready to wash. The curtains still hung down instead of being pulled aside to let daylight in.

The phone rang, its jangle cutting through the silence and making Martha jump. Thomas reached for it with a short laugh. "Just the phone, bride. Not a burglar. Hello, Thomas Blake."

Martha stood, then wandered to the key rack near the back door. She touched the skeleton key, now dangling from a hook, then with a sigh, returned to the table to collect the plates.

"No, it's fine. In fact, give us half an hour and we'll be there." Thomas grinned. "Okay, twenty minutes."

A plate in each hand, Martha tilted her head at Thomas, who got to his feet and took them from her. "Stop moping, Martha. There's little bits of her here everywhere, like the key to the trunk, but what good is it at Martin's house?"

"Who was on the phone?"

"If you'd like to have a hot coffee, Christie will be at Palmerston in a few minutes and promised to have one ready."

"Christie? Is she okay?"

"My darling, she has only been gone for one night, and she's done that before."

"I know, but..." Martha dropped her head.

Thomas put the plates down and took Martha into his arms, holding her against his chest, where she rested her head. "But she's not coming back. I know. And I'm every bit as sad."

"I'm selfish."

"Then so am I."

"I want her happy. And Martin makes her happy."

"Most of the time. He has his moments."

"Like you."

"What?" Thomas drew back to look at Martha's face. "Oh, you're joking. You are joking?"

"Anyway, we should be happy for them both. Together, and nothing is going to tear them apart. We won't let it!" Her voice went up a bit and Thomas pulled her against his chest again.

"We won't let it. Martha, nobody is going to conspire against them. In fact, this whole town is out there cheering for them and when they say 'I do' tomorrow, well, I believe it will be the happiest day not only of their lives, but of many others."

Martha smiled against Thomas' chest. "I agree. Deep down, I do. It's just that it took so long for Christie and me to find each other and I am a little bit selfish."

"Well, I'm a little bit coffee deprived, so stop moping and make yourself beautiful. There's a big day ahead and I, for one, am looking forward to dinner tonight."

"Of course you are, dear." Martha raised herself up to kiss Thomas' cheek. "Dinner is one of your three favourite meals of the day."

"Can't believe I left half my breakfast."

"Perhaps we can find something to fill you up at Palmerston House. Shall we hurry up?"

"Not yet. I want a kiss. And then we'll go and see the beautiful bride-to-be."

# 56

## A LOVE UNSPOKEN

*A*fter a quick coffee whilst it was barely dawn, Trev had grabbed a bottle of water and headed out for the beach in shorts and T-shirt.

Three and a half laps of the kilometre-long stretch later, he stopped to catch his breath at the lagoon, pulling his shoes off to cool his feet. He dragged the t-shirt over his head, then took a long drink from his water bottle.

As he twisted the lid back on, he noticed a person at the very end of the jetty.

*Charlie.*

Trev picked up his shoes and wandered in her direction. He'd barely seen her since they'd arrived back from the road trip to his mother's shop. She'd been amazing that night, talking to Elizabeth, Christie, and Martin once they returned from the hospital. Under pressure, Charlotte was the calmest and most coherent person he'd met.

One foot on the beach end of the jetty, Trev hesitated.

"It's a public jetty."

Without turning, Charlotte called to him. Shoes in one hand, t-shirt in the other, Trev wandered along the timber boards until he reached her side. "Hi."

"Hi. Christie and Martin will have the best weather tomorrow. Look at how clear the sky is. No sign of changing."

"How long have you been out here?"

"Ages. I like sitting on the edge to read but needed to stretch."

"So I ran past you a few times?"

"You did." Charlotte turned her head to look at him, her eyes going his chest, where sweat still lingered on his skin. "You have a good... technique."

Trev fought a sudden urge to gather her in his arms and demonstrate his kissing technique. Instead, he put the T-shirt back on, trying to ignore how wet it was in spots. "Thanks. Do you run?"

"Not unless I have somewhere urgent to go." Her eyes were amused.

*Or want to get away from me.*

"You look like you do. Run."

"Hot and sweaty? I'm teasing. I have lucky genes. At least where body shape is concerned."

"What about the rest of your genes?" Trev wished the words back as the humour drained from Charlotte's face.

"Any news about Bernie Cooper?" Her voice was strained.

"Charlie?"

She shook her head and walked away. "I have to get back. There's a lot to do today."

Trev caught up with her and adjusted his stride to match hers. "Me too. Need a shower then I'll be over to help."

She didn't reply, just nodded.

"Bernie is long gone. Last anyone saw of him was one of Lance's staff when Bernie picked up vodka from the bottle shop the day he hurt Angus. Sounds like about an hour later, so he was somewhere first. Nobody saw him leave town, but he'd already checked out of the motel when he went to Palmerston House."

"How much vodka? How many bottles?"

"Huh? Why?"

"Can't say."

"Charlie, stop for a minute. Please." Trev planted his feet in the sand. To his relief, she stopped as well.

"I haven't worked out what I'm thinking, which is why I can't say. I don't know, so quit imagining I'm withholding some valuable information." She'd put her hands on her hips and jutted her chin out.

"I was going to say I'd find out for you."

"Oh. Thanks. Are you sure he's gone, though? I mean... there's something he wants from Palmerston House, so why leave, even if he knew you'd be looking for him?"

"He's smart. Surely smart enough to know he'd crossed the line this time." Trev sighed. "I can't guarantee anything, Charlie. Wish I could promise it was the last we'd see of him but until there's confirmation of where he is—"

"Which could be anywhere." Charlotte began walking again, but not nearly as fast. "I worry for Elizabeth."

They followed the river, passing through the rift in the cliff and making it almost to the road before Trev thought of something to say to leave things between them on a better note.

"I spoke to Mum last night. She said to pass on her regards."

Charlotte's smile was worth waiting for. "How nice of her. Has she... well, found someone yet?"

"To work with her and eventually take over the shop? Not yet."

"She needs someone who can take on the chain stores and put her business online. Compete with the big boys by having the best customer service and all the hard-to-get books she specialises in."

"Isn't it hard to do? Set those sort of things up?"

"Not really. Do you think she'd mind if I suggested it to her?"

*Nurture it, because one day you'll want its shade and shelter.*

"I think she'd love to hear from you."

Charlotte gazed at Trev for a moment. "Are you okay? Does it make you sad talking about this?"

Somehow, Trev found a way to smile. "Give Mum a ring. I'll see you soon, okay?"

She nodded, then turned in the direction of Palmerston House. Trev crossed the road, unable to watch her leave.

# 57

# ONE WELCOME VISITOR. ONE NOT.

*S*ylvia arrived at Palmerston House a little before lunchtime, driving in with baskets of goodies for the workers and one very excited surprise. Almost before the car was parked, Belinda burst out of the passenger door and straight into Christie's arms, barely giving her time to put down the box of decorations she carried from a van.

"You're here!" Christie squeezed Belinda in delight. "I thought it wouldn't be until tomorrow morning."

"In which case, how would you possibly manage? Take now for example." Belinda let go of Christie to gesture to Sylvia. "Mum couldn't have prepared these delicious goodies for you all on her own."

"Yes, I could. But you can help carry them."

"We both will. Hi, Sylvia." Christie kissed Sylvia's cheek. "When did this one arrive?" She nodded in Belinda's direction as she took a basket from the now-open boot.

"Only an hour ago."

"Mum. In one single hour I've iced dozens of eclairs, filled apple turnovers, and packed a lot of these baskets."

"And talked non-stop about beauty school. Here, you can manage two of these." Sylvia passed the stacked baskets to Belinda. "I still blame you." This she directed to Christie, but with a smile.

"Sorry. Not sorry." Although Sylvia had originally panicked at the idea of Belinda moving to Melbourne to do a degree in beauty care, over time she'd become proud of her oldest daughter. Her anger at Christie for supporting Belinda's choice disappeared long before Belinda left home.

"You might be once I mess up your make-up tomorrow," Belinda, halfway to the front steps, called over her shoulder.

Sylvia put two more baskets on the ground and closed the boot. Christie grabbed one before she was told not to. "The decorations can wait because these smell so good. And I had no idea I was hungry until just this minute."

They followed Belinda into Palmerston House. By the time they reached the kitchen, Belinda was hugging Elizabeth, and then Angus. "And I'll set everything out buffet style so we can keep working on turning this marvellous establishment into a state-of-the-art wedding venue."

"Belinda, I'm sure everyone will enjoy a break." Sylvia relinquished her baskets to Angus. "Although there is a sink full of potatoes over there needing to be peeled. Perhaps something to keep you busy?"

Christie hid a smile at the way Belinda's face dropped. "Why don't we lay lunch out, let the others know, and have a quick catch up? Then we can work out what still needs doing today."

"Cool. Yes, Elizabeth, do you want lunch in here?"

"Yes, dear. Just use all of the table and we'll work around you."

"Excellent. Christie, you go and round up the rest of the crew. I can't wait to see Martin!"

"Yes, ma'am." Christie grinned and headed outside, Belinda's chatter following her out.

Today was flying past in a whir of activity and decisions. What seemed workable on paper wasn't always right in practice, so she'd taken a step back to reconsider some of the decorations. Not that any of it really mattered, because in just over a day she'd be married to

Martin. Christie's heart filled and she hugged herself. Nothing and nobody would stop this from happening.

Except, where was Martin? After a quick coffee in the kitchen this morning with Elizabeth, Angus, Thomas, and Martha – and Thomas helping himself to a second breakfast – Martin had kissed her forehead and said he had something to do.

Since then, he'd been absent. Unless he was down at the pond helping the boys. The pond came into view and Christie gasped. A white arch sat atop a circle of white timber boards, raised by a step all the way around. John and Trev were in the process of placing terracotta pots around it.

"I didn't think..." Christie blinked away sudden mistiness and swallowed. "Wow."

"No time for tears, young lady." John grinned at her and straightened. "It will be ready to decorate in a few moments."

"Is Charlotte helping you, Christie?" Trev's question was far too casual.

"She will. We're about to have lunch though, so come up to the kitchen when you want. Speaking of helping, where is Martin?"

The men shared a quick look.

"I saw that. Whatever is he up to?"

"Secret husband-to-be business."

"Maybe I should ask Daphne—"

"She doesn't know. So ask away." John was pleased with himself.

"Belinda's back." Christie decided to change the subject.

"Did she bring food? With Sylvia?"

"Yes, John. And yes. I'll need to let Barry know. Actually, where is he? Did you two do this all on your own?"

"It wasn't difficult, once we worked out which bit went where." Trev tossed his gloves into a pot. "We shouldn't keep those pies and— I mean, Sylvia and everyone else waiting."

"Go on. I'll be there in a minute." Christie smiled at John and Trev as they passed her. Then she walked down to the arch and stood in the spot where tomorrow she'd become Mrs Blake.

*C*oncealed amongst tall reeds on the far side of the pond, Bernie glowered at Christie. All ready for her big day and pretending to be something she wasn't.

He stretched out a hand and tapped each finger as he counted in his head.

*One.*

She wasn't the heir to Palmerston House because her ancestor cheated and stole.

*Two.*

Nor was she as loved amongst the locals as she believed. Nobody was as nice as she fooled people into believing. Most people.

*Three.*

Christie Ryan wasn't invincible. She might have survived her boat sinking, but it didn't make her some kind of saint.

*Four.*

If she thought her future marriage would work, she was mistaken. Her groom wasn't even here today.

He hesitated then tapped his thumb.

*Five.*

She wasn't safe.

Bernie opened a water bottle as quietly as possible and drank. He wasn't a violent man, a criminal. He simply needed to put things right. Harry died because of her. And her kin.

Christie stepped off the podium to stand at the edge of the pond. Bernie's heart almost stopped beating. Her eyes were directly on him. He froze. Not a muscle moved as she stared at him. Surely she saw him?

"Oh, there you are." Lottie appeared from between the trees, walking towards Christie.

The women talked for a moment before heading back toward Palmerston House. As they reached the shaded path, Lottie abruptly turned and shot a look across the pond. As if she could sense his presence.

They were connected, no doubt. Always were. Pity she took the side of the Ryan family.

Bernie crushed the bottle and tossed it into the reeds.

## 58

# CELEBRATION DINNER

"You do know I have a way of solving mysteries?" Christie grinned at Martin as they waited outside the pub. He'd finally arrived at Palmerston House in the middle of the afternoon looking pleased with himself and refusing to answer any questions. This was the first time they'd been alone since waking up this morning and Christie wasn't missing the opportunity.

Instead of answering, Martin pulled her into his arms and kissed her. She willingly returned the kiss, then drew slightly away. "I know what you're doing."

"Kissing my bride-to-be."

"Well, yes. But—"

"But nothing." He kissed her again. "All will be revealed when I'm ready." Another kiss. "Which is not now. So, behave."

"Aw... the lovebirds." Daphne giggled as she approached with her arm through John's. "At midnight you have to go separate ways."

"Or what?" Christie leaned against Martin, her hands tightly enclosed by his.

"Or your intrepid celebrant will delay the ceremony."

"I promise by midnight Christie will be in Palmerston House and

I," Martin winked at John "will be outside her window with a serenade."

"More like the sad wailing of a bunyip."

"Thomas!" Martha tugged at his arm as they approached from the opposite direction. "Martin has a lovely singing voice."

"If you say so, bride."

With a shake of her head, Martha reached out to kiss Christie. "Ignore him, Martin."

"Always have." Martin hugged Thomas. "Good thing he can paint."

"Actually, Thomas, been meaning to ask if you'd like some work." Trev stuck his head out of the pub door. "Need the station repainted."

"As long as you take care of those speeding fines."

Everyone turned to Thomas in shock. He burst out laughing. Trev stepped onto the pavement and held the door open. "Inside. The lot of you, before I have to arrest you all."

Lance greeted them as they filed into his upstairs function room, which was beautifully decorated with candles and flowers on a long, narrow table. The lights were dimmed and champagne chilled in ice buckets.

Sylvia – with Barry one side, and Belinda and Jess on the other – waved. George and Charlotte poured champagne into glasses at a smaller table near the window. Christie stopped just inside the doorway, overcome with happiness. Martin leaned down to kiss her cheek. "This is our time, sweetheart."

Yes, it was. Difficult times were behind them all. This weekend was a celebration for the town. A wedding. Lots of love and joy. An escape from the day-to-day and a hope for the future. In a couple of weeks, she'd open her new beauty salon and offer the people of River's End and surrounds a new approach to their health and wellbeing. They didn't know yet, but the first week was on her. Free for everyone to try.

"Earth to Christie. Come and sit down, okay?" Belinda held her hand out.

"Ha ha. Okay. Where?"

"Well, next to me, of course. Then, Martin can sit opposite and Martha beside you. Let the rest take care of themselves."

"What about Elizabeth? And Angus?" Christie glanced around.

"On their way. The phone rang as I left and Angus said they'd follow." Charlotte brought two glasses of champagne and handed one to Christie. "To you and Martin." She clinked her glass against Christie's and both of them took a sip. "How are you feeling?"

"Happy. Truly, deeply happy. Grateful for all the help and very thankful for the friends here tonight."

"Palmerston House already looks beautiful and by the time the guests arrive tomorrow it will be ready for a fairytale wedding."

"As long as there's no wicked witch involved."

"Or bad wolf roaming around the forest." Charlotte frowned.

Christie's stomach tensed. "Are you concerned about Bernie?"

Charlotte glanced around, her eyes resting on Trev, who chatted to George by the window. "Trev says not to be."

"What do you say?"

"He is obsessed with Palmerston House."

Trev smiled at Charlotte and she looked away.

*What is going on with you two?*

After the wedding Christie was determined to find out.

"Did he really believe he would get through the door with those tools? Dynamite would be a better choice."

"As the resident police officer, I'm going to have to ask you why you want to use dynamite, and where?" Trev appeared beside Charlotte with a beer and a big grin.

"We think you have too much time on your hands." Charlotte kept a straight face. "Small explosion at the back of the police station might give you something legitimate to take care of."

"In that case, I will require you to turn yourself in for questioning. After dinner."

Charlotte blushed and was suddenly very interested in her glass.

"We were talking about the door in the cellar at Palmerston House. Did you discover what's behind it?" Christie decided to give Charlotte time to compose herself.

"Isn't that your thing?"

"I've been busy. And I don't want to upset Elizabeth by asking too much until she feels a bit safer again."

Trev nodded, more serious now. "It isn't on the plans for the house. Hidden away for decades and no key to be found. Probably there's another small room behind it, perhaps for illegal grog or guns, but it certainly had Bernie Cooper interested."

"Any sightings of him?"

"Not a thing. Besides, how stupid would he be to show his face around here again? Ah, there's Elizabeth and Angus."

---

*A*s the evening wound down, it occurred to Trev this was amongst the best nights he'd experienced. To watch Christie and Martin together on this, their last day as single people, was a privilege. Such love he'd seen between his parents, and Thomas and Martha, but it was rare in a world of throw-away relationships.

Time and again he'd found himself gazing at Charlotte, who sat further down the table on the other side. What would she think of his musings? He knew she felt something for him, even though she kept him at arm's length. Her odd words at the beach this morning stuck in his head. "I have lucky genes. At least where body shape is concerned." Did she mean some other genes were unlucky? Prone to an illness? The thought made his stomach turn with worry.

Christie swapped seats and slid next to Trev. "Ask her out." It was a whisper but Trev's eyes shot to Charlotte. She was deep in a conversation with Daphne.

"I have."

"Then what's the issue?"

Trev moved closer to Christie. "She feels differently."

"Nope. Bet she doesn't."

"Christie."

"Okay. But don't be afraid to ask her again. Anyway, didn't she go with you to visit your mother that time?"

"She loves bookshops."

"Long drive to go shopping."

Trev leaned back and picked up the beer he'd nursed for most of the evening. "Might have been a mistake."

"Why? Didn't she get along with your mother?"

"Quite the opposite. They even chat on the phone sometimes. It's complicated and I'm not comfortable talking about this. She wouldn't like it."

"Sorry. You're right. I just want everyone as happy as I am. And you deserve to have love in your life, Trev." Christie dropped a kiss on his cheek and returned to her own seat.

He blinked, realising he was again staring at Charlotte and she was now regarding him. He quickly lifted his almost empty drink and smiled. She raised her own glass with a twitch of her lips, her eyes going to his beer. "Another?" Was that what she mouthed?

Charlotte stood and headed to the table near the window. A moment later, a beer and a glass of champagne in hand, she wandered toward Trev. By the time she reached him, he was on his feet.

"You look thirsty."

"I'm not overdoing it tonight. In case I have to arrest any loud party goers." Trev accepted the beer. "Thanks."

"I'll be sure to tell George to tone it down then." Her eyes sparkled. "You looked very serious talking to Christie."

*You were watching me?*

"You know Christie. She wants a world where her friends all enjoy life the way she does."

"Let me guess, then. She wants you to have a yacht."

"Not quite."

"A beauty salon? Trevor's Toning and Treatments."

Trev couldn't help himself. He burst into laughter. Charlotte joined in and for a moment, the connection was there, strong and deep.

*Anything is possible. You deserve love.*

He managed to control the chuckles. "And you'd be my first client?"

"Are you implying I need… improving?"

"You're already perfect, Charlie." The words came out before he filtered them, soft and sincere. Charlotte's smile dropped and her eyes suddenly glistened. Was she going to cry? Despite the sounds of laughter and talk around them, he could almost hear her breathe. Short, sharp intakes.

"But, I'm not perfect. And you shouldn't think… I shouldn't let you think…"

"I'm not thinking anything."

*No, it is all about feeling.*

"And you don't need improving."

"George is on his own. I might go… umm, I'm going to sit with him for a bit."

"Charlie—"

But she retreated with a sad smile and he was left with only the scent of her. He finished the beer in a few mouthfuls.

"Trevor, excuse me?" Lance appeared at his side. "I completely forgot I had this. Meant to hand it in ages ago and seeing nobody came looking, well, I forgot about it. You'd better have it."

"Sorry? What are you talking about?"

"This." Lance held out a leather bound book. "Somebody left it in a booth and there's no contact details in it. Being old, it might be of value."

"You have no idea who left it?" Trev took the book and flicked it open. Nothing to easily identify an owner. Just old. He slipped it into a jacket pocket.

"No. Sorry, it was a busy night. Shall I get you another drink?"

"Oh, maybe a sparkling water, thanks, Lance."

Lance hurried off and Trev glanced around to see where Charlotte was. She was next to George, listening to him, but her eyes were on Trev.

# 59

# THE KEY

The cottage was more of a challenge to get inside this time. The attic window had a new frame and lock so Bernie didn't even bother getting the ladder. He wasted ten minutes trying every door and window. Everything was locked, so he resorted to breaking the small window in the laundry. All he could hope was it wasn't discovered until after he'd got what he wanted from River's End.

Once he'd reached carefully through the broken window and unlocked the laundry door from the inside, he pushed it open. Before going any further, he found a dustpan and brush, then cleaned up the glass shards. He pulled the lacy curtain across the break. Might buy him some time. He took the glass to the bin around the back of the cottage and emptied the dustpan under some other rubbish.

Back inside the cottage, he began his search. Being an outcast for a few weeks had given him time to dig a lot deeper into recent events. Holed up in an empty house on the far side of town – up for sale and apparently on the market for years going by its neglected state – he'd spent a lot of time scouring the internet for anything from newspaper articles to social media mentions. A stroke of genius was becoming a Facebook friend of Daphne's, under a disguise of course.

In the archives of a local newspaper, he'd discovered an article about Thomas and Martha's wedding. Touted as the love story of the century, the reporter provided enough backstory to reassure Bernie he was on the right track. Christie was left a mysterious key and later found the trunk.

On his last visit to the cottage, the key wasn't with the trunk.

*Better to be sure.*

He went to the dining room but the trunk wasn't there. He found it in the front entry, tucked under the table near the door. With no key.

Although he'd looked there last visit, he headed for the kitchen. If it wasn't there, he'd go to the clifftop house in case she'd already moved in. There was enough light streaming through the window over the sink to see the key rack near the back door. It held a variety of keys but only one interested him.

An ornate skeleton key. Old and designed for the locks of the nineteenth century. Almost in disbelief, Bernie removed it from the hook and held it up. "I've got you. Harry, I found it!"

---

*B*ernie stood in the kitchen of Palmerston House. He'd once been welcome here. Given awful tea and very nice scones. Breakfasts he'd remember and some interesting conversations. All good times despite the circumstances.

Following Daphne on Facebook had paid dividends with her post about the celebration dinner tonight, even mentioning the guests. All he'd done was wait until the last person left, and now the place was his.

Backpack bulging with tools and water bottles, he sprinted down the steps and through the cellar.

Under torch light, the stone door mocked him. Bernie pulled the skeleton key from a pocket and with a shaking hand, managed to insert it. So far, so good. "Help me out, Harry."

The key turned with a loud click.

Bernie pushed the door – hard – and with a groan it swung open. Cold air rushed in from the darkness beyond. To celebrate, he opened a bottle of water and drank the whole thing with barely a pause.

Finished, he crushed the bottle, tossing it into a corner. "Guide me, Harry. I'm here to set things right." He had to duck to step through the doorway.

There was no keyhole on the other side of the door, so he pulled it almost closed and wedged a small rock to stop it locking him out. Bernie peered into the darkness beyond the torch beam. A long, slightly declining and narrow tunnel with a rough floor and damp sides.

Bernie could hear his own breath. Every footstep echoed. After a few moments he paused and glanced back. The door was only just visible and a lot higher than he expected. Trudging back up with a heavy load might challenge another man, but he had purpose.

The roof lowered and the tunnel veered to the left. Fissures in the walls suggested the tunnel was a natural formation Harry had refined. The diary mentioned it being done at the same time Palmerston House was constructed, but how he managed it without Eoin Ryan finding out was a mystery. Many more than one man must have done this and likely over a length of time. Was it possible the men he charged with the job of taking care of the grandfather clock were involved?

The tunnel was even steeper now, and small rocks skidded under Bernie's feet. His head brushed the roof. A lesser man would turn back, but Bernie was unstoppable.

*Harry would be proud* .

Understanding his diary, following the clues, overcoming every obstacle.

There was a new sound. Waves crashing against rocks. Heart pounding, legs shaking, Bernie stepped into the cave.

---

# 1 *853*

Legs dangling, Harry sat at the cave entrance, a glass in one hand and bottle of fine whiskey in the other. No reason to leave all the good drink here. He toasted the night sky and swallowed a shot, then refilled.

It must be only an hour or so before midnight. He was too tired to do more than drag himself back to Palmerston House. After some sleep, he'd bring the last load down, before Eoin Ryan evicted him. Sleep and food beckoned.

But for a few moments, he wanted to enjoy the peace of the night, here, alone. The ocean moved restlessly beneath an almost full moon. Waves smashed against the rocks. Sea mist wet his pants and boots.

Harry hurt all over. Physically, of course, with the sheer volume of carrying, dragging, and stowing goods. The tunnel was hard enough getting down, but then there was the long walk back. And his heart ached for Eleanor and his little girl. For the life they'd shared so happily until that fateful night.

He forced himself onto his feet, dropping the glass over the edge. It smashed on its way down and he shuddered. A person wouldn't want to fall. He took more care with the bottle, replacing its stopper and leaving it on top of a small, favourite side table. Good thing he did, for the key to the door beneath Palmerston House lay on the table and he needed to lock it behind himself.

The journey back to the house took a long time. Harry stopped frequently to rest, regretting drinking so much. Once this was all over, he'd give it up. He reached the stone door and closed it firmly, locking it.

There was only one thing left to take down and he'd do it when he woke. In his daughter's bedroom, he sat for a while on the bed as sorrow mingled with triumph. He might have lost a lot, but he'd stopped Eoin having the satisfaction of taking everything. One day soon, he'd be able to put these dolls back into his little girl's arms and see her smile. For now, they were piled in the trunk, waiting for the final trip to the cave.

Downstairs, the longcase clock chimed midnight. Harry closed the lid of the trunk and turned the key to lock it. Exhausted, he lay back on the bed and closed his eyes. Almost asleep, he imagined himself back with his family.

Until someone pounded on the front door and he sat bolt upright.

# 60

# WEDDING DAY...

*B*y mid-morning, Palmerston House was a hive of activity. Parked out the front was a florist van, its doors wide open as the florist, Christie, and Charlotte made trip after trip back and forth, arms filled with arrangements. Around the pond, Martin, John, Barry, and Trevor laid out staggered rows of white seats so all the guests would have a view of the ceremony, no matter where they sat. The arch waited for flowers as Daphne stood below it, practising.

Inside, Elizabeth, Sylvia, Belinda, and Angus worked on the food. Rows of platters covered the kitchen table and tiered plates lined one counter. The kitchen smelled divine with a curious mix of sweet and savoury. Delectable finger food and perfect pastries. Every time Elizabeth and Angus were close to one another, their eyes met with a smile. Belinda chatted non-stop.

In the foyer, trestle tables against one wall were piled with folded white linen to be laid out and decorated before the guests arrived. Ice buckets dotted all the main rooms, from the foyer to the living rooms and out on the verandah.

As Christie and Martin insisted Elizabeth be part of the wedding party, she'd allowed them to arrange for some of Lance's staff to run things. Once she was changed, she would hand the kitchen over and enjoy the evening from a guest's perspective. Before then, she had a lot to do.

"Would anyone mind if I do a final check on all the guest rooms?"

"Go and make sure everything is perfect, dear lady." Angus looked up from the oven, a mitt on either hand. "We'll have this done before you know it."

"That's if we don't eat all these preposterously fantastic creations."

"Child, if you eat one more—"

"Joking, Mum. Joking." Belinda giggled. "But wait until the reception and I will!"

"And you'll have deserved to." Elizabeth patted Belinda on the back. "As you all do. Such tireless workers, I cannot thank you enough."

Sylvia smiled over her pastries. "Our pleasure. Go and check on your rooms."

Elizabeth draped her apron on the back of a chair and hurried out of the kitchen. From her small desk near the sweeping staircase, she collected her clipboard with its list of soon-to-arrive guests and their allocated rooms. The front door was wide open and a giant armful of flowers, carried by Christie, juggled through.

"Oh, my! Wherever will you put all of these?" Elizabeth noticed one of the tables was already almost filled with flowers. "Shall I get someone else to help?"

Christie carefully place the flowers down and straightened, brushing hair from her eyes with a grin. "Is anyone not gainfully employed?"

"Perhaps Belinda might help. In fact, it may very well be good for Sylvia because she is… struggling, for want of a better word, with the endless talk."

"Send her out. Actually, I might get some water and some for Charlotte. I'll grab her if you really think it's okay? Thomas is doing the arch next."

"The more help you get the better. Watch the time, dear."

"I know. Once the clock strikes three I'll be upstairs. Promise."

Christie sprinted off in the direction of the kitchen and Elizabeth went upstairs.

Palmerston House was fully booked. Christie's best friends and past neighbours, Ray and Ashley, were expected soon and Elizabeth couldn't wait to meet them. They'd been there for Christie when she'd needed them in Melbourne and Elizabeth felt as though she already knew them herself, thanks to so many stories. There were also film producers and directors, names famous enough to make her heart flutter. On Martin's side, the principal from the youth camp he sometimes helped at, along with his wife, were on their way.

One of the front living rooms was already filling with wedding presents, off limits to Christie and Martin.

Elizabeth went into each guest room and checked her list. The very last was Christie's room. She'd stayed here last night and this was where she'd prepare for the wedding. At the very end of the hallway, it was actually two rooms, joined by a door. Perfect when couples stayed with children. The connecting door was a big, timber sliding one and was pulled back now. One side overlooked the front driveway, whilst the other provided pretty views through the trees to the glinting pond.

Hanging on a portable clothes rail was the wedding dress. So simple yet absolutely stunning. It was a replica of the one Christie's mother married in, at least as close as possible from the few photographs available. She'd opted for a circle of flowers on her head instead of a veil, and they matched her bouquet.

She fussed a bit with the curtains, until noticing a car turn into the driveway. Guests, no doubt. Elizabeth collected her clipboard and closed the door on her way downstairs.

By the time she reached the front door, Christie was racing to where the car had stopped. She threw her arms around a man with platinum, short cropped hair. A few second later, the driver climbed and she ran to him. Yes, it was all beginning. Tonight would be a wedding to remember.

*M*artin and Thomas wandered along the driveway of Palmerston House toward the gate, each carrying a bottle of water. "You didn't need to escort me off the property, Thomas."

"I'll finish helping Trev and Barry with the lighting in the trees. Give you a chance to have a nanna nap."

Martin spluttered out the water he'd just sipped, making Thomas laugh loudly. He stopped once Martin threatened to tip the rest of the bottle over his head, but his eyes were alight with amusement.

"Perhaps you should return to doing what you were doing, Thomas."

"I will, I will. But joking aside, maybe put your feet up for a bit, son. Sit out on the deck and let your mind wander for a while."

"Maybe. I have something to ask."

"Anything. Unless it entails an escape plan. Cold feet and all."

Martin stopped at the gates. "As you well know, I've waited my whole life for Christabel Ryan. There is no power on earth strong enough to stop me marrying her tonight."

Thomas nodded, his eyes suspiciously bright. "I'm proud of you, Martin. So very proud."

"Thomas... Granddad, for goodness sake." Martin hugged his grandfather, and for a moment they stood locked in embrace. A lifetime of shared grief, loss beyond comprehension, created a deep wellspring of emotion. Today though was about happiness.

"Right, then. Can't have my bride seeing me this way." Thomas let go and grabbed a handkerchief. "She relies on me to be tough as nails."

"Martha knows you're a big softie."

"Rubbish. Now, what were you going to ask?"

"Advise me. I've finished the painting and will give it to Christie. I'm stuck on timing though."

"It isn't your wedding gift to her though?"

"No, the counter and some paintings for the salon are."

"Then wait until after the honeymoon."

"What do you mean?"

"Better to sit down with her away from all the emotion and excitement of the wedding, in my opinion."

"Makes sense. But we're not going away, Thomas. Our plans are to stay around and help put Palmerston House back to normal."

"Well, change them. Christie doesn't know it yet, but she's driving the two of you to Melbourne tomorrow afternoon."

"What?"

Thomas grinned. "I'm going to be in so much trouble. Please tell Martha you forced this from me."

"Not a chance. Elaborate, please."

"Airport. Sydney for a few days. Plenty of time to visit some art galleries, do a show, soak up the harbour. You're welcome."

"But…"

"Don't thank me now. Anyway, you need to get Christie out on the harbour. Remind her how much she loves sailing now, before *Jasmine Sea* arrives back in Willow Bay. Yes?"

Martin reached out and again put his arms around Thomas. "I didn't expect this. Just having you both here is enough, but thank you."

"Enough of this." Thomas was impressed with himself as he stepped back. "Not a word until the official announcement. Now, go prepare yourself, son. I'll go check Angus is okay to keep an eye on my dog so I can go home and get ready."

"My dog." Martin walked away.

"We should let him decide."

"Then he'd choose to be Christie's dog, and she's about to become my wife. I win."

As he watched Martin go out of the gate, Thomas smiled to himself. "We all win, son."

## A DISTURBING FIND

*D*aphne strolled around the pond, reciting the wedding vows aloud. Confident of getting all the legal bits right, as she called them, there was a phrase or two of the beautiful vows written by Christie which she still got caught on. Mainly because of the emotion in her voice every time she read them out.

As the final touches were put on the arch, she'd decided to give the boys some space and surround herself with the relative peace of the opposite side of the stretch of water. But here the ducks quacked at her, following in growing numbers as she reached the far side. "I don't have any crumbs, so go and find something better to do." They took no notice.

*One more run-through.*

Then, she'd go home and rest for a short while before getting ready. A warm glow of excitement rushed through her. This was her very first act as a celebrant and what an occasion to choose! Two of her favourite people marrying, with her friends watching on. And John. Not to mention the famous people coming to share Christie's special day.

From over here, she could recite away without disturbing anyone.

Daphne planted her feet at the muddy edge, reeds tickling her legs. She closed her clipboard, took a deep breath, and began.

"Love weaves its gentle way of... no. Come on, Daph."

She was tired. Too many practice runs. Besides, she had notes and a podium so she wasn't going to make any mistakes, as long as she took her time. Perhaps the best course of action was a nice cup of coffee and one of the chocolate chip cookies she'd baked for John. In fact, he'd probably be home by now. After a full day helping here yesterday, he'd worked in the office this morning.

With a sigh, she turned and stood on something with a loud crunch. "Oh!" Daphne stepped back with a start, then giggled when she saw it was only an empty water bottle.

"My goodness, what are you doing out here?" With a grunt, she picked it up.

There was no lid, and as she made her way back to the path, something about this bothered her. From the look of it, the bottle was crushed long before she stood on it. But it was otherwise in new condition, its label undamaged and no sign of being out here for long.

Daphne mused over it, picking up speed once on the path. Crushed water bottles were hardly unusual. Most people did so before recycling them. But she'd never seen this cheap brand in Elizabeth's fridge. In fact, she'd only seen it on the shelf of the little supermarket in passing. And one other time.

"Trev! Barry!" Almost out of breath, Daphne called for them as soon as the arch was in sight.

"Daphne? Are you alright?" Trev jogged to meet her, Barry not far behind.

She stopped to draw in oxygen, holding the bottle out like an offering.

"Do you want to come and sit?"

"No... look what I just found."

Trev took the bottle and from his expression, Daphne knew he was thinking the same thing.

"I think Bernard Cooper was here!"

"Now?" Barry went to the edge of the pond and scanned the opposite side. "Did you see him?"

Daphne shook her head. "Stood on the bottle. But it's exactly like the one he threw on the pavement outside the bakery. I saw it after Jess picked it up. Remember?"

"I do."

"So should we go searching—"

"Hey, stop stressing." Trev squeezed Daphne's arm. "He really is long gone. No sign of him in the region and that includes using his credit card or his car being seen. I'd say he's back in Queensland."

"You're sure?"

"Sure as I can be. Look, you go home and relax for a bit. You have a big event to attend!"

"Well... if you think so."

"Tell you what, Barry and I will have a walk around. But Bernie's not about to gate-crash a wedding and risk getting himself arrested."

Trev was right. Daphne summoned a smile. "I might go and see if John is organised."

"Would you like me to walk you to your car?" Barry offered.

"How sweet, but no, I have to collect my bag and say goodbye. But I won't say anything to upset the others, don't you worry."

"We'll see you this evening?"

"Yes, Trev. And I look forward to seeing you both looking smart in your suits." Daphne giggled when they mock-groaned. "You'll both be so handsome." She turned away. "Yes, I can see myself officiating more weddings very soon."

The sounds behind her might have been the men choking. Or just her imagination.

---

*I*t was all Trev could do not to call the Dog Squad to thoroughly check the grounds of Palmerston House, but he and Barry couldn't find anything else to indicate Bernie was recently near the pond. Time was getting away from them and bringing police and dogs here was an overreaction.

"I can call up a few of my men who aren't coming to the wedding." Barry leaned against a tree. "See if they'll hang around tonight. At a discreet distance of course."

"Tempted to accept. But what do we tell everyone? No, we can't buy into Daphne's fear and intrude on what will be a perfectly safe and wonderful evening."

"Offer's there if you need them."

"Thanks, mate. We'd better head back."

"Yep. I want to give Thomas a hand with the last of the lights then we're done."

Back on the path, Trev's eyes roamed the surrounds of the pond. "I might get a couple of uniforms over from Green Bay to cover for me tonight, assuming some are available."

"You can have a few drinks, if nothing else."

"Won't have much. Need my wits about me."

"Why? In case one of the single ladies gets all emotional about the wedding and starts making plans for you?" Barry grinned widely.

"More in case I say something I shouldn't."

"Charlotte?"

Trev nodded.

"She'll come around. She likes you."

"As a friend."

"If you say so."

"Well, what about Sylvia?" Time to turn the tables.

Barry almost blushed. "Nothing to tell."

"Right. Noticed you're getting a little... wide around the middle. Wouldn't be from too many handmade pastries?"

"I'm trim and taut. But she does cook like nobody else."

"Better watch for the bouquet later on. If she catches it..."

"There's Thomas."

"I'll ask his opinion."

"About Bernie? I wouldn't."

"Nope. About you and Sylvia. Hey, Thomas—"

"Shouldn't you be doing some police stuff?"

They passed the arch and met up with Thomas, busy wrapping fairy lights around a tree. He viewed them with suspicion. "Where have you two been? Going to miss afternoon tea if we don't get this finished."

"Can't have that. Come on, I'll do the other side. Trev's got to go and make himself beautiful."

"Need more than a few hours."

"Thanks, Thomas. Thought we were friends," Trev said.

"And friends tell the truth to their friends. What were you doing over there?"

"Seeing what it all looked like from a distance. For photographs."

Thomas stopped what he was doing and stared at Trev. "For half an hour?"

"Those two will only get married once. Got to make things perfect. I do have to go so I'll see you both later on."

The further he got away from Barry and Thomas, the more Trev worried. He'd spend some time in the station, make a few phone calls. Bernie Cooper must be somewhere and it better be a long way from here.

## 62

# CALM. BEFORE A STORM.

"You've done a beautiful job, Belinda!" Christie stepped back from the mirror. "Absolutely flawless, sweetie."

"Really?" Belinda peered over Christie's shoulder. "I do rather like the eyes."

"You do rather like sparkles!"

"Oh, is it too much? I'll fix it—"

"Joking." Christie turned and cuddled Belinda. "I'm proud of you."

"You're not very funny."

"I know. But I am rather nervous."

"Now, how silly are you?" Belinda gently kissed Christie's cheek. "How can you of all people be nervous? In a short time you'll be walking along the path down there to meet one of the most handsome men in the region."

"Country."

"If not the universe. And in front of your closest friends and family you'll become Mrs Christabel Oliver Ryan Blake. Kind of a nice ring to it. Speaking of rings, I hope Thomas doesn't lose yours."

"Belinda!" Elizabeth stood inside the doorway, hands on hips. "Don't say such a thing!"

"Sorry. Sorry, Christie."

Christie laughed. "He isn't going to forget the ring. And with or without a ring, nothing will stop me marrying Martin." She squeezed Belinda's arm and then went to Elizabeth and dropped a kiss on her cheek. "Everything is perfect, okay?"

"You look so beautiful."

"All thanks to Belinda. And now it's your turn, so let her work her magic."

"Where are you off to?" Elizabeth asked as Christie slipped through the doorway.

"A cup of coffee and a sit on the verandah. Belinda, use the soft plum lipstick. Suits Elizabeth's lovely skin."

"Good thinking. Now, please join me here at the mirror and make yourself comfortable."

"Thank you, dear."

"What are your thoughts about glittery eyes for splendiferous occasions such as the one we are preparing for today?"

Christie almost turned back until she heard Elizabeth giggle.

*They'll be fine.*

Passing a mirror, she glanced at herself. Her hair was in a gorgeous, slick chignon. Small curls fell out around her face and would frame the flower garland she'd put on after the dress. For now she wore jeans and a loose buttoned shirt, her feet bare.

She almost skipped down the sweeping staircase, its mahogany balustrade colourful with flowers and fairy lights. In the foyer, the tables were set up ready for food and drinks, which would be brought out by Lance's staff during the ceremony. Everything was going according to plan. Even the arrival of Ray and Ash was perfect, except she longed to introduce them to everyone and show them every part of River's End.

The kitchen was empty for the first time today as Christie filled the kettle. The table almost groaned under the weight of all the prepared food and a peek inside the fridge left no doubt of the work done over the past two days.

*All for us.*

Coffee in hand, Christie wandered back through the foyer and outside. Although Palmerston House was now at capacity with guests, there were no cars in sight as Elizabeth had asked everyone to park around the side to keep the frontage clear.

"Come and sit with us." Angus called from the bench at the farthest end of the verandah. Beside him, Randall wagged his tail in greeting.

"What are you two doing out here?" She sank onto the bench.

"How lovely are you?" He leaned across and kissed her cheek. "Oh, I didn't just ruin your make-up?"

"Not at all, besides, everyone is kissing me. Belinda will do a touch up once I'm dressed."

"But first you wanted some time to yourself. We can leave you in peace."

"I'd rather you stay." Christie pulled her legs under her on the bench to sit cross-legged. "How are you holding up?"

"Me? Absolutely fine, my dear girl."

"You've done too much, you and Elizabeth, for Martin and me."

He chuckled. "A labour of love. Both of us, in fact, everyone involved, is so excited. You and Martin have given this little town something wonderful. And with your guests, a little bit of glamour."

"Will you go and have a rest for a bit?"

"I may do so, now Elizabeth is getting herself all pampered."

"When I left, Belinda was discussing glittery eyes."

"Oh, my."

"So, no matter what she says, don't let her trick you into a bit of make-up. She's full of mischief."

Randall stood and stretched. "Might be my cue to have a short lie-down. Eh, Randall? Care to join me upstairs?" Angus pushed himself to his feet and smiled at Christie. "You'll be alright alone for a bit?"

"Enjoy your rest and I'll see you in a couple of hours."

Soon she'd go upstairs and sort out Belinda's own hair and make-up. Martha would arrive and Belinda would no doubt fuss around her as well. Everything she'd longed for was happening. Her life with Martin was about to begin.

# 63

# TAKEN

*C*harlotte wandered into the kitchen as Christie put away her washed cup and saucer.

"Wow, you look stunning!"

"Belinda's done so well. Are you coming up to let her do your make-up?"

"Me? Oh, I don't want to intrude. And once I've had a shower it won't take me long to get ready."

"Not intruding. She needs practice for her course, and besides, I love having you around. There's still heaps of time, so please think about it."

"Ok, thank you. I'm going to get some water and then I'll shower."

"Cool. See you later." With a twirl, Christie danced her way out of the kitchen, leaving Charlotte with a smile on her face.

*You deserve such happiness.*

She filled a glass from the tap, not daring to open the fridge in case anything fell out. She'd seen how packed it was earlier and had no idea how Elizabeth made everything fit. With such delicious smells she regretted missing lunch.

Footsteps approached from the other side of the closed door to the cellar. The door handle began to turn and there was a muffled comment, something about "not enough hands".

"Hang on, I'm coming." Charlotte put her glass near the sink. She'd seen Angus bringing up wines today from a list Elizabeth kept adding to. She swung the door open. "There you go, shall I take something?"

He mustn't have heard her as he wasn't on the landing. She stepped through the doorway. "Need a hand?"

The door closed behind her and she reached to reopen it.

An arm whipped around her body.

"Shh, Lottie."

His hand covered her mouth as she struggled to free herself, but Bernie had her pinned against him. Charlotte kicked backwards, missing.

He laughed. "Not the movies. Now be a good girl and make things easy on yourself. Are you listening?"

The noise she made wasn't any sort of answer as fear turned to anger. She was going to have him arrested. Put away for years. How dare he—

"We're going to go down the steps and I can carry you. Or you can walk. Either way, we're going."

Charlotte made herself as heavy as she could, slumping against him. It didn't work. He picked her up with a grunt, releasing her mouth. "You make a noise and something bad will happen."

Bernie paused at the bottom of the steps, drawing in breath heavily. Then he went through the cellar and pushed another door open with his foot. They were in the storage room, where he'd hurt Angus. Nausea rose in Charlotte's stomach.

In an abrupt move, he put her down, gripping her shoulders. "Go through the doorway. Quickly."

At first she couldn't see what he meant, then her eyes adjusted to the low light. The stone door was open, a key inserted into its lock.

"Do it!"

"No, Bernie. Let me go."

"I'm not telling you again. Or would you prefer I tie you up here and go back upstairs – in time to attend the wedding?"

Dismay flooded into Charlotte. He wouldn't hurt her, of that she was certain. Whatever he was up to, she'd talk him through it. Nobody was going to ruin Christie's wedding. She ducked her head and stepped through. The temperature dropped.

"Where are we?"

Bernie followed and turned on a torch. "Tunnel." He flashed it around, the light picking up a pile of boxes lining a rock wall.

"See these? Mine. All left by Harry for his family."

"Where were they?"

"You'll see soon enough."

Bernie brushed past, flicking the torch onto a framed painting. "There's Harry."

Charlotte glanced at this side of the door. No keyhole. A small rock stopped it closing on itself. It was a one-way door.

"Are you sure?"

"Of course. Look at the likeness." Bernie reached for the painting.

"Is there a signature?"

"Yes. It was painted by... umm... let's see." He peered at the bottom corner.

In an instant, Charlotte was at the stone door. Bernie grabbed at her and she fell heavily on her stomach but free of his grasp. She scrambled forward, arms extended to push the door with all her might.

"No, you don't!"

He was almost upon Charlotte as she shoved the rock aside and forced the door shut with a thump. She slid down face forward.

"No!"

Bernie pulled the door. Then hit it. "What have you done?"

*Stopped you.*

He roughly turned her over, his face close to hers, breath rancid and anger radiating through the tunnel. "You're gonna regret that, doctor."

# 64

## WHEN DANGER COMES

*B*arry and Martin had finished the reception counter in Christie's salon. The base was mirrored steel beneath a whole piece of mountain ash, stained and highly polished. It retained most of its original shape including interesting imperfections.

"Truly unique." Barry had admired it once they wiped it down. "One of a kind. She'll love it."

"I'll bring her down in the morning. She has enough to worry about this afternoon without me dragging her away."

"According to Daphne, it was bad enough you seeing her this morning so probably best not to mess with tradition anymore."

"By seeing, you mean us being in different parts of the property and only having time for a quick kiss in passing?"

"Yup. She mumbled something about it being bad luck."

"As if anything will spoil today."

And nothing would. Back at his house, Martin rested both hands on the jasmine covered railing surrounding the deck. Less than a year ago, under a moonlit sky, he'd wanted to kiss Christie at this very spot. They weren't together then, not even as friends. He was protecting Thomas and she was determined to unravel the secrets her grandmother left in the cottage. Yet the attraction between them was so strong, he'd struggled to keep his hands to himself.

Soon, he'd stand near the arch and watch her approach with Angus. Their friends and family there to share this most special day.

Out at sea, yachts dotted the water, some under spinnaker and others simply idling along. *Jasmine Sea* was undergoing final safety checks before making her way home to them. Whether Christie would ever step aboard again was another matter, but they'd face any residual fears together.

Martin selected some long strands of jasmine, going down onto the other side of the railing to pick the ones he liked. If he could get them to Martha or Belinda once he arrived, he hoped Christie might wind some through her hair, or in her bouquet.

A sound drifted up from the cliff face. Seabirds no doubt, squabbling over some morsel on the path. But when it happened again, Martin stopped picking jasmine and listened. It surely wasn't a person calling?

There it was again, nothing clear but definitely a person's voice. A woman. Sometimes visitors to River's End started up the narrow, winding path to the top of the cliff, only to find themselves lost. Hopefully not today. He strode across to the cliff edge and looked down.

"Help!"

Martin dropped the jasmine and ran down the track to where it forked.

"Where are you?" Martin took the right fork.

"Get... help."

He forced his way through the bushes, stopping where the sides crumbled. A rope trailed over, tied to the base of one of the larger bushes. What on earth was anyone doing climbing? There were signs at the bottom not to go off the path.

"I'm coming. Hang on." He checked his pocket for his phone before remembering it was on the bed. "Are you hurt? I'll go and call for assistance. Stay as still as you can."

"Martin?" It was Charlotte

"Charlotte! Are you hurt?"

Martin reached for the rope. The knot was good, but there was nobody on it. He braced his legs and used the rope to let him see further over. "Charlotte?"

"Help—" Her scream was cut off and Martin found himself over the edge, his feet on the rocks and using the strength in his arms and shoulders to lower his body.

How she'd got herself down there, let alone why, was forced into the back of his mind. Within minutes, sweat poured down his back and arms, which ached under the tension. His breath was shallow, rushed.

*Idiot. Should have got help.*

He knew better than to climb like this with no protective gear and all alone.

He rested, feet finding a crevice to support him and give his muscles a brief respite. Not far below was the entrance to a cave. But no sign of Charlotte. And with a shock, he realised he was almost at the end of the rope. It wasn't long enough.

He pushed himself away from the wall, checking the terrain between his position and the cave. There were hand and footholds within reach. Going back up would take too long, so at the very end of the rope, he locked his fingers into a crack.

A yacht sailed past, not far out. Every ounce of his strength concentrated on moving one hand, then one foot, over and over, until he was close enough to drop onto a small ledge outside the cave.

Where was Charlotte? He looked down to an ocean crashing against jagged rocks.

*No. Surely not.*

Fear gripped him. Then a sound from inside the cave. A shuffle.

Martin stepped inside, trying to see into the murky depths. "Charlotte?"

This time he heard her, close by. Not words, but definitely Charlotte. He followed the sound, blinking to make his eyes focus in the darkness. Against a wall, she sat on the floor, feet tied together, arms behind her back, and a rag wrapped around her mouth.

Her eyes darted to her left, toward the back of the cave and she shook her head. Before Martin could reach her, Bernie stepped between them, an old revolver dangling from one hand. "Wouldn't go any closer, mate. In fact, why don't you take a seat right there. You look tired."

# 65

# PLAN C

*N*ow he had two of them to worry about.

It should have gone to plan. He'd worked through the night moving Harry's treasures through the stone door. Load by load, he'd crept through the kitchen and out to the old, unused residence behind the garage. His original idea of hauling everything up the cliff was stupid once he was in the cave and saw the rocks below. One slip and they'd crash down and be destroyed.

Once the reception was underway, all he needed to do was back up the SUV and fill it. Nobody would notice if he crossed a paddock and moved quickly.

Already safely stashed were several paintings, two small cases which annoyingly had no keys, five wooden crates filled with spirits of a vintage so old they must be worth thousands, and several firearms.

After sleeping until midday, he'd eaten a lunch of pastries stolen earlier from the kitchen, followed by a couple of bottles of his special water. He'd waited for the right moment for another run. Even in broad daylight, he knew he'd be safe if everyone was upstairs. So, he'd managed another wooden crate as far as the stone door, then heard

Christie come downstairs. Once she left the kitchen, he tried to move another, which was where he ran into problems.

*Lottie.*

Plan B was going to have to work.

Except here he was with Plan C.

"You're Bernie, aren't you? What's going on, mate?"

"I told you to sit down. Do it."

Martin made no sign of moving from his wide-legged stance and crossed arms. Sweat dripped down his face and he inhaled unevenly.

"You climbed down? Unbelievable. Sorry to make you do that on your wedding day."

*Not sorry.*

"Turned my back on her for one minute and there she was, waving at yachts and screaming like a banshee."

It was satisfying seeing Lottie shake with rage. So good she couldn't speak. Made a change for him to be heard. Him to be in control. From the corner of his eye he saw Martin move toward him. Bernie spun to face him and raised the gun. "Sit."

This time, Martin Blake did what he was told and sank to the floor on his knees.

*Nice touch.*

Almost begging to be spared. Thing was, the gun – as pretty as it was – might not even fire after all those years in a cave.

"Marty, all I want is to get the rest of my treasures and leave. Palmerston House might be lost to me, but Harry wanted me to have the contents of this cave."

"Harry?"

"Harry Temple. I'm his direct descendant. Your thieving wife-to-be thinks she'll get her hands on it, but I have something she wants now. I have you."

"I assume there's a tunnel back there, leading to the locked stone door."

"Except I have the key, thanks to the carelessness of the owners of the cottage."

"You broke in? What, for the second time, or more?"

"I'd watch my tone." Bernie took a few steps back to an empty crate, and lowered himself on it. "You're my prisoner, remember."

"And I have a wedding to attend, so let's get this sorted quickly. You need a hand removing the rest of this junk, and taking it somewhere to gloat over. I'll tell everyone to let you pass. Give you a head start before Trev arrives. Let's go."

"Junk!" Bernie yelled. Lottie jumped. "Did you hear what he said?"

She nodded, eyes on him. No point getting upset. There was a water bottle within reach and he picked it up with one hand, still training the gun on Martin. He managed to open it and took a swig.

"Thing is, Marty, our friend here thought it funny to close the stone door. No way to open it from this side."

Did Martin Blake actually smile? "You're stuck here."

"We all are."

"You didn't think this through very well."

"I know what you're trying to do. Make me angry enough to make a mistake. And maybe this gun is too old to work, or not loaded. Can you get to me before I get to her?"

Lottie was scared, she'd huddled up more and stared at the ground. Good. After everything she'd put him through.

*Good.*

"Maybe I should take the gag off and let you tell our guest what you did." He had her attention now. She shook her head. "Yep. I might enlighten him with a bit of back story."

"Cut it out, Cooper."

"Got herself in trouble. You know, I was her patient for a while. Thought I could trust her with anything. But so did the poor woman she reported for something she didn't do. Broke your doctor-patient confidence, didn't you, Lottie?" He smiled at her. Were those tears in her eyes?

"And there's more. You want to tell him? No. Okay. She had her own mother committed to a psychiatric hospital. Permanently."

Lottie struggled to stand, but the way he'd tied her feet made her fall back, tears streaming down her cheeks. He almost felt sorry for her. Almost.

"Enough! What is it you want from me?" Martin hadn't moved, but his anger took all the fun out of teasing Lottie.

"I want to get out of here, with the rest of my possessions. I suggest you climb back up and make it happen. Shouldn't be hard to unlock the door and make sure nobody stops me."

"You let Charlotte go and I'll show her how to climb up the cliff. The groom arriving early will raise suspicion, but not a resident. While she's gone, I'll help carry everything you've got left to the door."

*He thinks I'm stupid.*

Bernie extended his arm toward Lottie, pointing the gun at her, and cocked it. "I don't trust her. Don't trust you, either, but you've got a lot to lose today. I'd be climbing back up that cliff because my patience is almost gone, Mr Blake."

# 66

# THE MISSING

*T*rev tapped a pen against the keyboard as he waited for the computer to respond. For the past hour he'd sent queries about Bernard Cooper and his SUV to every agency he could access. Everything was coming back the same as his own department. No sightings of the man or vehicle since the purchase of vodka at the pub the day he'd hurt Angus.

It was impossible. No credit card use. No photographs from tollways. Queensland police had spoken to past connections, other photographers, magazines he'd worked for, even the staff at the cemetery where his mother was buried. Nobody recalled seeing him in months.

"Where are you?" He ground the words out.

"Sir?"

Trev turned his chair. "Sorry, constable. Forgot I had company."

Constable Jacqui Prentiss grinned as she carried two cups of coffee to the other desk. "Talk to yourself all you want, sir." She put one coffee in front of Constable Gareth Greetham and sipped the other.

"I will. I do. You are both going to be bored silly today. Most of the town will be at Palmerston House and just about everything else is good."

"Except for the elusive Bernard Cooper. Are you sure I can't make you a coffee, sir?"

"Thanks, no. I'm going to get ready soon. And yep, he's bothering me no end. Would love to have a long chat with him again."

"Do you want us to keep an eye on Palmerston House tonight?"

"Can't see the need. Have a bit of a drive around town if you will. Make sure nobody is lost."

"Sir? Who'd get lost around here?" Jacqui asked but got no answer, so turned back to her partner.

*Who indeed?*

Trev would never forget the first time he saw Charlotte, lost in the back roads of the town. And now she might be lost to him, if she moved away. Well, tonight he'd ask her to dance and try for one last time to break through the wall she kept up between them. What better place than a wedding?

"Right, I'm off to get ready. Help yourself to whatever is in the fridge."

"Any chance of excitement like last time, sir? Quite enjoyed arresting Derek Hobbs that night."

"Constable Greetham, if you see Derek Hobbs then please arrest him again. Otherwise, I expect a peaceful evening."

Why the nagging feeling in his gut? As he prepared for the wedding, he worried. The empty water bottle near the pond might have been there since Bernie's time as a guest.

He reached for his tuxedo but accidentally pulled out the suit he'd worn last night. And stood there, staring at it.

*Get your act together, Sibbritt.*

All this talk of bad guys and weddings was messing with his brain. In the inside pocket was the book Lance gave him. He removed it, returned the suit, and took the tuxedo out to lay on the bed.

Lance had said this book was left behind by a customer. It was a diary, with the year 1853 engraved into its brown leather cover. He deciphered the flowery dedication. This once belonged to Harry Temple, if he was reading it right.

*Bernie's infamous diary.*

Interesting he hadn't come looking for it. He'd drop it on the constables' desk on his way out, get them to do some digging.

---

"*D*ear, have you seen Charlotte?" Elizabeth popped her head around the doorway of Christie's room. Belinda was in there alone, dressed in an ankle length, sea green dress and doing small twirls before the mirror.

"Now you mention it, not for ages. Christie invited her up here for hair and face, but maybe she changed her mind."

"I wonder where she's got to. Probably found a quiet spot to read and time has got away from her."

"Do you need help with something? I'm going to be dressing the beautiful bride once she emerges from the bathroom, and her matron of honour arrives, but can give you a hand first."

"Oh, no need. It is more a case of me keeping track of everyone. I'll send Martha up once they're here."

"We'll be waiting. The glorious dress, the spectacular bride, and fabulous me."

Elizabeth chuckled to herself as she made her way to the top of the staircase. Belinda had a way of making everything sound more interesting and exciting than it was. Although today there really were no words to properly describe the joy and anticipation surrounding Palmerston House.

The front door was wide open to welcome the guests. Once Angus was ready, he'd join her in the foyer to greet each one and ensure they had a drink before the ceremony. In the kitchen, Lance and two of his staff were fussing around, ready to have the tables filled by the time the ceremony ended.

Martha came in, followed by Thomas. They stopped and stared around, then smiled at each other. "Not so long ago this was our reception, my bride." Thomas kissed Martha as Elizabeth rushed over.

"You both look wonderful!" She hugged each in turn. "Your dress is perfect."

As with Belinda's, Martha's sea green dress swirled around her ankles from a narrow waist.

"She's like a model, isn't she?" Thomas was openly admiring and Martha shook her head with a blush. "Now, where's my dog?"

"Martin's dog is with Angus so they'll be down shortly. Martha, dear, go upstairs. Belinda will need your steadying hand or she'll cover Christie's dress in glitter, or butterflies."

"And I'll stay here and keep an eye out for the groom. Shouldn't he be here?" Thomas glanced around.

"Soon, I'm sure." Martha lifted her skirt as she headed for the staircase. "I'll see you at the ceremony."

"Give Christie my love."

"Would you care for a glass of something? Champagne perhaps?" Elizabeth reached for a bottle on ice near the door. "I might have one myself!"

"Let me." Thomas poured two glasses and handed one to Elizabeth. "To Palmerston House, its rich heritage, perfect location for weddings, and gracious owner."

She smiled. "What a sweet toast, thank you."

They sipped champagne in the quiet of the foyer. Outside, the sky was darkening and lights flickered on along the driveway. A car turned into the driveway, and then another.

"And so it begins." Elizabeth put her glass down on a windowsill. "Would you like to help me meet and greet until Angus comes down?"

"Honoured to. Then I'll give the boy a ring if he's not here. Can't have the groom late for his own wedding."

# 67

# NOW... FOR THE GROOM.

Several unanswered phone calls later, Thomas went looking for Trev, Randall at his heels.

Trev was on the phone in seconds. "Goes to voicemail."

"Told you. Now, will you come and help find him?"

"Calm down, Thomas. Most likely he's left the phone at home and is taking his time walking down. Big thing, getting married."

"He's late. He's never late."

"Okay, I'll send the constables up to give him an escort." Trev dialled.

Martha joined them. "Do you think we should look for him?"

"Where's the groom? I need to make sure he looks good enough to marry Christie." Belinda breezed past, then stepped back. "Why do you all look upset?"

Trev hung up. "They'll call back in a couple of minutes. Everyone calm down."

"Is Martin not here?" Belinda glanced up at Palmerston House. "Christie's watching us."

"Act natural," Thomas said. "Why haven't they phoned yet?"

Martha grasped Thomas' hand. "He's not going to miss his own wedding, dear. There'll be an explanation."

"Besides," Belinda added, "there is no real start time of the ceremony. It isn't even dark yet."

Randall whined. Thomas drew in a long breath, and scratched
behind the dog's ears. Belinda disappeared to find Elizabeth and
Angus and brought them over, filling them in on the way.

"Should we go and speak with Christie?" Angus asked, noticing she
was at the window.

"Let's not worry her at this point." Trev's phone rang and everyone
stared at him as he answered. He walked a few feet away, giving
instructions. When he hung up and returned, his expression was
stony. "We might need to tell her now."

*I*t took Christie less than three minutes to get out of her
wedding dress with the help of Belinda and Elizabeth, and
into jeans. By the time she reached the bottom of the staircase, Trev,
Angus, Thomas, and Martha were waiting.

"It's Bernie Cooper," Christie burst out before anyone else spoke.
"Trev, you need to find Bernie."

"But, dear, why and how would Bernie be able to stop Martin
coming to his own wedding?" Martha took Christie's hand. "Martin is
strong, and wouldn't just go with the man."

"There's something else." Everyone turned to look at George, who
walked in stiffly, his walking stick taking much of his weight. "Our
Charlotte hasn't been seen in a couple of hours."

"Charlie?" Trev paled. "She's not here?"

"I saw her mid-afternoon. She was going to get some water then
shower, and I expected to see her for make-up," Christie said. "We
need to find Martin. And Charlotte. Trev, what do we do?" Christie
grabbed Trev's arm. "I'm going to the house."

"Not alone. In fact, I'd prefer everyone stay here. My constables
are on their way... and they're bringing something. I don't know if it
will help."

Christie's legs wouldn't hold her as coldness gripped her stomach. She sat on the steps. Belinda dropped next to her and rubbed her shoulders. She was barely aware of Trev calling for assistance from Green Bay, a few muffled words drifting back. Missing. Presumed dangerous. Emergency.

She knew Belinda was there, but couldn't feel her hands.

George spoke. She didn't hear him, only saw his mouth move.

Angus reached out a hand. Her own hand floated to his of its own will.

Her eyes roamed until stopping on Martha. Her arms were tightly around Thomas, whose face was white.

"Thomas." Christie forced herself to her feet. "Listen." He struggled to focus. "We're going to find Martin and he's okay. You know in your heart he is."

"Sir?" Jacqui appeared through the open front door, Gareth not far behind. "Is this it?" She held out the diary.

"Yes. Listen, we have two missing people now. Charlotte Dean hasn't been seen for approximately the same time as Martin Blake." Trev took the diary from her hand and offered it to Christie. "It's Henry Temple's."

"Umm, sir, if they are both missing, perhaps…"

"Constable. Start a search immediately." He guided them away from the group.

"They didn't run away together," Belinda announced. "Silly police person. She obviously has never seen you two together because there is no greater love."

"It's okay. Police stuff. That's all." Christie sat again and flicked through the diary, forcing tears down. Somewhere, Martin was dealing with Bernie. Probably Charlotte was there as well. But where? "Was I definitely the last person to see Charlotte?"

"I think so, dear. Shall we ask around?" Elizabeth, hands gripping each other, stood apart from Angus. He stepped closer and she moved away. Christie frowned. What on earth was going on there?

"I'll run and ask everyone. Even the people who don't know her." Belinda was off without a backwards glance.

Martha lowered herself beside Christie on the step. "I'm good with puzzles, child."

"Thomas needs you."

"Thomas is going to find Randall," Thomas said. "And we will make ourselves useful. Somehow. So solve the puzzle and tell me where to go looking for my boy." He turned and walked off to the back of the house.

"Okay, Auntie. We need to find them. I'm only getting married once, and the groom had better be here before the night is through."

# 68

# A STAND-OFF

"*I*'m not going anywhere." Martin stretched his legs out and leaned against the wall of the cave to prove his point.

Bernie stalked to the front of the cave and stared out, gun dangling again. It was an old revolver, probably made in the 1840s or 50s. Martin knew a bit about these from George, and didn't believe it would fire, even if Bernie had managed to load it.

"Charlotte is ill, Bernie." He caught Charlotte's eyes, willing her to follow his lead. "The gag is interfering with her breathing. She has asthma. Come on, mate, take it off, and for that matter, untie her."

"You think I'm stupid."

"Hardly. In fact, I'm impressed you've persisted under such opposition."

Bernie turned around.

"I don't know how you know you're Harry's descendant. Nevertheless, you've had a goal and stuck to it. Most people would give up."

"Not me."

"Not you. Let me untie her and we can plan how to get out of this. Okay?"

"Lottie likes to analyse me."

"Don't think it's on her radar right now. She needs to breathe."

"Fine. Untie her. But one word of wisdom and I swear I'll push her over—"

"Yeah, yeah, we get the point. Thanks, mate." Martin was at Charlotte's side before Bernie could change his mind. He worked on the knots. "You're a good man. Just in a situation out of your control."

"My mother used to say something like that." Bernie lost interest and returned to gazing at the horizon.

As Martin untied Charlotte, he whispered, "Just agree with him."

She nodded. He pulled the gag off and helped her up.

"No way out through there?" Martin gestured toward the tunnel.

"Locked from the other side. You should go."

"Not without you."

"Instead of plotting against me, I'd suggest you work on a way to get me and my treasures safely out of here."

"Not a lot of options." Martin placed himself in front of Charlotte. Her eyes were afraid and he'd felt how shaky she was on her feet. "We can go up or down. Unless you have some dynamite in one of those boxes for the stone door?"

"I looked before. Harry obviously didn't see a need at the time."

"It was a joke. But is there rope? Any tools?"

Bernie glared at Martin. "There's nothing funny about this. If she hadn't shut the door I'd be on my way and you'd be at your wedding. And if your thieving fiancée had done the right thing, I'd be hosting the wedding with Palmerston House rightfully restored to me."

It took every ounce of self-control for Martin to stop himself responding how he wanted to. Once Charlotte was safe he'd make sure he had a nice talk with him. One on one.

"Is there rope? Tools? Anything useful?"

"I told you to climb back up and open the door from the other side. That's the way out and its time you did it."

"Not unless Charlotte comes with me."

"This is loaded. Mate." Bernie raised the gun. "I'm done with you stalling. Make the right choice."

# 69

# THE DIARY

"I hope this will help us, Auntie." Christie frowned at a page in the diary. "Henry Temple admitted to losing Palmerston House to Eoin Ryan in a poker game. His wife left him. He hid some of his favourite belongings in a secret room – presumably on the other side of the door we can't get through. Eoin claimed the house earlier than expected and Henry left with little more than his clothes."

"And came back a few times, breaking in, from what you read out earlier." Martha stretched one leg, then the other.

They still sat on the stairs, poring over the diary. Belinda had reported back that nobody had seen Charlotte since Christie did. This sent Trev into a huddle with his constables and they quickly left. Angus and Elizabeth were outside, quietly relaying the need to delay the ceremony to Daphne without causing the guests to worry.

"The final time he was caught near the pond. He'd come back for a key." Christie turned the pages. "Which explains why Bernie spent half a night in the pond. It has to be the key to the stone door."

"Can we simply get a locksmith?"

"George said probably not. He was going to take a look but I'm not sure how he'll go with the steps."

"What does it have to do with Martin and Charlotte though? Surely, if they were in the room, we'd hear them?" Martha said.

"This is interesting. There was a longcase clock belonging to Palmerston House. That's a grandfather clock? Harry Temple gave it away! Yes, here... oh, he charged two brothers with the care of the clock, for it to remain in their family for all time. I wonder where it is now."

"In my shop."

Martha and Christie looked up in surprise as George hobbled across the foyer. "It was given to my predecessors and right or wrong, they protected it for all these years."

"The clock that was in the cottage?" Martha asked.

"Yes. My father and Tom's kept it there for a while, and then it came to the shop. Bernie Cooper recognised it and tried to make me admit my part in the deception. He believed it was rightfully his as well as Palmerston House." He leaned on his cane, his face lined with regret. "Only a few days ago, I made the decision to return it to where it belongs. Right here, and against this wall." He pointed to its original position. "Elizabeth doesn't know yet."

"George, is this why you were having problems with Bernie? Did he threaten you?"

"He made certain statements, Christie. I did wonder if he'd break in at some point, so Trev and I made up a story about getting new security cameras."

"When were you last at the shop?"

"Yesterday. You don't think—"

Christie leapt to her feet, handing the diary to Martha. "Keep reading, in case I'm wrong."

"Dear, you're not going looking for them there?"

"I have to look somewhere, and it makes sense if the clock was important to Bernie. Maybe he wants them to help steal it." She ran up the stairs. "I'll just grab my bag."

"I'll get my car, Christie." George patted Martha's shoulder. "I doubt they'll be there, but it gives her something to hope for. Perhaps you can update Trev?"

"Yes. Yes, of course. Please take care and phone as soon as you know anything."

As George went through the front doorway, Belinda burst from the hallway. "Is there any news?"

Christie sprinted down the stairs and past Belinda. "Not yet."

"Wait. Where are you going? You're the bride, you can't leave."

"Martha will explain."

"And she's gone. Just like that." Belinda joined Martha and threw herself onto the step at her side. "Should I be following her?"

Martha shook her head. "George is with her. They're going to look in his shop, but I don't think they'll find anyone."

"Fill me in on the clues and I'll become a super detective with you."

# 70

# MARTIN'S HOUSE

*T*rev managed to keep a tight control on his emotions, right up to the time he stepped into Martin's bedroom.

The tuxedo was laid out, ready to be worn. A crisp white shirt hung off the corner of a cupboard. Beside the tux was Martin's phone, which suddenly rang, showing Christie's smiling face.

He reached out to answer, then stopped himself. She'd believe, for an instant, it was Martin answering. He couldn't do that to her. She looked so happy in the photo on the phone, a different Christie from the one he'd left at Palmerston House, lost and confused by all of this.

And Charlie.

*Where are you?*

Was her disappearance connected to Martin's, or coincidental? His hands curled into fists as he gulped down unwanted fear, planting his feet further apart to keep himself steady.

"Sir?"

With a deep breath, Trev forced himself into action. "Find anything, Gareth?" He'd searched the house whilst the constables checked the shed and studio.

"Nothing out of the ordinary. Can't get into the studio but it is virtually all windows. Nowhere to hide in there and no sign of anything other than paintings on easels."

"Shed appears undisturbed," Jacqui said. "Surfboards on stands, an old motorcycle, everything neat."

"So his bike's there. Let's fan out and check the property. I'll take the cliff boundary."

Trev started at the gate. On the other side were two patrol cars, the constables' and his. He'd gone to the station to collect it, along with his kit, although he still wore everything for the wedding except the jacket. With his belt on and a radio, he was in a better position to do his job. Whatever that meant today.

From there he moved to the far corner of the property, where fence gave way to cliff. Recently, Martin mentioned to him he'd be building secure boundary fencing once they were ready to start a family.

"Where are you?"

He worked his way to where the path to the beach began. An early evening breeze rustled through the grass, lifting a clump of jasmine off the ground. Trev scooped it up. Fresh, long strands.

"Martin! Can you hear me?"

Nothing.

Trev cupped his hands on either side of his mouth. "Martin!"

"Sir. Have you found him?" Jacqui and Gareth ran from different directions.

"Look."

"Flowers?"

"Yes, Constable, flowers. Jasmine, freshly picked. And left in a pile here. As if he had picked them and dropped them." Trev started down the track, the constables on his heels. At the fork, he gestured for them to go to the left and he followed the right.

It was a dead end of bushes and cliff. But under a bush was a bottle. He pulled it out. Crumpled, empty. The same brand Bernie drank.

Trev pushed his way through the bushes, careful not to go straight over the edge. More bottles. And a rope tied to a large bush hung over the cliff face. He dropped to his stomach and looked down for a moment, then got up again and tapped his radio.

# 71

# WHERE ARE YOU, MY LOVE?

*T*he jewellery shop was a waste of time. Christie and George checked every corner and the rooms out the back with growing dismay. They met back at the grandfather clock.

"I'm sorry, Christie. I've led you on a wild goose chase."

"I jumped to the wrong conclusion. You've nothing to be sorry about."

"About this I do." He nodded at the clock. "If I'd spoken up about Bernie's questions, we might have worked out earlier he is a troubled man."

Christie's phone rang and she grabbed it out of her bag, then her shoulders slumped. "Thomas. Any news?"

"Not about Martin, but I'm at the cottage. Thought I'd try here, in case."

"I'm at the jewellery shop for the same reason."

"Someone broke in."

"What?"

"Through the laundry window. Nothing is missing, but it was Bernie. I know it. Randall went nuts as soon as we walked in."

"Are you okay? Have you called Trev?"

"Next job. Do you think he's looking for something? What about your salon?"

"I'll go check. Then I'll come up to you."

Once she disconnected the call, she filled George in and asked him to go back to Palmerston House. As she sprinted across the road in the near dark, it crossed her mind she was going against everything Martin always told her about personal safety. But, without him, nothing would ever matter again.

She unlocked the door. Empty. To be certain, she ran to the to the back, but it was secure. On her way out, she saw the counter. With a trembling hand, she touched the smooth timber top. Martin's artistry was unmistakable. And now she knew where he'd been all those hours yesterday.

"Where are you, my love?" Even as she whispered the words, tears flooded her eyes and she could no longer deny the fear in her heart. She sank to the floor and wept.

The phone might have rung for a while before she heard it through the sobs and when she answered, it was to Martha. "Christie? Are you there, child?"

"… yes."

"Have you heard something?" There was sudden alarm in Martha's voice.

"No. No, Auntie. Just… sad."

"Alright then. Belinda and I found something in this diary. About the key."

"Which is lost."

"Perhaps not."

"Auntie?"

"I'm a very clever detective." Belinda's voice chimed in from a distance.

"Yes, she is," Martha continued. "Henry Temple wrote about the night he was evicted. He desperately wanted to go to his daughter's bedroom."

"Whatever for?"

"Dear, her bedroom, from the description, is the one Dorothy had as a child. She loved her old dolls, handed down over the years and kept in—"

"The trunk." Christie jumped to her feet. "Oh, how did I miss it? The key is the one to the trunk. I have to go. Phone Trev."

Fingers trembling, Christie somehow dialled Thomas.

"No news, but can you look at the keys next to the back door please?"

"What am I looking for?"

"The trunk key."

"Other end of the cottage. Come on, Randall, this way. Why am I looking for it?"

"Theory. And then you need to go to Palmerston House with it."

"I was about to go anyway. Problem. Key isn't here."

"You're sure?" There was hope in Christie's voice. She let herself out of the salon.

"Eyes aren't that bad yet. Is that what he broke in for?"

"Yup. And I think I know where Martin and Charlotte are. Hurry. But drive carefully."

# 72

# KEEPER OF SECRETS

"*W*here's Trev?" Christie burst through the doorway into the foyer, startling Martha, Angus, and Elizabeth, who huddled around the diary.

"We don't know, exactly." Angus said. "Don't look at me like that, he's not missing but the calls are going to his message bank."

"Well, would someone try again please? Tell him he needs to get over here." Christie hurried through the foyer.

"Where are you going?"

"Downstairs, Auntie. Come on, we've got to see if the door is open."

"No! Christie, you can't. Angus, don't." With a tremor in her voice, Elizabeth continued. "I'll go. This is my house and it is up to me to face whatever danger there is—"

"Elizabeth, dear lady, stop." Angus took her hands in his. "Look at me."

She pulled her hands away, and refused to meet his eyes. "Nobody else is going to be hurt because of me."

"It is not your fault Bernie pushed me over. This is why you've gone all quiet and distant, isn't it? Elizabeth?" Angus gathered Elizabeth into his arms.

She shook her head, her body language defensive.

Christie turned around. "Oh, Elizabeth, you are not responsible in any way, shape or form for the terrible behaviour of Bernie Cooper! Did you blame me for what Derek did to this town?"

There was no response, but Angus smiled at Christie as Elizabeth relaxed against him, and he mouthed 'thank you'.

"People, I have a wedding to attend. I'd really like to find my husband-to-be, so...?"

"Sorry, Christie." Elizabeth's words were muffled against Angus' chest. Her arms wrapped around him for a moment.

Martha got off the phone as Christie passed her. "I've left a long message. He must be out of range. Do you know where Thomas is?"

Christie glanced over her shoulder. "He'll be here soon. Why don't you stay here and bring him down."

"Forget that. I'm coming to find Martin and Charlotte!"

As she rushed through the house, Christie found herself trailed by Belinda, John, Daphne and Sylvia, as well as Martha, Angus, and Elizabeth. Sylvia said something about Barry going to the beach but it didn't make sense to Christie and she kept going.

After grabbing a torch from the kitchen, Christie tore down the steps into the cellar, then into the storage room. At first sight, all hope drained away, for the stone door was still firmly shut. Tears rushed into her eyes and she impatiently brushed them away.

"Oh... it's still closed." Belinda put her arm around Christie's shoulder. "It's okay, we'll find another way."

"I believe I'm the oldest person here and apparently the only one with good vision! For goodness sake, Christie, turn the key!" Martha reached the door as Christie did.

In the lock was the key from the trunk. First, the keeper of Ryan family secrets, and now, of Palmerston House.

# 73

# DEADLY DESCENT

"One of you, give Palmerston House a ring. Tell them to stay put but we might have some news soon. There's a heap of messages on my phone so let's update them a bit." Trev fitted himself into a climbing harness.

Barry was out in his dinghy with one of his men. They'd take a look around the cliff face from a distance and report back to Trev. From here, their search light was visible as they rounded the farthest point of the cliff, so they'd only be a few minutes with the outboard motor driving them through the swell.

"All set, sir?" Jacqui checked the buckles on the harness. "The line's secured and good to go."

"Great." Trev shoved a helmet on. "Is Gareth ringing Elizabeth?"

"Yes. He'll be back down in a sec... couldn't get a signal here."

Trev checked his firearm. It was all business now. "As soon as he's back, you go to the top and field calls and direct any backup. Whatever happens, don't allow any of the wedding party down here."

"I won't. Sir, I can't imagine how distressing this is for the bride."

"We'll get her groom back. And Charlie."

Gareth burst through the bushes, panting. "Done. But Elizabeth said Christie found a key. Something about the stone door."

"Jacqui, liaise with the patrol car on its way from Green Bay. Tell them to get a move on and to investigate this key Christie has. Right, off you go, and Gareth, throw the gloves on and grab the rope."

As the constables followed his orders, Trev backed to the edge of the cliff, feeling the rope tighten to support his weight. His radio crackled and he hit the button. "Barry?"

"Yeah, Trev we can see the mouth of the cave and there's some movement there. Don't want to spook anyone so will go past at a distance."

"So there's people there?"

"Two. Or, three maybe. Too far really. There's a lamp or something in there but nothing is clear."

"Thanks. I'm going down now. Nice and slowly."

CRACK!

The sound cut through the air, echoing across the water.

"Sir... that was—"

The worst sound. Dreaded by police everywhere. "Hold tight, constable. It was a gunshot." Trev pushed off from the edge.

# 74

# TUNNEL TO THE SEA

*T*he stone door opened. Christie held up her torch. Behind her, Belinda, Martha, and now Thomas, peered into the gloom.

"It's a tunnel!" Christie stepped through the doorway and Thomas joined her. "Look at the those paintings, and boxes. And bottles."

"Christie?" Elizabeth looked through the doorway. "Oh my. A tunnel."

"It is. But you need to go back. We'll follow it as far as we can. Okay, Thomas?"

"Wait, dear. The nice constable called to say Trev is making his way to the cave down the cliff."

Christie spun around. "Near Martin's house? But it's so dangerous."

"I'm sure he knows what he's doing. But anyway, he wanted you to know there might be some news soon. And to stay upstairs."

"I can't. All of these things," she flashed the light on the boxes, "they are so old. Look at that painting. Isn't it Henry Temple? They didn't just get here on their own."

"You're right. There's drag marks as far as I can see. Someone's been moving them recently." Thomas had his own torch. "Can you smell the sea?"

Now he mentioned it, Christie recognised saltiness layered beneath the dank smell of stale air and dirt. "Do you think this goes to the cave?"

"One way to find out." Thomas ducked back through the doorway and spoke to Martha. She kissed him and then he returned. "Shall we retrieve the errant groom?"

"Shall I come with you?" Belinda popped her head through the doorway. "I can be the trailblazer."

"Thanks, but I need you here. Please look after everyone and tell Daphne to stay close by because she'll be busy soon."

"Be careful. You're going to be my cousin-in-law, so I need you back safely. And the others."

Christie blew a kiss to Belinda, then took Thomas' hand. "Ready?"

He grasped her hand and nodded. She glanced at his set face, worried about the strain around his eyes. "We'll find them."

For a while, they walked beside each other. Their footsteps were the only sound, until they turned a sharp corner. Then there was the ocean. Waves pounding in the distance. They stopped and exchanged a glance.

"How could nobody know this existed?" Christie asked.

"There were rumours. When I was a kid, George and I and some of the others would climb a bit. Which is why I sent Martin off as a kid to learn to do it properly because he is as bad as I was. Curious. Always pushing boundaries. Anyway, George and I almost got to the cave once but the cliff was crumbly and the waves scared us. Rocks below, sticking up out of the water. We scrambled up and never tried again."

"But Martin knows how to climb."

"Like a mountain goat. He's strong and quick and can see the safe spots. Why?"

"Charlotte was in the kitchen when I last saw her. What if Bernie thought the kitchen was empty?"

"And found her there? Took her down this tunnel to the cave?"

They reached another bend and stopped. Thomas was breathing heavily. The tunnel was steep here and staying upright a constant struggle.

"Rest. I'll go ahead."

"Give me a second." He forced his air intake to slow.

"Maybe Charlotte called out and Martin heard her."

"From the house?"

"I'm being silly. I just want…"

Thomas patted her arm. "Me too. Let's go."

Christie led the way as the tunnel not only narrowed, but lowered. The waves were louder and there was a little more light. Yet the sun must have set, so where was the light coming from? Her feet slipped and Thomas steadied her.

"Don't do it!"

Martin's voice stopped them in their tracks, his voice echoing through the tunnel.

BOOM!

A scream. Charlotte.

Then silence.

Christie ran blindly, falling and scrambling to her feet more than once. She'd dropped her torch the moment the shot rang out. Thomas was somewhere behind. Light from his torch flashed on the sides, the roof, the ground. He might have called her name, but she couldn't stop.

*Martin.*

Silence ahead. Perhaps the waves had stopped to mourn.

"Martin!" It was a sob, a desperate, heartbreaking cry she could no longer contain.

She slid into the side of the tunnel, her feet losing traction and pain screaming through her as her thigh scraped along the rock. On her hands and knees, she lost her sense of direction.

Light surrounded Christie. Thomas was there, his hand outstretched, eyes frantic.

Somehow she was on her feet.

Thomas was ahead now and she held the back of his shirt, tears coursing down her face, hair loose and sticking to her skin.

By the narrow light of his torch, they went around yet another corner.

The sea was ahead. An open cave. A sky not quite dark, pink and gold ribbons suggesting everything was normal.

Thomas stopped. Christie bumped into him, then laid her head against his strong back, her heart broken.

She'd seen.

At the entry of the cave, silhouetted by the sunset, a man lay on his side. Charlotte crouched beside him.

Christie's knees buckled and she fell.

From nowhere, Trev appeared at the cave entrance, attached to a rope.

Thomas reached down and touched her face. "It's over."

*Why are you smiling?*

Now, her eyes couldn't see. Only blurred images. Charlotte hugged her. "Come on, are you okay?"

She wasn't okay.

*How could I be okay?*

Warmth surrounded Christie. Warm, strong, comforting arms enfolded her, lifted her, and carried her to the entrance. She was gently lowered onto a firm, familiar lap. Sea breezes lifted her hair from her forehead and she rubbed her eyes.

"Sweetheart, Belinda will have to redo your make-up." Martin pressed her against his chest, his heart pounding. Alive.

# 75

# TOWN FULL OF LOVE STORIES

"*I* have no idea what you did you spoil all my lovely work, but at least I know how to fix things." Belinda threw her arms around Christie. "Even in this dressing-gown you look fantastic, so imagine how splendorous you will be in your actual wedding dress. And this time, you will stay in it until after the ceremony."

"Yes, ma'am," Christie giggled, perhaps from the half empty glass of champagne or possibly the after effects of the earlier events. Either way, she wanted Belinda to hurry up and make her presentable so she could go and marry Martin.

"Finish the champagne. I'm surprised it's still cold, but then again, Lance is pretty good at this catering stuff. Not quite up to Mum's standard, but not bad. Now, seeing as you are in a vulnerable state, I shall take advantage and cover your eyelids with glitter."

"Glitter away."

Belinda powdered Christie's face until they both coughed. "Okay, that'll cover the teary stuff. How much did you actually cry?"

"Too much." Charlotte wandered in with her own glass of champagne. "He was never at risk, your handsome man. Martin is so brave and very, very confident."

Christie took Charlotte's hand. "I'm so happy you're safe."

"Bernie has some issues. I mean, a smart person doesn't load a century plus old pistol and fire it at a passing boat. When the whole thing exploded he was lucky it only knocked him off his feet, not over the edge."

"And Martin was right there to tie him up. Close your eyes, please." Belinda was armed with a palette of eye colour.

"Hurry. I need to get married. What is the time?"

"Not midnight so you'll be fine," Charlotte laughed. "your guests are amazing. Although I am hearing talk of a movie. About tonight. Apparently there are not only producers and directors in the crowd, but screenwriters."

Christie groaned. "I'll ask Ashley to speak to them."

"He's the one behind it all," Belinda announced. "Okay, you'll have to do. But don't let anyone credit me for this lot of make-up. There's only so much a professional can do."

When Christie opened her eyes, it was straight into the mirror. There was no sign of the tears she'd shed before and after Martin took her in his arms in the cave, no sign of the deep lines of worry she thought would never go. Her eyes were bright and excited. But her hair was now loose and curling around the flower crown which somehow included fresh strands of jasmine.

"I adore you, sweet Belinda. Thank you for more than the make-up, little cousin-in-law." She kissed Belinda's cheek and reached for her glass but Belinda grabbed it first.

"Not now. You have perfect lipstick and I am actually quite over fixing you up. So be a good bride, stay in your dress, with your outstanding hair and make-up, and get married."

"Aren't you my bridesmaid? Shouldn't you be letting people know I'm on my way?" Christie grinned as Belinda tore out of the door. Then she turned to Charlotte and took both her hands. "Thank you."

"Whatever for? If I hadn't shouted out at the cliff, you'd already be Mrs Blake."

"And you'd be lost."

Charlotte took a deep breath. "Trev would have found me. Eventually."

"I thought he'd cry when he found you. Charlotte, he—"

"No. Don't say it, please don't."

"But you know it's true. And I see it in your eyes."

"You know, tonight is about you and Martin. And I will dance with Trevor and who knows. Maybe the incredible love in this town, between you and Martin, Thomas and Martha, John and Daphne... and if I'm not mistaken, Angus and Elizabeth—"

"You're not mistaken."

"Perhaps even Barry and Sylvia?"

"It sounds like River's End is filled with love stories."

Charlotte handed Christie the champagne flute. "I won't tell."

"Nor will I. But at some point, you need to talk to Trev. He deserves that."

"Come on, child. Let's take you to your groom." From the doorway, Angus extended his hand.

# 76

# A ONE AND ONLY WEDDING

"*L*ove weaves a web of magic around those it touches, heightening the senses, reawakening long forgotten dreams."

Under the starry sky, amongst the most patient and understanding friends and family imaginable, Christie and Martin faced each other beneath the flowered arch, their hands entwined.

"It unites two people, two individuals of independent thought and action..."

The pond was a shimmering surface reflecting the moon. The guests barely moved, many of them holding hands with the person at their side.

"...giving them the desire, and the courage, to share their lives." Daphne paused for effect.

These moments were beyond precious.

"Learning about the other, learning about themselves. Developing trust and understanding."

Martin mouthed, "I trust you."

Against her will, tears of joy filled Christie's eyes. She whispered, "I understand you."

When Martin raised an eyebrow, happiness bubbled over and she giggled.

Daphne stared at her quite solemnly and Christie grasped Martin's hands more tightly.

"Ahem. The enchantment of love can be kept vital and strong by nurturing each other through sadness and difficult times."

*And kidnapping and sinking of yachts.*

It must be a reaction to the events of the day but Christie wanted to laugh and burst into song and dance around the pond. She was certain Martin would not approve so reined herself in. This was, after all, her one and only wedding.

Daphne continued, unaware of Christie's almost overwhelming need to take the vows she'd written herself and turn them into a love song. Martin understood. His eyes steadied her but with humour. He did understand her. Love her. But nobody was never allowed to be in danger again.

"Love is the final challenge, ongoing and ever-changing. A wonderful partnership that offers happiness. When simply being together is enough. And a shared smile means more than the answers of the universe."

The universe was finally in step with this wonderful night. Above, the velvet sky sparkled with diamond stars and when she stole a glance Christie recognised Vela and Carina. A soft breeze rippled across the pond and Christie suddenly knew her parents would always watch over her. There would be no more fear or holding back.

"To be cherished and respected, and knowing that laughter is the purest gift of all… Martin, Christie, this is the love your marriage celebrates."

Randall trotted onto the platform and sat between Christie and Martin, his tail wagging as he looked from one to the other. There were muffled giggles from the guests, then Daphne's mouth quivered and all of a sudden, everybody was laughing.

# 77

# ONE DAY YOU'LL WANT ITS SHADE

*P*almerston House was ablaze with lights and filled with music and laughter. Outside, the path to the pond was covered with confetti and lit by only the fairy lights. Trev and Charlotte wandered toward the pond, not touching, not speaking. They found the bench against the old tree and sat.

Trev extended his hand and, after a moment, Charlotte placed her hand in his. The warmth radiated through him, a tiny taste of what might be. But tonight belonged to Christie and Martin Blake, without doubt the happiest couple he'd ever known.

"They deserve it."

"The newlyweds?" Charlotte nodded. "They are relishing every second."

"Had some doubts about the wedding going ahead. When I heard the shot ring out..."

"Gave us a scare in the cave. Bernie was waving the gun around for ages and then he spotted the boat and before Martin could reach him, sort-of aimed and fired."

"The paramedics said he'll be okay. Hand is pretty messed up though."

Charlotte gazed out at the water. Trev watched her.

*What are you thinking?*

Eventually, she looked at him, her face serious. "I can't do this."

"Do what."

She squeezed his hand.

Disappointment replaced the glimmer of earlier hope. "Charlie, I thought I'd lost you—"

"You never will. But I have stuff to figure out. Family stuff."

"You're leaving."

"I'm… yes. Your mother thinks I'm perfect to work with her for a while. See what happens. I love books."

"River's End doesn't have a bookshop. What about opening one here?"

*Plant a seed, let it grow into whatever it will be. Nurture it, because one day you'll want its shade and shelter.* He'd planted the seed of opportunity, watered it, cared for it. Now he wanted to take it all back.

"Nice thought, but Trev, your mother needs help. I can help her."

"I might need to visit her more often."

Charlie's smile broke through the pain in his heart and she touched his face. "I think you should." She leaned toward him and kissed his lips, just a touch.

He drew her against him and she rested her head on his shoulder.

*She isn't saying goodbye.*

He was patient. She was worth it.

# 78

# FINALLY HOME

*C*hristie sat at the top of the staircase, swaying slightly to the music as she watched the guests dance and mingle. She'd taken off her shoes and they were on the floor behind her. The exhaustion in her bones was creeping back and her thigh hurt where she'd hit the rocks in the tunnel. But her heart was full and she'd remember the last few hours for her whole life.

Martha and Thomas danced slowly, eyes on each other. It wasn't long ago this was their reception, a time Christie knew she loved Martin but was convinced he didn't feel the same.

"I think you'll need this." Martin dropped onto the step beside Christie, holding out a crisp, white handkerchief.

She viewed it with suspicion. "Why?"

"Always a question. Because you cry a lot. And because I had a whole lot made for you." He unfolded the fabric to reveal the initials C. B. in one corner. "Okay?"

"Oh thank you! I needed it earlier."

"Nothing bad happened to me, sweetheart."

"Right. You always disappear just before your own wedding. Climb down a dangerous cliff and only partly with a rope. And refuse to do what the man with the gun tells you."

"I don't do as I'm told."

"You're a married man now."

"And?" Martin ran his hand down Christie's spine, sending a delicious shiver through her body from head to toe.

"I love you."

"Good answer." He kissed her lips lightly. "Shall we have one more dance?"

"And then?"

"And then, Mrs Blake, I intend to take you home. To our home."

The promise in his eyes spilt tears from hers and with a smile, he gently used the handkerchief to dry them.

Randall bounded up the stairs and stood there looking at them, mouth open in something like a doggie smile.

"Hello, dog." Martin held his hand out to pat him, but Randall lay down on the step beneath Christie. "I knew this would happen."

"He still loves you."

"I'm a dismal third on his list of people. But at least I married the one who is first."

"Oh. That's why you married me?"

"Yes."

Christie climbed onto Martin's lap. "The only reason?"

His arms tightened around her. "You smell nice. Really nice. And cook well."

"You cook better. In fact, you should do all the cooking."

"Then you'll have to grow everything I cook in the fancy new glasshouse John and Daphne gave us."

"So, I smell nice, can grow stuff, and the dog loves me."

"People marry for a lot less— ouch!"

"Sorry, did my elbow accidentally poke your ribcage?"

"You used to be so nice."

"We're married now. You'll get to see the real me." She giggled.

Martin raised her chin and held it. His dark eyes reflected her love. "I've known the real you since the first time we met, Christabel Blake. I love you now and forever, and I think we might miss the dance and go home now."

"I am home, Martin. Wherever you and Randall are, I'm home."
Her heart was held within his. Forever.

# ABOUT THE AUTHOR

Phillipa lives just outside a beautiful town in country Victoria, Australia. She also lives in the many worlds of her imagination and stockpiles stories beside her laptop.

Apart from her family, Phillipa's great loves include music, reading, growing veggies, and animals of all kinds.

She loves hearing from readers and sends out a monthly email with news, competitions, author recommendations, and lots of other goodies.

www.phillipaclark.com

Printed in Great Britain
by Amazon

39614921R00192